# Applications of Anthropology

# Studies in Applied Anthropology

General Editor: **Sarah Pink**, University of Loughborough
Reflecting the contemporary growing interest in Applied Anthropology this series publishes volumes that examine the ethnographic, methodological and theoretical contribution of applied anthropology to the discipline and the role of anthropologists outside academia.

**Volume 1**
*Anthropology and Consultancy:*
*Issues and Debates*
Edited by Pamela Stewart and Andrew Strathern

**Volume 2**
*Applications of Anthropology:*
*Professional Anthropology in the Twenty-First Century*
Edited by Sarah Pink

# Applications of Anthropology

Professional Anthropology in the Twenty-First Century

Edited by

**Sarah Pink**

*Berghahn Books*
New York • Oxford

First published in 2006 by
*Berghahn Books*

www.berghahnbooks.com

© 2006 Sarah Pink

**Library of Congress Cataloging-in-Publication Data**

A catalog record for this book is available
from the Library of Congress

**British Library Cataloguing in Publication Data**

A catalogue record for this book is available from the British Library

Printed in the United States on acid-free paper

ISBN 1-84545-027-2 hardback
ISBN 1-84545-063-9 paperback

# CONTENTS

# LIST OF ILLUSTRATIONS

# ACKNOWLEDGEMENTS

*Applications of Anthropology* has been above all a collaborative venture, and those who have contributed their ideas and energies to it go far beyond the set of authors listed on the contents page. This book is based on the Applications of Anthropology seminar series, a project I developed as Networking Officer of the Association of Social Anthropologists (ASA). Indeed I was inspired to develop this project as a result of being invited to take up this role by the ASA committee, keen at that time to develop closer links with anthropologists working outside the academy. My first thanks must go to the ASA committee for their support and feedback in the development of my proposal to the ESRC who with the ASA and the Centre for Learning and Teaching Sociology, Anthropology and Politics (C-SAP) co-funded the seminar series.

Most of the chapters in this book are from our first seminar, which aimed to survey the contemporary field of applied anthropology. The exception is Adam Drazin's chapter, presented in the second seminar. Due to the constraints of time that so often plague applied anthropologists, two further contributions, from Genevieve Bell and Chris Loxley, both of which were very important to our discussions during the seminar could not be published here. This seminar was a highly stimulating event driven not solely by the stunning and excellent set of presentations from our speakers, but equally by the discussion and comment from the seminar participants. This enthusiastic, critical and collaborative set of people ranged from undergraduate, masters and doctoral students to established senior applied and academic anthropologists. Their contributions have inevitably influenced the ways these chapters have been rewritten for publication. In particular our discussions helped me shape my own perspective on the issues and questions I have raised in the introduction to this volume. Without these participants the seminar and this book could not have developed as they have, and this volume would be incomplete without an acknowledgement of their exceptional contribution.

Finally, I would like to thank those who have helped in and supported the process of producing both the seminar itself and this book: Sue Jeffels and Ann Smith for their secretarial assistance; John Postill for his help in organising our first seminar; and Marion Berghahn for her enthusiasm and support in the publication of this volume.

# PART I

# THE HISTORY AND DEVELOPMENT OF APPLIED ANTHROPOLOGY IN THE U.K.

# INTRODUCTION:
## Applications of Anthropology

*Sarah Pink*

In a recent guest editorial in *Anthropology Today* (19(1)), Paul Sillitoe urged anthropology to 'promote its professional identity beyond the academy' in what he saw as the obvious areas 'such as development ... forensic science, the media, the 'culture' industry, heritage work, museums and galleries, teaching, intercultural relations, refugee work and the travel industry' and what were to him the less obvious occupations 'such as law, banking, social work, human resources, retailing, management and the armed forces' (2003: 2). This, Sillitoe hoped, would help anthropology to develop a profile as a profession and in doing so increase student numbers and prevent non-anthropologists from posing as members of our profession. Two years earlier, in 2001 I was invited to become the networking officer for the Association of Social Anthropologists[1] (ASA) committee, and as part of that role I endeavoured to develop links between anthropologists working inside and outside academic departments.[2] Through this came the idea for the Applications of Anthropology seminar[3] from which this book has been developed. At this time the scope for anthropologists' involvement outside academic departments was growing and shifting. The seminar unfolded in a context of expansion of the use of anthropology in business, education and the public sector, while in overseas development the demand seems to be shifting to meet a different set of needs. Likewise in visual anthropology the application of anthropology to television in the *Disappearing World* and *Under the Sun* documentary series of the 1970s and 1980s has diminished. A contemporary applied visual anthropologist is more likely to be using a camera to do consumer ethnography for a multinational company or medical anthropology research than taking a television crew to Africa (see Pink 2004b).

Sillitoe (2003) lists a good number of areas in which anthropologists might work. In fact some of those that he considers less likely as well as those that he classifies as likely were represented during our seminar series. We learnt not only about what anthropologists are actually doing in these areas, but also how their involvement is developing, what new roles they are presently involved in, and how they envisage the future of applied anthropology in their field.[4] More specifically our focus was on how the developments are unfolding in the socio-cultural and political context of contemporary Britain and how they are part of a particularly British experience of applied anthropology. As well as its particular place in the global political economy, Britain also has its own unique experience of applied anthropology. In the United States there are well-established associations of applied anthropologists[5] and a substantial literature for teaching, professionals and career guidance,[6] some of which I refer to below as point of comparison and as the 'existing literature' that this work contributes to. In Britain no such associations are currently active (although they have been in the past) and no similar body of literature exists (with the exception of the *Anthropology in Action* Journal and e-mail list discussed in more detail by Susan Wright in Chapter 1).[7] It is however clear that in Britain at the beginning of the twenty-first century the demand for anthropological approaches, understandings and methodologies outside academic departments is shifting and changing. This is happening in relation to developments both internal and external to the discipline. Wider changes in British culture, society and politics within a global context, changing approaches within anthropology, not to mention a situation where there are more anthropology Ph.D.s than academic jobs, all contribute. The contributors to *Applications of Anthropology* explore this new context where anthropologists, anthropological approaches and ethnographic methods are increasingly important in the public sector and in industry. For example, in organisations as diverse as television production companies, multinationals such as Unilever and Intel, as expert witnesses in legal cases, as public health service researchers and as employees of or consultants to government in the Ministry of Defence (MoD), Department for Education and Skills (DfESS) and Department for International Development (DfID).

Although it may as yet lack the public profile that Sillitoe urges it to develop, applied anthropology is beginning to thrive in Britain. It also has a history (see also Pink forthcoming). In Chapters 1 and 2 respectively Susan Wright and David Mills outline this historical context.[8] Some early missionaries and colonial administrators can be said to have practised applied anthropology of a sort, although it was not named as such (Mills personal communication; see also Van Willigen 2002: 20–25 for a North American perspective). As for some other western national anthropological traditions (see Hill and Baba 1997), the roots of British applied anthropology were as Shore and Wright put it, embedded in its 'Colonial Gaze'. They note how Evans-Pritchard's (1951) and Firth's (1981) writings tended to define applied anthropology 'in the rather narrow terms of its value for government' (1997: 141). During this time the Colonial Social Science Research Council (CSSRC) (1944–1962) funded applied anthropology in the colonies until it was wound up in 1961 (Mills 2002; see also Pink forthcoming). Rather than dwelling on this well-versed colonial history here I would direct the reader to the detailed historical work of David Mills (especially 2002, 2003 and this volume) and Adam Kuper (1996).

In this volume Mills draws from archival materials to offer us an insight into how, after the colonial period, a new form of applied anthropology – what is today sometimes called 'business and industrial anthropology' (see McDonald 2002: 378–421) – was flirted with and finally abandoned by the leading anthropologists and institutions of the 1950s. Mills' chapter also provides an important historical context for the question of the relationship between the 'pure' (academic) and 'impure' (applied) anthropologies of the ensuing years (see below), as well as a delightful contrast to the contemporary blossoming of the relationship between anthropology and industry reported both in the media (see for example Hafner 1999) and in the contributions to this volume. Susan Wright's chapter provides our second stage of the historical context, drawing from, amongst other things, Wright's own experience of being one of the people central to developing and promoting applied anthropology in Britain in the latter quarter of the twentieth century. Indeed it is particularly important that we take heed of her commentary as it has happened all too often in Britain (but not in the U.S.) that proponents of more systematic attention to Applied Anthropology become caught up in a cycle of reinventing a wheel which gradually stops spinning, awaiting the momentum of the next generation of enthusiastic seminar and network organisers. However one encouraging factor regarding the particular wheel that this present book spins is that it has been fully supported by the key institutions involved in the development and representation of anthropology in Britain today: the Association of Social Anthropologists (ASA); the Royal Anthropological Institute (RAI); and the Centre for learning and teaching in Sociology, Anthropology and Politics (C-SAP).

In the ensuing chapters, through a set of case studies of anthropologists' experiences of working with diverse organisations, this book revisits historical debates about applied anthropology, defines existing issues and explores possible futures. In doing so it develops a series of themes that by way of introduction I begin to unravel below: the relationship between the 'pure and the impure' – academic and applied – anthropology; the question of anthropological identities in new working environments; innovative methodologies appropriate to these new contexts and the new research questions they involve; the skills needed by anthropologists working in applied contexts where multidisciplinary work is often undertaken; issues of ethics and responsibility; and how anthropology is perceived from the 'outside'. It reflects on the implications of these for the future both of the application of anthropology outside academic departments and of the new generation of anthropologists who might be involved in this.

# The Pure and the Impure – or the Academic and the Applied

The question of the relationship between academia and applied anthropology never ceased to rear its head during the Applications of Anthropology seminar series. As Mills (2002, 2003 and this volume) shows, it was a key issue in the era of applied colonial anthropology and persisted to fudge the chances of any relationship between anthropology and industry in the 1950s. Indeed as Mills describes, soon after the ASA was founded in 1946 the debate was represented in two proposals circulated to the membership by Evans-Pritchard (its first Chairman and Secretary General): 'Nadel urged that the association should address the issues of applied anthropology, and provide some "scope for discussing colonial problems so far as they come within the purview of social anthropology". Gluckman, on the other hand, was adamant that "in the present situation there is a grave danger that the demands of colonial governments for research workers may lead to the detriment of basic research and the lowering of professional standards"', arguing that the theoretical development of social anthropology should be the priority (Mills 2003: 10). Wright (this volume) describes how the debate over the acceptability of an applied anthropology was played out in the following years, through to the present, as applied anthropologists were sidelined by those who opposed it. Nevertheless, practising applied anthropologists and their supporters with academic posts held their ground. Their presence through GAPP (Group for Anthropology in Policy and Practice) and Anthropology in Action made a powerful impact and established them sufficiently for the academic/applied dichotomy to persist as it indeed has. Now in the twenty-first century some recent anthropology Ph.D.s who have opted for a career outside the academy still comment on the negative responses they received from their ex-tutors, echoing Shore and Wright's characterisation of the 1990s situation where 'when anthropologists have gained employment outside university departments, the discipline has tended to slough them off and no longer define them as "real" anthropologists' (1997: 142). While the climate has definitely changed to some degree, some practising anthropologists still feel they are considered to have left the profession.

To consider what might be specifically British about this situation we might take recourse to one of anthropology's 'traditional' endeavours – cross-cultural comparison. Hill and Baba (1997) compared the status of applied anthropology internationally in the 1990s. According to them, 'The relationship between anthropologists who practice anthropology and those who work in traditional academic settings often is an uneasy one in many countries'. In Britain (c.f. Shore and Wright (1997)) and elsewhere (such as France, Canada and Australia) 'the usefulness of anthropological knowledge is being held hostage by the culture of the discipline itself'. Comparing this with Central America, Mexico and Israel they note how 'the practice of anthropology in these countries dominates the discipline, and, in effect, *is* the discipline' (emphasis in original) (Hill and Baba 1997: 10–11) in these 'countries that have a tradition of using anthropology to solve their problems' (Hill and Baba 1997: 12). The status of applied anthropology is particularly bound up with its relationship to theory which in the 1990s in Britain, as in most western/westernised nations, was one of a 'traditional linear model' whereby a 'one way flow from theory to practice is reinforced by various distancing mechanisms that separate theorists and practitioners -- they work in different types of institutions with little interchange between them, they dwell on different ends of the disciplinary status hierarchy and they clash almost obsessively over ethical issues' (Hill and Baba 1997: 16). There was, they note, an 'absence of a strong feedback loop from practice to theory in the West', whereas in non-Western nations (Costa Rica, India, Mexico, Nigeria and Russia) 'anthropological theory often was embedded consciously in larger state-level political and economic theories that were used broadly to construct and implement national policy over many decades' (1997: 17).

In the context of British social anthropology in the 1990s Shore and Wright described this in terms of Mary Douglas's (1966) work on classificatory systems. There was, they propose 'a characteristic preoccupation with the purity of academic boundaries, where "purity" is associated with academic theory, neutrality and detachment', thus maiming applied work 'not only "untheoretical", but also "impure", even "parasitical" and "polluting" to the discipline' (1997: 142). Moreover, the discipline was conservative and reluctant 'to accept that knowledge generated from work in policy and practice can constitute a legitimate basis for constructing theory' (1997: 143). This assessment is still accurate to some extent, and the cross-cultural comparison Hill and Baba engage in demonstrates how the relationship between applied and academic anthropology in Britain is part of a specific national context, providing a background that situates chapters 1 (Mills) and 2 (Wright) globally.[9] Currently, however, with the expansion of applied anthropology in Britain an increasing number of anthropologists are beginning to bridge the gap between making a theoretical contribution to the academy and applying their anthropological approaches to practical problems. My book, *Home Truths* (2004a), a monograph, based on a video ethnography of 'Cleaning, Homes and Lifestyles' carried out for Unilever Research, is an attempt to achieve just this. Contributors to this book also combine theoretical and applied work relating to the same project. In chapter 9 Marvin describes how his academic work on the fox hunt has involved him in filmmaking and report writing and in chapter 10 Schwander-Sievers discusses how as an academic she also plays a role as an expert witness in legal cases. Further examples of projects that combine academic and applied components can be found in Gellner and Hirsch's (2001) edited volume *Inside Organisations: Anthropologists at Work*. However, it should be noted that when they have engaged in work that has had both applied and theoretical import, most anthropologists involved have been employed by academic institutions. Practising anthropologists working full-time outside the academy have less time to develop and publish theoretical work to contribute to academic anthropology. Indeed they have less motivation to do so as their own career development does not depend on academic publications, unlike for academics publishing for Research Assessment Exercise (RAE) success. This however does not mean that practising anthropologists have no need for theory, that they are incapable of producing it or that their work has no theoretical implications. Indeed, the need to establish and maintain a dialogue between applied and academic anthropology was emphasised throughout our seminar series. There are various ways to bridge the gap between the academic and applied and different arrangements (e.g. seminars, training and updating workshops, invited speakers) will suit academic and applied anthropologists in different working situations.

Wright (chapter 1) describes how, in the 1980s and 1990s, GAPP steered away from dichotomy between pure and applied anthropology (not least in its decision to use the term 'practice' rather than 'applied' in its title, but also to emphasise the importance of practice for anthropological teaching and researching).[10] By the early twenty-first century it is clear that any mutually exclusive dichotomy between applied and academic anthropology is not only now undesirable for a great many contemporary anthropologists from both 'camps' but also clearly misinformed. In many areas of practice the two are fundamentally related: academic anthropology nowadays often has an applied or 'user' focus (and indeed this appears to be encouraged by the Economic and Social Research Council who asks applicants to name potential users of their research in their grant application forms); and applied anthropology is inevitably academically informed in that it draws from and represents the theoretical and methodological concerns of academic anthropology. The current problem is that these links are often not sufficiently consolidated in the training, work practices, publications and networks of applied and academic anthropologists. A questionnaire survey as well as the qualitative materials noted from the seminar and workshop sessions showed that there is a need for updating in academic theory and methods for applied anthropologists and for training in applied anthropology skills for both postgraduates and academics considering doing applied work.[11] Such connections are more likely to be made in the work of university-employed academic anthropologists who also carry out applied work. Nevertheless, most important is that the relationship between academic and applied anthropology be recognised and nurtured from both inside and outside academic departments. I take this idea up again at the end of this introduction in the section about the future of applied anthropology. I think it is now difficult to say that The Academy in any general or unanimous sense is opposed to applied anthropology for a number of reasons. First, because it is being taught at undergraduate level in several departments (e.g. at the University of Durham and University of Wales, Lampeter). Second, it is not so unusual for academic anthropologists to do applied consultancy work. Finally, as noted above, the key institutions of academic anthropology in Britain have tabled their support for applied anthropology.

## How do Anthropologists Define Themselves?

In 2003 a lively discussion developed on the 'Anthropology in Action' e-mail list. The topic was the question of when and with what credentials might one consider or call oneself an anthropologist? The themes discussed – such as having an anthropological way of thinking and one's work being theoretically informed, as well as having a Ph.D. or M.A. in anthropology – resonated with the issues raised at the Applications of Anthropology seminar. The question of anthropological identities is furthermore crucial because it is not only a question of how anthropologists feel about and define themselves to one another, but crucially how the discipline and the unique skills and advantages offered by anthropology are represented externally by both the academy and practitioner groups.

The question of the identity of applied or practising anthropologists has for a long time been a contested identity. As I noted above, the history of applied anthropology in Britain has been characterised by the opposition of 'the academy'. In the past applied anthropologists have not only felt invisible, as many continue to feel today, but it was made clear to them in no uncertain terms that leading academics of the day had little sympathy with their project to use anthropology to solve problems in the real world. However, present day anthropologists who undertake applied work, whether anthropologists in academic posts, working freelance, or within organisations, continue to insist on their anthropological identities and the anthropological nature of their work. Indeed their work as individuals has contributed greatly to the process by which anthropology is becoming increasingly established as a discipline that can respond to practical questions and provide unique insights. It is through their individual efforts and persistence combined with the support offered in the past by BSAPP, GAPP and Anthropology in Action that British applied anthropology has progressed as far as it has.

Anthropology has always been hard to define, be it academic or applied. Indeed the authors of leading introductory anthropology textbooks have found it difficult to arrive at a satisfactory definition for undergraduates, often skirting around the issue by describing what anthropologists do (i.e. long-term fieldwork) rather than what anthropology *is* (e.g. Hendry 1999, Eriksen 2001). This is even more unsatisfactory if we want to extend the definition of anthropology to include the work of applied anthropology. The work of applied anthropologists is often undertaken in new contexts, it involves researching new topics, asking different questions and requires innovative methodologies. As such this means a shift from the idea that anthropology might be defined by its method – of long-term participant observation – to defining anthropology as a type of approach, paradigm or a set of ideas that inform our understandings (applied methodologies are discussed in more detail below). The contributors to this book demonstrate that doing anthropology might take a variety of different forms that include doing *ethnographic research*, doing *anthropologically informed research*, or taking *anthropologically informed decisions* in the role of manager or policy maker. They show how one aspect of being an anthropologist is about having a particular way of constructing and analysing a problem, producing and critically reviewing 'evidence' and reflecting on the wider social and cultural contexts that impinge on this. As the contributors to *Applications of Anthropology* insist, we should not essentialise anthropology and what anthropologists do as being only one thing, rather the discipline needs to accept that there are in fact many different ways one can be or call oneself an anthropologist in and out of 'pure' academic contexts.

Academic anthropology has avoided essentialising itself (although sometimes perhaps by default). Definitions of the discipline are vague and contested, even more so when characteristics that have been used to define it – such as cross-cultural comparison, relativism, long-term fieldwork, its object of study, and forms of representation – have been systematically critiqued and redefined. It would be difficult at any rate to find agreement about the purpose, theory and method of anthropology amongst all anthropologists. Applied anthropology perhaps needs to resolve this problem more urgently. Again universal agreement over a definition of applied anthropology (especially over ethical issues and questions of range and method – see below) is very unlikely. Nevertheless to 'sell' anthropology, to develop its public profile, applied anthropologists need to make its unique benefits clear and known. Indeed, one of the key issues that occupied the seminar participants was how to 'sell' anthropology outside the academy. What is it about anthropology that is unique? How does it provide understandings that other disciplines cannot and what are the advantages of this to a client. To some degree North American writing on applied anthropology has already attempted to answer this question. For example, in his guide for students contemplating a career in applied anthropology Nolan identifies a series of advantages that an anthropology graduate has which can be paraphrased as follows (Nolan 2003: 78):

> ability to 'define the shape of the world of work';
> skills in researching and evaluating existing literature;
> can understand local 'languages' and subcultures;
> skills in interviewing and liking interview data to other materials;
> used to contradiction and complexity and flexible to revise ideas as new meanings emerge.

Recommending how graduates might convince employers that their anthropology skills give them advantages over other candidates Nolan suggests the 'anthropological advantage' is that they: 'understand that culture is key to many of the patterns we see and to many of the problems we try to resolve'; gain their understanding inductively from the ground up rather than by imposing theories beforehand; 'are holistic in their approaches and perspectives'; are comparative; 'are interactive' and realise the importance of formal and informal relationships (Nolan 2003: 119–120). Nolan's set of generic skills that one would also hope anthropology students in the UK to graduate with (and academic anthropologists to have gained during the course of their own training and experience) is notably different from academic attempts to define anthropology by means of long-term fieldwork methods and a comparative perspective. It reminds us that there are two sides of the coin: one where anthropologists might usefully operate in contexts where they work not as anthropologists but apply anthropological approaches and methods; and another where anthropologists are employed as consultants or in salaried posts to actually provide anthropological research, insights or expertise. In this book we will be looking at mainly the latter, although most of the contributors also use what Nolan calls their 'anthropological advantage' not only to do applied anthropology but in their everyday work practices as individuals interacting with and in organisations and institutions. As the seminar participants emphasised, an anthropological approach inevitably involves one not simply using anthropology to do the job one is paid to do, but informs one's whole approach to understanding and operating in the organisation or industry one is working in/for. Such an approach is implicit to the contributions to this book, and is most explicitly expressed in Drazin's analysis of the market research industry in chapter 4. In this sense applied anthropology almost always becomes an anthropology of organisations, and fieldwork in itself as the anthropologist learns how to speak the language of the organisation, understand its power hierarchies, and social and cultural systems.

## Ethics, Rights and Responsibilities

New working contexts, methodologies and research sponsors all have implications for ethics in anthropological research and representation. When one does applied work one is confronted with a series of ethical choices. First one can decide whom to work for. Some types of applied work are perhaps more universally morally justified – for instance Good suggests that 'Acting as an expert in the asylum courts is easy to justify morally, all the more so in view of the manifest failings in Home Office procedures' (Good 2003a: 7). This view of what we might call 'applied anthropology as a moral corrective' is quite a common approach to policy research. Some anthropologists would feel uncomfortable working for the Ministry of Defence, for multinational companies that are integral to global capitalism or for organisations involved with fox hunting. However the idea of anthropology as a moral corrective is also suggested in some of these more controversial contexts. For example Lucy Suchman, reflecting on the role of corporate anthropology, has suggested that 'As anthropologists and consumers, our problem is to find the spaces that allow us to refigure the projects of those who purchase our services and from whom we buy, rather than merely to be incorporated passively into them' (Suchman 2000). Regarding his work in the MoD, Mils Hills argues 'Unfortunately, if one has no stake in this domain, no participation in the evolution of policy and plans; no commitment to improving the knowledge base that sustains decision-making, one can hardly complain about malformed outcomes' (this volume). The contributors to this volume show that such questions as 'should anthropologists work for this or that organisation?' are actually more complex than they first appear. Applied anthropology inevitably constitutes a social intervention, in whatever context one is working, be it commercial, public sector or for another independent organisation. Ethical questions do not only apply to the choice of who to work with/for, but also to the question of to whom one is responsible when involved in an applied project. A Ph.D. anthropologist may feel her or his main responsibility is to her or his informants. But when an anthropologist is employed by a university to carry out a consultancy for another organisation, and simultaneously finds her or himself doing research with a set of informants with whose lives her or his own becomes intertwined, this becomes combined with new sets of responsibilities. As such applied anthropologists can become tied up in complex series of loyalties and moral responsibilities. To whom, and under what circumstances are anthropologists responsible?; to the consumers, to the institution, to the film production company, to their own university or to the company who is the client paying for results? All of these relationships must be clearly set out at the start of a project. They will make the way information is produced, used and shared differ from the way it is managed in academic work and will inform how consent and informed consent and the ownership and control over research materials are negotiated.

In the U.S., NAPA and the SfAA have published relevant sets of ethical guidelines on their web sites.[12] The NAPA ethical guidelines have been developed collaboratively with practitioner groups and were first published in 1988. They address 'general contexts, priorities and relationships' since 'No code or set of guidelines can anticipate unique circumstances or direct practitioner actions in specific situations' (NAFA web site). To gain a full sense of their coverage the reader should consult the guidelines. Briefly they cover issues of: welfare and human rights; disclosure of research objectives and confidentiality; competent communication of ethical priorities and commitments to employers; commitments to students and colleagues; and making a contribution to and publicly representing the discipline. The SfAA guidelines are broadly similar with perhaps more emphasis on preventing harm to communities studied and anthropologists' duty to 'communicate our understanding of human life to society at large' (SfAA web site). These approaches to ethics encompass the different levels of ethical involvement discussed above. They identify not only what might be ethical practice. Simultaneously they construct applied anthropology itself as an ethical project with a mission. It should contribute anthropological insights to society and might serve as a moral corrective.

The contributors to this volume describe their own experiences of making ethical and personal decisions in a range of applied research contexts. Their descriptions bring these general principles into view as real experiences. In doing so they set out some types of dilemma any applied researcher may encounter. They draw out the personal nature of ethical decision making in a discipline where the personal and professional lives of anthropologists become so easily merged, even in applied work. Moreover they stress the personal responsibility felt by anthropologists whose work leads to interventions that change other people's lives.

## Re-thinking Ethnography

For applied anthropologists ethnography remains a key anthropological method. Nevertheless the new contexts and questions applied anthropologists research also invite a re-thinking of what we mean by ethnography. Is the research done in business research (and other areas) really ethnography? Some would say it is not. It is not long-term fieldwork in a so-called community context, but is more likely to be multi-sited and/or multi-researcher and we can even now find out much of what we need to know on-line – either on the Internet or by e-mail. Such ethnography is likely to involve much shorter periods of participant observation than the typical 1–2 years of the traditional doctorate in anthropology. But does this necessarily render it less anthropological? The contributors to this volume argue that it does not. First because such work is still equally informed by anthropological theory and interpretation (even if this theory is not explicit in one's final report to a client), the knowledge it produces and scrutinises is still subjected to anthropological critique. Second, because once an anthropologist has been doing applied work in the same area for some time it becomes her or his field. One might have less time for participant-observation but past ethnographic work informs one's current anthropologically informed research with shorter periods of participant observation. Finally such methodological developments might also be understood in terms of changing approaches to methodology in academic anthropology – the ideas of multi-sited work (Marcus 1995), ethnography on-line and the anthropology of home (Miller 2001) all approach ethnography in new ways that have particular relevance for practitioners of applied anthropology.

Existing North American applied anthropology textbooks normally outline a series of established methodologies that their authors identify as part of the skills set that makes up the portfolio of an applied anthropologist. This list includes participant observation, key informant interviewing, surveys, questionnaires, participatory action research, rapid ethnographic assessment, needs assessment, social impact assessment, focus group research, and social network analysis (see, for example, Ervin 2000, Gwynne 2003: 36–42). Moreover, applied researchers, including those who draw from anthropology (e.g. the Everyday Lives group[13]), are increasingly using visual and digital methods and media as methods of research and representation. In my own work with Unilever Research I have developed video ethnography methods (see Pink 2004a, chapter 2) and worked with documentary video and hypermedia representations. Similar uses are being developed in other companies and hypermedia reporting on CD-ROM or on organisations' own intranet systems is an increasing phenomenon (Pink 2004c). Added to this, the new contexts anthropologists work in require new forms of anthropological representation to communicate anthropological understandings to colleagues and clients. Contemporary anthropologists might be writing business reports, making policy recommendations to DFID or the NHS, running seminars for senior MoD staff or presenting their knowledge on TV or in the law courts. This might mean learning the appropriate terminologies and vocabularies, using pictorial representations or material forms, communicating verbally, and delivering information in a two-hour stretch or in sets of five bullet points in ten minutes. Learning to operate in this way often means not simply doing an anthropological study of a particular problem or question. Rather in the absence of existing manuals or guides to how to operate in these institutional or organisational cultures, it means applying one's anthropological eye to the institutions for whom one might work or carry out consultancies in order to inform our own actions and practices of representation within them.

## The Profile of Anthropology in Multi-disciplinary Contexts

To those 'purists' who have rejected applied anthropologists as 'lost' to the discipline, the new contexts and methodologies outlined above might seem contrary to the identity of anthropology as an academic pursuit. But as one of the postgraduates at our seminar posed: Are there 'jobs for life' for anthropologists any more?[14] Do we need to be able to be more adaptable? As the contributors to this book outline anthropologists in applied contexts often work in multidisciplinary teams, some do multidisciplinary work themselves. They need to be open to and to understand, if not be able to practise, other methods and approaches. They might be working with for example, engineers, designers, lawyers, television producers, public health officials or psychologists. Anthropologists are well placed to understand the different 'world views' of other disciplines – we might say that is another strand of the anthropologically informed approach. In addition in many applied contexts anthropologists need to understand quantitative methods and in some cases produce statistics. There are debates about whether this means it should be mandatory for postgraduate anthropology students to take courses in statistics as part of the 'skills' packages they are required to acquire as part of their methodology training.[15] It might well be the case that such training should be available when relevant to each individual student's career trajectory, rather than on a routine basis.

Some applied contexts require anthropologists to make skilled uses of information and presentation that are specific to that situation. Tony Good's (2003a) article written as 'a basic primer for those involved in' work as an expert witness in asylum cases in courts (2003a: 3) provides a good example of what an anthropologist might need to know in order to be able to function effectively in a particular consultancy context. Parallel to the Hindmarsh legal case detailed in the following section (see Peace 2003), one of the issues regards recognising legal (and journalistic) assumptions about evidence and truth and how these differ from anthropological approaches to truth. If anthropologists cannot manage these types of knowledge and work with them in such applied contexts their evidence will not be taken seriously. As Good explains:

> ... anthropologists are well accustomed to evaluating and interpreting informants' statements – but whereas in academia 'consistency', 'plausibility', and 'credibility' may seem virtually interchangeable terms, in legal circles 'reliability' is a term of art, denoting a judgement which only the court is entitled to take. There is therefore a world of difference between stating that an account is plausible or consistent with objective evidence, and judging it to be credible. Many experts simply do not realize that while the first two judgements are permissible, the third is not. The court may respond by devaluing a report which they see as attempting to usurp its authority. (Good 2003a: 7)

Situating anthropology in multidisciplinary work has a further implication. We need to be able to define anthropology and its contribution in and to particular working contexts, as well as 'the *intellectual* contribution that anthropology can make' (Ingold 2003) and moreover to be able to communicate this to others. This adds up to not only finding ways to convince one's immediate colleagues of the value of anthropology, but also (as Sillitoe (2003) has stressed) highlights a need for us to work at the public profile of anthropology in Britain. Some of our speakers found that when they gave business presentations, often their audiences did not know what an anthropologist does. Although the contributors to this book definitely show that professional anthropology is becoming increasingly established as we move into the twenty-first century, there is still work to be done to develop anthropology's public profile. This book is intended to play a role in that process as well as serving as a source book for any postgraduate student or academic anthropologist considering working in an applied context.

## The Public Profile of Anthropology and Anthropologists as Public Figures

It is hard to define exactly what the public profile of social anthropology in Britain is. First impressions indicate, however, that compared with disciplines such as psychology, sociology and history the mention of anthropology in any but an academic context brings mainly blank stares or the assumption that one is interested in bones. In the past (1970s and 1980s mainly) anthropology was given a space on television, notably in the BBC's *Under the Sun* and Granada Television's *Disappearing World* ethnographic documentary series, and in its heyday 'British television invested at least £10 million in programming based on anthropological research' (Henley, this volume). Nevertheless, currently the presence of anthropologists and anthropology in the British media (audio-visual and print) is minimal, either in the form of documentary film representations of anthropological work or topics or in anthropologists taking the role of public commentator. This is a stark contrast when compared with countries such as Norway, where, as Eriksen (2003) outlines, anthropologists play key roles as commentators on public issues and current affairs and, as was noted in our seminar discussion, Catalonia where a pool of anthropologists provide anthropological analyses of current issues on television new programmes.

There are reasons why anthropology needs to reinforce its public profile: not only to help create jobs for its Ph.D.s but also to be prepared to protect itself in situations where its profile is about to be created in a less positive light by others. A brief example from overseas makes the point. Adrian Peace's (2003) discussion of the Hindmarsh Island case in Australia, where 'the boundary between consultancy work and university-based research is repeatedly traversed' (Peace 2003: 2), demonstrates how anthropology might be brought into disrepute when applied work becomes a public issue. Brought to the public domain by Margaret Simons (an investigative journalist), the Hindmarsh Island case involved a legal dispute over whether or not some Aboriginal women's objections, made on spiritual grounds, to the construction of a bridge as part of large marina project, were authentic or a hoax. Opposing anthropologists became involved as advocates on both sides – for the Ngarrindjeri women who argued against the building of the bridge on the basis of their Aboriginal traditions *and* for other Nagarrindjeri women who denied any knowledge of such beliefs. Thus the evidence given by anthropologists was 'often complex and contradictory' and 'a major thread running through this episode concerned the rivalries between different anthropological camps' (Peace 2003: 2). This was picked up on in the media and resulted in a series of critical articles that sought to discredit anthropology as a discipline – rather than the few consultants who had been involved in this case. There are two interesting points to be made here. First, the media critique entailed a slippage between applied and academic anthropology. That the reputation of the latter might be damaged by problems generated by the former might well fuel arguments that echo the mid twentieth century pleas in British anthropology to prioritise the academic over the applied. Second, however, as Peace points out there is a further issue related to the way the discipline reacted to this case. In general, the anthropological profession 'has been slow to involve ourselves seriously in public discourse and we have evaded engaging the media on complex issues, even when the discipline's status and integrity are under question' (2003). As this case shows, to develop and maintain a positive public profile that will promote both the use of anthropology in applied contexts and the (academic) discipline as a whole, anthropology does need to be involved. It is important for anthropology and its professional associations to develop the means to participate effectively in such situations.

It is not only at the level of producing an appropriate media profile for anthropologists that the reputation of the discipline might be advanced. For example Hills argues that by proving themselves in policy contexts anthropologists can demonstrate the worth of the discipline. In his view, 'through our empathetic understanding of others, our ability to enhance the robustness of thinking; tailoring/improving policy anthropologists can achieve a lot for the benefit of policy and decision-makers, the lot of those that Government exists to serve and, finally, the recuperation of the reputation of anthropology' (Hills, this volume).

## How Can Anthropology Have an Influence?

To begin with an example from one of the best established domains of applied anthropology, in the first paragraph of his edited volume (Sillitoe *et al.* 2002), Sillitoe's rallying cry to anthropologists of development states that:

> The time has come for anthropology to consolidate its place in development practice, not merely as frustrated post-project critic but as implementing partner. There are growing demands for its skills and insights to further understanding of agricultural health, community and other issues, and so contribute … to positive change in the long term, promoting culturally appropriate and environmentally sustainable interventions acceptable to 'beneficiaries'. (2002a: 1)

He urges the discipline of anthropology to 'build on its maligned applied tradition' and 'bid to become the intellectual home of participatory development' as such 'offering it disciplinary pedigree and coherence'.

Within the context of development practice, Sillitoe's agenda focuses on the 'new field of specialism called, among other things, "indigenous or local knowledge"'. Although he develops a more complex discussion of the terminology and its meaning later in the volume (Sillitoe 2002a: 8–13; Sillitoe 2002b), indigenous knowledge can more simply be described in terms of the 'proposition that an understanding and appreciation of local ideas and practices should inform development work' – something that is not new to anthropologists and that 'puts anthropology on the development team' (Sillitoe 2002a: 2). In the twenty-first century a new 'action approach, as opposed to a purely academic one' (italics in original) to development 'pioneering ways to facilitate others' expression of their understandings of the rapidly changing world, while informing them about our thoughts (e.g. the scientific understanding that underpins the technology that drives development and its implications from our experience)' (Sillitoe 2002a: 5). This, however, needs to be balanced with the account that Green (this volume) offers in her outline of her experience as an anthropologist consultant to DFID. In this context, Green's 'competencies' that 'in practice, centre on an understanding of the policy process, and the ways in which programme documents can be used to further its objectives' (Green, this volume), are more in demand than her ability to represent specific instances of 'others' culturally conditioned knowledge and expectations' (Sillitoe 2002a: 5). Indeed, what remains unclear to me from the Sillitoe et al. (2002) volume is how, and the extent to which, his otherwise excellent agenda for an anthropological engagement with indigenous knowledge development will come to fruition. As Ellen (2002: 254–256) points out anthropology's relationship to development remains difficult. Rather than being intellectually purist, anthropologists need to seek ways to integrate their perspectives with those of the other disciplines involved in development. However, in addition to this, anthropologists need to find a way of ensuring that development agencies and the projects they run take note of anthropology's argument: that anthropological ideas and practice become part of development practice and policy. Some, like Michael Schönhuth, doubt that this will be possible. Paraphrasing Sillitoe he questions his assumptions that the present is 'a revolutionary new era for the practice of anthropology with development' and there are 'new opportunities for local communities through the marriage of participatory and anthropological research'. The basis for these doubts are that academic anthropology's relationship with development and with applied research is unresolved and there are 'fundamental inconsistencies between participatory and academic anthropological research traditions' (2002: 139–40).

This brings me back to the wider question of how applied anthropologists might work in organisations and the benefits anthropology might bring. The indigenous knowledge in development argument offers a particular take on what anthropology can contribute to a particular area of practice. Perhaps because the subject-matter of anthropology and development have often coincided anthropologists have had a long-term involvement in the critique of and participation in development and development projects, and this means that a sophisticated debate has developed about the relationship between the two. The situation for other policy arenas in which anthropology is practised, such as defence and education, is far different. For example, Mils Hills contribution (along with Collinson 2004) to this volume is one of the first publications to outline the role of anthropology in contemporary defence work in government. Whereas the anthropology of conflict does exist (and is taught at M.A. level at the University of Sussex), there has to my knowledge developed no parallel debate about the relationships between the anthropology of conflict and the contemporary role of anthropologists in defence policy and research in Britain.[16] As applied anthropology expands in these areas it will be interesting to monitor such developments and the extent to which they run parallel to the question of anthropology and development. Hills answers the question of how anthropology might influence government policy in a number of arenas related to the work of the MoD in defence and 'at home'. Working as an anthropologist in government is important because 'If we are not part of decision and planning processes, decisions and plans will still be made, and decision-makers and planners will remain convinced of the belief that they understand the effects of their actions' (Hills, this volume).

## The Future of Applied Anthropology in Britain

It is impossible to predict, but the future of applied anthropology in Britain will depend not only on a growing demand from users/clients, but also on the actions of university-based and practising anthropologists. This means networking and forging links between academic and practising anthropologists, promoting the applied strand of the discipline inside and outside academia, teaching applied anthropology in universities and providing methodological training and theoretical updating for applied anthropologists.

The U.S. provides an example of a context where applied anthropology has two professional associations – the Society for Applied Anthropology (SfAA) and the National Association for the Practice of Anthropology (NAPA). It is taught in many Universities as a Masters degree and there is a substantial literature on the topic both as student texts and in journal form. The public role of anthropologists in the U.S. might be lacking in that public interest anthropology and the advocacy role attached to it are not developed enough to make anthropology a key force in public debates (see Nader 2002). However, it has applied anthropology as teaching and professional agendas. I am not suggesting that we replicate the U.S. model – applied anthropology in Britain has its own history (see above and Mills and Wright, this volume). However surely there are some lessons to be learnt. With this in mind we were pleased to welcome Riall Nolan (University of Cincinnati) as a speaker in our final Applications of Anthropology seminar. We learnt that for a student or academic in the U.S. seeking a career in applied anthropology, a wealth of resources and contacts already exist (training, literature, professional associations) (see also Nolan 2003). Nevertheless networking is still one of the key ways to create the right circumstances through which to both judge and be selective within the applied anthropology jobs market and to find employment. 'Practising anthropologists need a talent for building networks. Although they tend to be jacks-of-all-trades in their research and implementation skills, they cannot do everything' (Ervin 2000: 219). For job seeking Nolan emphasises the importance of networking ('… a systematic method of creating and managing a web of professional relationships' (2003: 79)) for career planning and development in applied anthropology. It is such strategies that enable one to access the individuals, organisations and knowledge that are needed to begin and develop a career in applied anthropology (see also Gwynne 2003: 306). In Britain there is no standard career structure for applied anthropologists, and given the diversity of the fields in which we work it seems unlikely that one will emerge. Here too networking is crucial. Some training in applied anthropology is provided by the ASA courses (previously GAPP). However personal contacts and networking seem set to remain the key way that individual applied anthropologists will find their niches outside academia. Nevertheless, there are institutions that might be put in place that will smooth this path: taught Masters degrees in applied anthropology; an active association of applied anthropologists that provides regular meetings, seminars, a web site and a mentoring system. As result of the Applications of Anthropology seminar a group of us are working towards establishing these through the ASA Applied Anthropology Network.

The above initiatives, combined with the favourable context I described at the beginning of this introduction (where recognition that anthropology can provide methodologies, insights and understandings that are not only unavailable from other disciplines but that also really matter, and demand for applied anthropology is increasing across the public and private sectors), indicates a bright future for applied anthropology in Britain.

## The Book

The book is divided into four Parts. Part I situates the contemporary applications of anthropology discussed in this book historically. In Chapter 1

Susan Wright sets the scene by recounting the recent history of applied anthropology in Britain. This is a history in which Wright herself has been an active advocate of applied anthropology. Indeed it is Wright (amongst the others she mentions in her Chapter) we have to thank for her initiatives that have carried applied anthropology through to the present. Then in Chapter 2 David Mills takes us back to the mid twentieth century. Through a case study of a brief encounter between the leading anthropologists of the day and representatives of industry, he demonstrates how anthropology's relationship to its application is always historically contextual.

Part II focuses on applications of anthropology in industry. Chapters 3 and 4 are written by anthropologists who are actively involved in developing consumer ethnographies and design anthropology for and in collaboration with clients that include multinationals. Simon Roberts is an anthropologist with experience of working for a range of business clients and who has set up Ideas Bazaar, an anthropological research agency. In Chapter 3 Roberts discusses both the practical questions of undertaking commercial anthropology and how such work can enrich the relationship between applied and academic anthropology. In doing so he raises a series of practical and methodological issues that need to be addressed in order for this field to develop to its full potential. In Chapter 4 Adam Drazin writes on the basis of an anthropologist who, as a freelance anthropologist who has also been a market researcher, has a different relationship to industry. Analysing his experience of these contexts, Drazin suggests applied anthropologists understand 'research' as a product. Through an overview of the roles anthropologists might play in industry he provides an informative and analytical perspective (taking an 'anthropology of' approach) that situates the potential contributions of anthropology and anthropologists within a multidisciplinary research context.

Part III takes us to the public sector. The contributors discuss their experiences in three quite different areas of work covering the Department for International Development, the National Health Service, and the Ministry of Defence. In Chapter 5 Maia Green writes about the changing role of anthropologists in overseas development. Drawing from her experience in social development, working both seconded to and as a consultant to DfID, Green describes how in this context an anthropologist's work becomes anthropologically informed, rather than based on her expertise with a particular culture or region. In Chapter 6 Mils Hills who works for the MoD discusses how an anthropologist might contribute to the work of government and have an impact on policy. Although for some working for the MoD raises ethical questions, it is, Hills argues, important for anthropologists to engage their skills and insights in such areas. In Chapter 7 Elizabeth Hart takes us through a series of key projects in the story of her career as an anthropologist commissioned to do research for the NHS. In this context ethnography is still part of the basis upon which policy recommendations are made. However as Hart shows any one project is unlikely to fund long-term fieldwork. Rather the anthropologist's experience of fieldwork in any one type of setting is cumulative.

Finally Part IV examines the application of anthropology in the media and public sphere. Chapters 8 and 9 focus on different aspects of the roles played by anthropologists in television. Chapters 9 and 10 also overlap in their discussions of how anthropologists represent their expertise to others as forms of evidence. In Chapter 8 Paul Henley reflects on the changing relationship between anthropology and television since the 1970s. Combining this with his experience of having, since 1988 directed the Granada Centre of Visual Anthropology at the University of Manchester, Henley shows how the opportunities for visual anthropology graduates to work in television have shifted as the context of television production has altered. In Chapter 9 Garry Marvin writes from the perspective of an anthropologist who worked in television before returning to the academy. Marvin discusses the ethical issues, rights and responsibilities that developed as he became involved in making a television film based on his anthropological research about fox hunting. Marvin's work on fox hunting, however, also led him to another application of anthropology as his research became of interest to policy makers and lobbying groups concerned with the issue of banning fox hunting in Britain. The involvement of anthropologists with the law is developed more fully in Chapter 10 by Stephanie Schwandner-Sievers in relation to her work as an expert witness in cases concerned mainly with Albanian asylum seekers. Drawing from her experience of using her expertise in this field Schwandner-Sievers demonstrates the complex ethical issues and knowledge of the legal system involved in representing 'culture' in this context.

Of course there are areas of work in applied anthropology that one volume cannot cover. However, by selecting a set of case studies that draws from the private and public sectors and examines the increasing work of anthropology in the media and public sphere, this book presents a set of insights into the academic and applied practices and issues that contemporary applied anthropology involves.

## Acknowledgements

Many of the ideas discussed in this introduction emerged from my experience of the Applications of Anthropology seminar series and would have been impossible for me to develop without the contributions made by the other participants in those events and the lively discussions that characterised them. In addition, particular thanks are due to Susan Wright for her reading and comments on this introduction.

# Notes

1.   The full official title of the ASA is The Association of Social Anthropologists of Britain and the Commonwealth.
2.   This is worthy of note since in 1994 Grillo (1994: 311) characterised the ASA as a professional association that has traditionally recruited from inside the academy. However in 2003 the Applications of Anthropology seminar series was initiated and co-funded by the ASA.
3.   The Applications of Anthropology seminar was funded by the ESRC, and co-funded by the ASA and C-SAP. Its overall aims were:
     1.   To review and report on existing debates about the role of anthropology outside academic departments, including ethical issues.
     2.   To review the range of professional areas and activities that anthropologists are currently engaged in outside academic anthropology, and explore and report on the implications of this for the 'shape' of anthropology as a profession and as a discipline.
     3.   To explore existing links between anthropologists working in and outside academic departments, and to investigate and report on how such links might be developed further to create stronger and sustainable working relationships and collaboration between academic and professional anthropology.
     4.   To explore the implications of these findings for the training needs of postgraduate anthropologists: to report on and recommend what provisions might be appropriate to offer postgraduate anthropologists; training in skills needed to develop anthropological careers outside academia; to develop a range of appropriate pedagogies and the best methods of course delivery.
     5.   To examine and report on the needs of current and potential users (business, NGO and public sector) and make recommendations concerning how these might be met.
     6.   To examine the ethical issues raised by such collaborations and recommend, where necessary working methods, guidelines and a code of conduct.
     7.   To promote the profile of anthropology and ethnography to potential users and other bodies through a range of activities and media.
4.   Each speaker was given a brief to cover in her or his own way and as relevant to their area, the following themes: how anthropology and its uses are viewed in their professional context; the advantages and limitations of anthropology in their field, and its use in multidisciplinary work; examples and case studies of successful (and otherwise) uses of anthropology; anthropology and ethnography; ethical and methodological issues; a vision for the future of anthropology in their area.
5.   The National Association for the Practice of Anthropology (NAPA) http://www.practicinganthropology.org/, accessed 19 July 2004 and the Society of Applied Anthropology http://www.sfaa.net/, accessed 19 July 2004.
6.   This is developed to the extent of having career guides such as Riall Nolan's (2003) *Anthropology in Practice: building a career outside the academy*. This book sets out for students a series of chapters that introduce applied anthropology, explain how to choose a career, find a job, keep a job and advance the profession. Other North American applied anthropology texts contain more modest outlines of a similar nature. For example, the final chapters of Margaret A. Gwynne's (2003) *Applied Anthropology: a career orientated approach* are dedicated to 'Finding a Job'. Other North American texts (cited by McDonald 2002 in his *The Applied Anthropology Reader*) include: Blythe Cameson's (2000) *Great Jobs for Anthropology Majors* (Lincolnwood, IL: VGM Career Horizons) and John T. Omohundro's (1998) *Careers in Anthropology*, Mountain View, CA: Mayfield.
7.   Anthropology in Action http://www.angelfire.com/rpg/anthropologyinaction/, accessed 19 July 2004.
8.   Although it is perhaps not customary to describe two of the chapters at this stage in the introduction, leaving the rest for their usual slot at the end, here it is important to do so to set the stage for the discussion.

9. As I write, Baba and Hill's (1997) volume is being updated into a new and expanded edition, to which I have contributed myself (Pink forthcoming). This new volume is unfortunately not available in time for discussion in this chapter. The reader is recommended to consult Baba and Hills forthcoming volume for more information about the global context of applied anthropology.
10. Susan Wright, personal communication.
11. The results of the skills survey and workshop on skills developed as part of the Applications of Anthropology seminar series are available on the ASA Applied Anthropology Network web site at http://www.theasa.org/applications/index.htm, accessed 19 July 2004.
12. These can be found for NAPA and the SfAA respectively at the following sites http://www.practicinganthropology.org/, accessed 19 July 2004. http://www.sfaa.net/sfaaethic.html, accessed 19 July 2004.
13. Details of this company are on the web site at http://www.edlglobal.net, accessed 19 July 2004.
14. Susan Wright has pointed out that in the 1980s and 1990s when academic posts were not available, applied anthropologists tended to work on short-term contracts and consultancies and often in doing so cross sectors, for example from overseas development to health. What seems to be new about the current context is the number of anthropologists now working outside academia on permanent contracts within one sector (Wright, personal communication).
15. As argued by Richard Vokes at the 3rd Applications of Anthropology seminar (see Vokes 2003).
16. Although Susan Wright notes a special issue of *Anthropology in Action* on Development and Conflict was edited by Mark Bradbury and Mark Adams with seven articles in winter 1996 3(3) (Wright, personal communication).

# References

Baba, M. and C. Hill (eds). 1997. *The Global Practice of Anthropology*. Williamsburg, VA: Department of Anthropology, College of William and Mary.
Cameson, B. 2000. *Great Jobs for Anthropology Majors*. Lincolnwood, IL: VGM Career Horizons.
Collinson, P. 2004. 'Anthropology in the Ministry of Defence', in S. Pink (ed.) *The Pure and the Impure*, a special issue of *Anthropology in Action*.
Ellen, R. 2002. '"Déjà vu All Over Again" Again: Reinvention and Progress in Applying Local Knowledge to Development', in P. Sillitoe, A. Bicker and J. Pottier (eds) *Participating in Development: Approaches to Indigenous Knowledge*, ASA Monographs 39, London: Routledge, pp. 235–258.
Eriksen, T. 2001. *Small Places, Large Issues: An Introduction to Social and Cultural Anthropology*. London: Pluto Press.
———. 2003. 'The Young Rebel and the Dusty Professor: A Tale of Anthropologists and the Media in Norway'. *Anthropology Today*, 19(1): 3–5.
Ervin, A. M. 2000. *Applied Anthropology: Tools and Perspectives for Contemporary Practice*. Boston: Allyn and Bacon.
Evans-Pritchard, E. 1951. *Social Anthropology*. London: Routledge and Kegan Paul.
Firth, R. 1981. 'Engagement and Detachment: Reflections on Applying Social Anthropology to Social Affairs'. *Human Organisation*, 40: 193–201.
Gellner, D. and E. Hirsch (eds). 2001. *Inside Organisations: Anthropologists at Work*. Oxford: Berg.
Good, A. 2003a. 'Anthropologists as Experts: Asylum Appeals in British Courts'. *Anthropology Today*, 19(5): 3–7.

————. 2003b. 'Anthropologists as Expert Witnesses: Political Asylum Cases Involving Sri Lankan Tamils', in Richard Wilson and J. Mitchell (eds) *Human Rights in Global Perspective: Anthropological Studies of Rights, Claims and Entitlements*. Routledge: London, pp. 93–117.

Grillo, R. 1994. 'The Application of Anthropology in Britain, 1983–1993', in C. Hann (ed.), *When History Accelerates: Essays on Rapid Social Change, Complexity and Creativity*. London, Athlone Press.

Gwynne, M.A. 2003. *Applied Anthropology: A Career Orientated Approach*. Boston: Allyn and Bacon.

Hafner, K. 1999. 'Coming of Age in Palo Alto', *The New York Times*, 10 June, Section G, P1, Column 6, available at http://www.ahasolutions.org/articles/ComingofAgeinsiliconv.pdf, accessed 19 July 2004.

Hendry, J. 1999. *An Introduction to Social Anthropology: Other People's Worlds*. London & Basingstoke: Macmillan Press.

Henley, P. 2004. 'Putting Film to Work: Observational Cinema as Practical Ethnography', in S. Pink, L. Kurti and A.I. Afonso (eds) *Working Images*. London: Routledge.

Hill, C. and M. Baba. 1997. 'The International Practice of Anthropology: A Critical Overview', in M. Baba and C. Hill (eds) *The Global Practice of Anthropology*. Williamsburg: Department of Anthropology, College of William and Mary, pp. 1–24.

Ingold, T. 2003. 'Response to Paul Sillitoe'. *Anthropology Today*, 19(2).

Kuper, A. 1996. *Anthropology and Anthropologists*. London: Routledge.

Marcus, G. 1995. 'The Modernist Sensibility in Recent Ethnographic Writing and the Cinematic Metaphor of Montage', in L. Devereaux and R. Hillman (eds) *Fields of Vision*. Berkeley: University of California Press, pp. 35–55.

McDonald, J.H. (ed.) 2002. *The Applied Anthropology Reader*. Boston, MA: Allyn and Bacon.

Miller, D. 2001. 'Behind Closed Doors', in D. Miller (ed.) *Home Possessions*. Oxford: Berg.

Mills, D. 2002. 'British Anthropology at the End of the Empire: The Rise and Fall of the Colonial Social Science Research Council 1944–1962'. *Revue d'Histoire des Sciences Humaines*, 6: 161–188.

————. 2003. 'Professionalizing or Popularizing Anthropology?: A Brief History of Anthropology's Scholarly Associations in the UK'. *Anthropology Today*, 19(5): 8–13.

Nolan, R. 2003. *Anthropology in Practice: Building a Career Outside the Academy*. Boulder, London: Lynne Rienner Publishers.

Omohundro, J.T. 1998. *Careers in Anthropology*. Mountain View, CA: Mayfield.

Peace, A. 2003. 'Hindmarsh Island and the Politics of Anthropology'. *Anthropology Today*, 19(5): 1–2.

Pink, S. 2004a. *Home Truths: Changing Gender in the Sensory Home*. Oxford: Berg.

————. 2004b. Introduction to *Applied Visual Anthropology* a guest edited issue of *Visual Anthropology Review*.

———— (ed.) 2004c. *Applied Visual Anthropology*, a guest edited issue of *Visual Anthropology Review*.

————. forthcoming. 'From the Colonies to the Modern Organisation', in M.L. Baba and C.E. Hill (eds) *The Global Practice of Anthropology*, 2nd Edition, NAPA Bulletin.

Schönhuth, M. 2002. 'Negotiating with Knowledge at Development Interfaces: Anthropology and the Quest for Participation', in P. Sillitoe, A. Bicker and J. Pottier (eds) *Participating in Development: Approaches to Indigenous Knowledge*, ASA Monographs 39, London: Routledge, pp. 139–162.

Shore, C. and S. Wright. 1997. 'Colonial Gaze to Critique of Policy: British Anthropology in Policy and Practice', in M. Baba and C. Hill (eds) *The Global Practice of Anthropology*, Williamsburg: Department of Anthropology, College of William and Mary, pp. 139–154.

Sillitoe, P. 2002a. 'Participatory Observation to Participatory Development: Making Anthropology Work', in P. Sillitoe, A. Bicker and J. Pottier (eds) *Participating in Development: Approaches to Indigenous Knowledge*, ASA Monographs 39, London: Routledge, pp. 1–23.

————. 2002b. 'Globalising Indigenous Knowledge', in P. Sillitoe, A. Bicker and J. Pottier (eds) *Participating in Development: Approaches to Indigenous Knowledge*, ASA Monographs

39, London: Routledge, pp. 108–138.

———. 2003. 'Time to be Professional?' Guest Editorial in *Anthropology Today* 19(1).

Sillitoe, P., A. Bicker and J. Pottier (eds). *Participating in Development: Approaches to Indigenous Knowledge*, ASA Monographs 39, London: Routledge,

Suchman, L. 2000. 'Anthropology as "Brand": Reflections on Corporate Anthropology', published by the Department of Sociology, Lancaster. University at: http://www.comp.lancs.ac.uk/sociology/soc058ls.html, accessed 19 July 2004.

van Willigen, J. 2002. *Applied Anthropology: An Introduction*, Westport and London: Bergin and Garvey.

Vokes, R. 2003. Untitled paper presented at Applications of Anthropology III: Future Visions, Hosted by C-SAP at the University of Birmingham.

Chapter 1

# MACHETES INTO A JUNGLE?
A History of Anthropology in Policy and Practice,
1981–2000

———— ⌬ ————

## Susan Wright

In the early 1980s, there were about a 100 anthropologists with doctorates in the U.K. whose education was based entirely on the assumption that they would want to become university lecturers. Yet, at that time, only 1–2 academic posts were advertised in a good year. This chapter presents a history of the organisations set up in the early 1980s and continuing to the late 1990s which aimed to provide anthropology graduates with the additional knowledge and skills, and the contacts, they needed to use their anthropology in policy and practice. It especially traces the development of GAPP (Group for Anthropology in Policy and Practice) which was founded in 1981, transformed into BASAPP (British Association for Anthropology in Policy and Practice) in 1988, and renamed Anthropology in Action (AinA) in 1993. Anthropology in Action ceased to be a membership organisation with a programme of activities in 2000, although its journal of that name, a website and its vocational training courses continue. This history is based on the archives of, and interviews with, some of the key people; minutes, published newsletters and reports; and my own notes of meetings I attended first as a participant then as convenor of GAPP (from 1987) and finally as founding convenor and committee member of BASAPP and AinA (from 1988 to 1996).

Established academics in the early 1980s maintained a very tight boundary around what counted as 'anthropology' and many wanted a clear separation between themselves and anthropologists who worked outside academia. Indeed, when I got my first job as an anthropologist on a university-based but government-funded project to research the impact of policies and decision making on rural areas in the UK, a generally sym-

---

Notes for this chapter begin on page 52

pathetic Oxford don received the news with the comment: 'It's a shame you will be no longer an anthropologist'. Many of us were not just impelled for economic reasons to seek employment outside anthropology departments; we actively wanted to use our anthropology to contribute critically to international development or to improve the operation of the British welfare state. We did not think of ourselves as 'no longer' anthropologists, even if we did not fit within the tight confines of academic anthropology.

In every previous generation, anthropologists had found work outside the academy, in government and voluntary agencies, in planning, housing, community work, health and social services, in international development, and in the private sector in industrial businesses and consultancies. In doing so, these practising anthropologists disappeared from academic view. There were no institutional links or effective ways of networking between them and the next generation of students. Unable to follow in their footsteps, we, the next cohort, had to cut a new path for ourselves into these areas of employment – like taking a machete into an overgrown jungle.

During the twenty-year existence of these organisations, there have been changes in the employment markets for graduates and postgraduates, transformations in the purpose and funding of universities, developments in university curricula and pedagogy, and in the discipline of anthropology itself. The context is quite different now from that when GAPP started. Currently almost 100 Ph.D.s in anthropology are completed every year in the U.K. (Mills 2003: 21). For students who now seek to use their anthropology in employment outside academia, is there access to networks, training and academic debate involving practising anthropologists? Or are the paths growing over again?

## Postgraduate Unemployment in the Context of 1980s University Crises

The post-war expansion of universities came to a shuddering halt during the first Thatcher government. In 1980/1 the University Grants Council (UGC, the vice chancellors who distributed the government's grant for universities) warned there would be cuts to universities' funding. University managers looked to make savings, and anthropology was among the 'minority' subjects that were vulnerable. At the same time, Sir Keith Joseph established the Rothschild Commission to look into the future of the Social Science Research Council (SSRC). It was widely rumoured that the Minister felt that the social sciences had no future at all in post-socialist Britain. Anthropology was picked out for particular attack, as a subject born of a colonial age which had outlived its time. Anthropology was faced with a very real fear that it would lose its research funding and postgraduate awards, without which it could not survive. At the same time, anthropology departments were producing postgraduates with no hope of university employment.

Anthropologists in the academy were split over how to react. Some thought the talk of crisis was overblown and would never happen. One interviewee remembered a professor at a meeting say 'the UGC is a paper tiger', only to find that the UGC had meanwhile deleted funding for an entire department at his university. Some perhaps shared the widespread disbelief that the Thatcher government would ever turn into reality its speeches about rolling back the public institutions of the 'nanny' state and freeing people to look after themselves in an enterprise culture; or like many at the time, they perhaps did not grasp the enormity of the transformation that was in store for all the sectors of the post-war welfare state and their associated professions.

Others decided to mobilise to defend the discipline. The Association of Social Anthropologists (ASA) was chaired by Bill Epstein, professor at Sussex, in 1980 and by Edwin Ardener, from Oxford, in 1981. But few other leading anthropologists from the well-established departments were involved with the committee. Those active on the ASA committee, whom some called 'the Young Turks',[1] included Ralph Grillo from Sussex but were otherwise from small, peripheral or joint departments – Nancy Lindisfarne (then Tapper) who taught anthropology at the department of religion at Kings College London, Anne Akeroyd from the joint sociology/anthropology department at York, and Lorraine Baric from sociology/anthropology at Salford. Grillo and Akeroyd were on the Senate of their institutions and Baric was a pro-vice chancellor. They were well attuned to the policy environment and were reading the runes of the times. This did not necessarily help them protect anthropology in peripheral locations – for example it did not survive a 45 per cent cut in UGC funding at Salford – but their actions did help save anthropology in the main departments and as a discipline.

There was a further division over whether to be concerned about the employability of postgraduates. Paul Stirling, professor at Kent, argued that if departments stayed solvent by producing more postgraduates than they needed to reproduce themselves, then they had a moral duty to provide their students with the skills, experience and contacts needed for employment elsewhere. Some pragmatists were prepared to consider problems of postgraduate employment outside the academy on the grounds that, if anthropology developed a reputation for producing unemployable postgraduates, it would affect their department's future student intake and viability. Others, including many professors of leading departments agreed that the ASA should concern itself with the funding and viability of university departments, but they were adamant that it should have nothing to do with the employment of postgraduates outside the academy. One of my interviewees recalled one Cambridge don saying

'If the chaps are any good, they won't be hawking for jobs'. An apocryphal story was widely quoted, that Malinowski had said to Lucy Mair, 'Applied anthropology is for the half-baked'. Edmund Leach, professor at Cambridge, referred back to the founding of the ASA in 1946 when he, among others, had battled successfully to reserve membership of the ASA for only 'pure' anthropologists. Those who had taken a training in anthropology or ethnography (e.g. the Oxford diploma in ethnology) as preparation for work in the colonial service, on their return to the U.K. with the end of colonialism, were excluded from membership of the ASA. As membership was essential to be considered for an academic job, applied anthropologists were excluded from employment in anthropology departments. Leach now argued strongly against the ASA concerning itself with the employment of graduates outside the academy. At the 1983 ASA Annual Business Meeting, Stirling proposed that the ASA committee should

> Investigate ways of persuading the main departments to adopt a more concerned attitude regarding the future employment of their students, more especially their graduate students. (ASA Annals 1983: 10)

The minutes record 'Leach dissented strongly from this view' (ibid.). The Young Turks were therefore up against senior members of the ASA who wanted to maintain the ASA as an exclusive preserve of university anthropologists.

The Young Turks were faced with contrary pressures, both to preserve the boundary around academic anthropology in their negotiations with SSRC and to break it down in their concern for graduate employment. In relation to the SSRC, they joined in the overall campaign to defend the social sciences, whilst trying to protect anthropology in particular. This meant laying claim to a special academic expertise clearly located within university departments and bounded from the 'outside'. At the same time, the unemployment of postgraduates, and perhaps the ability to recruit students in the future and maintain the viability of departments, involved transgressing that boundary and making links to applied anthropologists working beyond the academy. The Young Turks tried to make both moves at once. They succeeded in producing an excellent submission to the Rothschild Commission which preserved research funding for the discipline. In November 1982 they also held the first meeting of Heads of Anthropology Departments to survey each department and the national scene and to examine the likely impacts of UGC cuts to university funding. This spurred successful lobbying for the survival of at least the bigger departments, even if the discipline lost the more peripheral locations where anthropology had been taught. Thus the ASA committee was very effective in mobilising the discipline for its survival within universities. In contrast, a very real split opened up over the employment of graduate students outside the academy.

# ASA on Postgraduate Employment Outside the Academy

On behalf of the ASA committee, Lindisfarne organised a conference, funded by the SSRC, and held at SOAS in London on 25–26 September 1980, on 'The Training and Employment of Social Anthropologists' (RAIN no 41: 5–7, Dec. 1980). The aim was 'to reduce the current estrangement between academic and applied anthropology'. The conference was attended by 40 people, including representatives from all 13 departments which received SSRC awards. There were sessions on three areas of employment. For each session they drew on practising anthropologists as speakers, identified employment opportunities, and discussed what knowledge, skills or training anthropologists needed for employment in that sector:

- **Employment of anthropologists in development**
*Speakers*: Sean Conlin, Kevin O'Sullivan, A.F. Robertson, Terry Spens
*Skills*: Anthropologists' strength is their knowledge of other cultures. But anthropologists also need a further specialist training so as to be a technical expert in a particular field e.g. nutrition. If not, they have little to offer employers.

- **Commerce and industry**
*Speakers*: Dan Gowler, Gerald Mars, Michael Nicod
*Skills*: Anthropologists do not need to be technical experts. What they 'sell' is intrinsic to all anthropological training – participatory methodology, a holistic approach, a lack of dogmatism. Undergraduate courses need more on organisational theory and on the anthropology of work. The growth of evaluation research in industry offers employment prospects for anthropologists.

- **Public sector**
*Speakers*: Gaynor Cohen, Nicholas Deakin, Malcolm Young
*Skills*: The sector was receptive to social inquiry in the 1960s and 1970s but this is currently in decline. Anthropologists need to know more about British society – the culture of Whitehall, local government and the institutions of social control.

If attendance at the meeting was mainly motivated by concern for the economic viability of departments, there was little agreement about the extent to which degrees, posts or departments were under threat, and whether from UGC, SSRC or university councils. The next session on how anthropology courses needed to change in order to attract students and help graduates find jobs provoked 'marked differences and conflicting opinions' (ibid.). Some whose departments were not threatened felt no need to engage with applied anthropology. Others made practical suggestions about including placements in postgraduate courses to give students work experience preparatory to entering the job market; about gaining experience of working in multidisciplinary teams; and about the idea of a national training course. Ethical issues about working for government or capitalism were also raised, with a call for anthropologists to commit themselves to an active moral stand and to use their expertise for human-itarian purposes. This was parried with the usual, unsatisfactory, response that anthropologists do no harm because their advice is often rejected any-way: employers often found anthropologists failed to conform to their expectations about the causes of problems and their solutions, and unless anthropologists were able to influence the research agenda at its earliest stages, their results were often dismissed as irrelevant or disruptive (ibid.).

Two firm proposals were, first, that the ASA should set up a joint work-ing party with the Royal Anthropological Institute (RAI) on the public image of anthropology. Second, that the ASA should support the develop-ment of training and careers in applied anthropology. The ASA was asked to support the professional status of career anthropologists working out-side the academy, to change its membership rules to include such anthro-pologists and to involve them in its activities. The ASA was also asked to provide publicity about departments that wanted to develop specialist training; about publications on applied anthropology, and about careers in applied work. This conference raised the issues and set the agenda that dominated much of the 1980s.

There was a follow-up meeting at the LSE in November 1980, attended by 50 people, where a joint RAI/ASA working party was proposed to pur-sue the two fields of public relations and of training and careers in applied anthropology. The joint committee consisted of Grillo (Chair), Akeroyd, Lindisfarne, Baric, David Butler of the Overseas Development Agency (ODA), and Sean Conlin. They established a programme of work. Akeroyd compiled a bibliography on applied anthropology and made a survey of applied anthropology training programmes in the U.S.A., she listed the knowledge and skills they covered, and gave details of their practical training, practicums, placements, internships and study service schemes (Akeroyd 1983). This report was meant to form the basis for a conference which was postponed several times and eventually cancelled (Mills per-sonal communication).[2] Lindisfarne began work on a leaflet about careers in applied anthropology which was finally produced in December 1983 when 2000 copies were printed, and another 5000 were printed the fol-lowing February (Mills personal communication). Arising from the first conference, Dan Gowler and Graham Clarke (1982) were commissioned to write a report for the SSRC entitled 'The employment and training of British social anthropologists'.

The joint working party produced valuable work for the ASA and the SSRC, but little that was visible or made much impact from the point of view of a postgraduate student. From my current reading of the historical records, the joint working party continued to face a contradiction which limited their effectiveness. They had succeeded in mobilising general support for lobbying universities, the UGC and SSRC to protect departments and the discipline. They needed the support of senior figures in the discipline for this endeavour,[3] but among these figures there was fierce opposition to the allied strategy to secure the future student intake and viability of departments by widening the concerns of the ASA to include graduate training and employment. The next event in the story, an unexpected move to set up an independent organisation for graduate students and applied anthropologists perhaps gave the joint committee a little release from the contradictory pressures, whilst it also opened the danger of fragmentation within the discipline, which everyone at that stage wished to avoid.

## Group for Anthropology in Policy and Practice

On 12–17 April 1981, the U.S.A.'s Society for Applied Anthropology (SfAA) held its decennial conference at Edinburgh (Eades 1981). Alan Rew (Development Studies, Swansea) organised a session called 'Anthropological involvement in development team work' and British anthropologists concerned with the training and employment of postgraduates attended. Paul Stirling convened a meeting and proposed the establishment of a new organisation, tentatively called Applied Anthropology Group (RAIN 1981: 15). Stirling was not one of the Young Turks, but he was exasperated at the blocking tactics of the old guard. He was energetic and excellent at making things happen, although, as he freely acknowledged, he was not good at running organisations. He had already set up a company, called SA4, to match anthropologists with vacancies in development consultancies.[4] The organisation he now proposed was for applied anthropologists and students ineligible for ASA membership and it would hold events to put them in contact with each other and improve the quality and quantity of anthropological participation in social analysis (Stirling 1981).

The inaugural meeting of the new organisation was held at the RAI on 23 October 1981. My notes record how the meeting decided on the name Group for Anthropology in Policy and Practice (GAPP).[5] This was specifically to avoid the term applied anthropology. The new name implied that anthropologists, when active in contexts of policy and practice, were still part of the one discipline of anthropology. 'Applied', in contrast, carried connotations of a separate profession, parasitical on 'pure' academics for ideas which they 'applied' without making contributions to the development of the discipline themselves. 'Pure' academia was supposedly untainted by real life whereas applied was polluted with practical action and politics (Wright 1995). The new name not only aimed to steer away from the pure/applied dichotomy but to suggest that those involved in policy and practice generated insights that would give a needed stimulus to anthropological theory. David Marsden (Development Studies, Swansea) suggested 'Anthropology in Praxis' to convey this interdependence between theory and action, but praxis was rejected for its association with Marxism. So Conlin's proposal of GAPP was accepted. With echoes of 'Mind the GAPP', the refrain of London tube stations, this title was a constant reminder of the need to mind and overcome the gap between the university and practising wings of the discipline.

GAPP quickly established an ethos which was self-consciously different from the ASA. Membership was open to anyone with a self-defined interest in anthropology (I became member number 49). The fee was a very modest £2, or £10 for high income academics – soon there were 150 members. No titles were used in meetings or publications. Committee meetings, in London on the last Friday of each month, were open for anyone to attend and contribute. The core of the committee, the GAPP activitists, included academics and practitioners.[6] They drew on their contacts for workshops and training events. Importantly, they also invited postgraduates to organise conferences which gave students experience in planning, budgeting, making presentations and writing reports – the very skills they needed to gain employment. Some of them, in time, played important roles on the GAPP Committee.

## Workshops

The first workshop, Anthropology at Work, funded with a Nuffield grant and organised by Stirling, was actually held at the RAI on the two days following the inaugural meeting. It was similar to the ASA's earlier conference, but this time the 44 people who attended were mainly practising anthropologists and anthropology postgraduates. Practising anthropologists described their work, employment opportunities and requisite skills.[7]

On 8–9 May 1982, Lydia Morris (then a research officer) organised a conference called 'People, Trouble and the State' which focused on anthropological work in the social services (Morris and Stirling 1982). It was attended by 37 people and funded by the SSRC. The conference had a strongly comparative perspective but was also a good response to the call from the ASA's earlier conference for postgraduates to learn more about state systems in Britain.

On 22 January 1983 Stella Mascarenhas-Keyes (then a Ph.D. student, SOAS) organised a Forum on the Employment of Anthropologists, funded by the Nuffield Foundation. The report of this meeting was sent to anthropology departments and circulated widely (Marcarenhas-Keyes 1983). The 59 participants included 'some concerned academics', but were mainly students, unemployed and underemployed anthropologists. Three panels, with three speakers each, concerned with Development, British Industry, and Health and Social Services in Britain, brought together the information so far accumulated on job prospects in those fields. The meeting also identified new employment areas including the behavioural aspects of medicine and community care, and the emerging leisure studies. As the report put it, 'a concerted effort' was also needed to ensure that anthropologists' abilities to conduct mini-fieldwork, crack codes of social systems, act as interstitial people, and think widely came to be used in market research, personnel management, sales and public relations, and running organisations (ibid.).

The meeting identified action that was needed regarding postgraduate training: students appear overqualified and they should identify aspects of their doctoral research and experience that is relevant to applied work; applied work requires methodological flexibility and doctoral training should include a wider range of methods than participant observation; policy professionals work under tight time constraints and have to use available information with flair and imagination; they have to write concise reports comprehensible to a non-academic audience; they usually work in multidisciplinary teams, not in isolation. Students and university departments were urged to establish links with public and private organisations in their area, to encourage students to do applied research, and organise placements. Postgraduates should form networks and self-help support groups. Many of these points shaped the development of GAPP's training courses.

This meeting also decided to establish subgroups on particular sectors. The ASA/RAI joint working group picked up this idea and invited Peter Lloyd (professor at Sussex) to set up Social Anthropology and Social and Community Work (SASCW). He made a survey of anthropologists working in these fields and held very informal meetings to network and exchange ideas and information. By then a rural community worker, I organised a SASCW event on this subject (Wright 1984). Following the Griffiths Report, SASCW organised a sequence of meetings on community care.

*Training*

Meanwhile, other GAPP activists had set up training events. Carol Mac-Cormack ran a whole day workshop on research methods for social investigation into the health services. This took us through a repertoire of research methods, including my first encounter with how to design a questionnaire. Indeed, bearing in mind that I did my Ph.D. at Oxford without methods training, it was the first time I learnt about how systematically to design a methodology suited to the issue under investigation. It was also an excellent demonstration of how to organise a workshop and the range of teaching methods to use – all new to me.

On 25 September 1982, Alan Rew ran a 'Simulation Workshop on Development'. This also used a teaching method I had not previously encountered (Wright 1982). Rew pre-circulated a prospectus for a development project and participants were asked to submit in advance a draft bid for the work. These responses would be discussed at the meeting, chaired by someone called Wedgewood-Tebbitt. Not only did I not get the joke, but I could not tell when Rew was role-playing and when speaking in his own voice, and why. I was too scared to send in my views to these unknown people, and I found the whole event, fiercely scrutinising draft proposals, terrifying. But it offered insights into how a different world worked. In retrospect, the idea was excellent but was maybe so daunting because the pedagogy was not explained.

By 1983 Sean Conlin had learnt from these two events and he developed a pedagogy that became standard for GAPP training, with modifications, for the next 15 years. He invited practitioners to turn a project on which they had worked into a case study. Each case study set the students tasks which simulated the actual work of the original project. For example, at the first workshop there were case studies on development, education, health, social services and rural planning (Conlin and Mascarenhas-Keyes 1983). The last, an analysis of rural deprivation, I based on my rural policy research, with Rosemary Lumb another anthropologist/rural community worker as the expert. The students worked on one case study throughout the weekend in a team of 6–10 people, facilitated (rather than taught) by the practitioner who had done the original work. The students had to work out how to investigate the issue, and think what they would draw from anthropology to do so. They had to design a practicable methodology and a plan of work. They had to present their ideas, usually in the form of a proposal or a report, to a visiting expert from an organisation relevant to the case study. Thus they had to explain their approach, and how it was informed by anthropology, but in language an employer could understand. The students experienced team work and worked to a brief within tight deadlines. This form of experiential learning used simulations of real projects and of real working conditions, and built in the concepts and skills which students were not gaining from their postgraduate training but were needed in applied work.[8]

## ASA Cambridge Decennial Conference and Grillo Report

Whilst the GAPP activists engaged in a flurry of workshops, training events and newsletters, progress on the RAI/ASA Joint Committee slowed down. Grillo had become one of the organisers of the ASA Decennial conference on 4–8 July 1983 at Cambridge, entitled 'Anthropology in the 80s'. It was attended by 200 people including, for the first time, people like myself, who were ineligible for ASA membership and were working in applied fields.

> The programme and the atmosphere differed markedly from the second decennial conference held at Oxford. In 1973 the mood was one of optimism, of expansion and 'new directions' in anthropological creativity; in 1983 there was no more expansion (at least within the Academy) and optimism had

been replaced by sober realism and intellectual consolidation, a concern to apply anthropology to policy research fields, and for the employment prospects of young graduates. These themes dominated the entire meeting. (ASA Annals 1983: 17)

A substantial part of the programme concerned anthropology and policy with sessions on the politics of anthropological advice, social factors in rural policy, social anthropologists as policy professionals, and issues in industrial societies. It was a major achievement to hold such a conference, especially as an ASA Decennial.

A second major achievement was the ASA Annual Business Meeting where it was agreed to change the membership rules. The ASA committee convened a meeting of postgraduates at the conference and reported to the Annual Business Meeting that graduates felt strongly 'that academic and applied anthropologists needed to be kept together as a single discipline' (ASA Annals 1983: 10). This meant making intellectual connections between the work of practising and academic anthropologists; it also meant including both wings in one professional organisation. A survey of members had yielded 100 responses overwhelmingly in favour of a change to the membership rules. The minutes record a 'lively discussion' and a feeling that the association would lose much of its character if it were to be swamped by a large number of new members as a result of changes in the rules. Nevertheless, the changes were agreed 'provisionally and in principle'. Henceforth, anthropologists with doctorates or substantial publications could be considered for membership not only if they held a university post, but also if they 'held a non-academic employment utilising his or her training in anthropology' or were 'unavoidably unemployed'. In practice, as I found later when I was on the ASA committee, each non-academic case had to be fought hard for and the way the rules were applied, and therefore the composition of the membership, did not change greatly.

Despite these changes, graduate students expressed frustration at the lack of progress. The Young Turks, and especially Grillo, had not only run the conference but been involved in the response to the Rothschild Commission, and in surveying the impact of the UGC cuts on departments. It looked as if the work of the joint committee had stalled. Stirling proposed to the ASA's Annual Business Meeting the establishment of an 'Action Committee' to investigate:

1. Ways to improve employment prospects in applied and policy-related fields and in general outside academic departments.
2. Ways of improving the public image of anthropology among potential employers.
3. Ways for departments and applied anthropologists to cooperate, and an institutional framework to encourage interaction.
4. Problems connected with teaching and training in applied anthropology, e.g. syllabus design. (ASA Annals 1983: 9)

The Action Committee was to be set up by the ASA but to include representatives from the RAI and GAPP. It was to report to the Heads of Departments meeting in the autumn of 1983. The regulation of professional and ethical standards was deemed too complex a matter for the Action Committee and was to be considered by the ASA main committee. In effect this revived the Joint Committee chaired by Grillo, now renamed the 'Action Committee for Employment and Training in Applied Anthropology'. It made an interim report in autumn 1983 after which it was reconstituted as a Working Party, [10] funded by the Nuffield Foundation, and finally published its report (known as the Grillo Report) in July 1984. Four of its six conclusions and recommendations were:

1. 'Existing graduate and undergraduate courses are largely based on a traditional view of the professional anthropologist as an academic researcher, and do not provide adequate training for the new fields which anthropologists must enter' (Grillo 1984: 2). Graduate training needs to include:
   (a) Background knowledge on contemporary society and international organisations.
   (b) Theoretical and practical grasp of bureaucratic processes, decision making and policy making.
   (c) Work skills, working to a brief, managing time, and giving professional advice.
   (d) Team work, including multidisciplinary teamwork.
   (e) Ethical and professional responsibilities.
   (f) Understanding when to use a range of research methods including surveys and quantitative methods.

2. There is a backlog of doctoral students who are overqualified but poorly prepared for employment and are in urgent need of training in skills for non-academic work. The appendices included draft curricula for 'remedial' training which could be either one course or separate events:
   (a) A five-day residential 'Vocational Practice in Anthropology' course for which ASA-RAI-GAPP should take responsibility. Based on the GAPP model, this would involve four case studies and 20–30 students.
   (b) Training in research methods and computing.
   (c) How to write a job application and cv, and prepare for an interview.
   (d) Work skills, team work, professional responsibilities.

3. New Vocational Masters courses should become a necessary and sufficient condition for entry into employment, and should replace the view 'of the Ph.D. as the anthropologist's trade union ticket' (ibid.). They should include courses on organisations, have a strong method-

ological focus, and make use of projects, placements and practica. To enhance graduates' prospects, senior members of the profession should be more actively involved in policy research (ibid.: 13).

4. To overcome the shortage of U.K. academics with the knowledge and experience to provide this innovative training, there should be greater use of those with expertise outside the academy.

The report had two main results. First, there was an efflorescence of specialist Masters courses over the next decade in areas of applied anthropology e.g. medical anthropology, development, environment, childhood, visual anthropology. When I reviewed these courses in 1996,[11] it was clear that, while of a high academic standard, many engaged principally with the academic literature; very few investigated how organisations and policy making in their specialist field worked, or considered the professional and ethical responsibilities of working in these contexts. Apart from for recruitment purposes, few departments had built links with relevant government and not-for-profit organisations in their area, or used professionals from the relevant field in their teaching. A very few included projects and placements. The full import of the Grillo Report for Masters level teaching was very rarely realised.

The second result was that Adrian Collett (Graduate student at SOAS) made a successful application on behalf of GAPP to SSRC for £10,000 and the first week-long residential vocational practice course was held in 1985. Designing the curriculum, working with practitioners to prepare the case studies, and publicising and arranging the event was a major enterprise for GAPP's volunteer activists. It replaced the weekend workshops which ceased thereafter. The Grillo Report aimed for the ASA and RAI also to be responsible for the course but 'little further mention is made of the course in ASA committee meetings during the remainder of the 1980s' (Mills personal communication). By 1986, according to Mills, the ASA 'committee that had been so active in the early 1980s had been completely replaced and vocational and employment issues appeared no longer to be a key concern of the ASA' (ibid.).

## GAPP and Anthropology in Action

By the mid-1980s, the activists who ran GAPP were also exhausted. Stirling was away doing fieldwork in Turkey for two years. Peter Loizos (LSE) chaired for a year whilst the committee trawled for a new chair. They wanted a senior academic who had the gravitas to pursue GAPP's agenda with the ASA and RAI and stand up to any complacent diehards. In the end the committee admitted failure. They agreed to Sarah Ladbury using the remainder of GAPP's resources to hold a conference called 'Society and Information Technology' in June 1987 at UCL. If all else failed, this would

be a major event on which to end GAPP. Optimally, out of the junior lecturers she involved as speakers and chairs, they would find someone who
had, if not the gravitas, then the energy and commitment to keep GAPP
going. I had learnt so much from GAPP about policy research, methodology and pedagogy, that, now I was a newly appointed lecturer at Sussex,
I agreed to become Convenor in 1987. I reassembled the GAPP committee,
with a core membership, but holding open meetings. Many long established GAPP activists lent us their experience and, as a programme of
events got underway, many new lecturers, practitioners and students
became actively involved (Wright 1988).

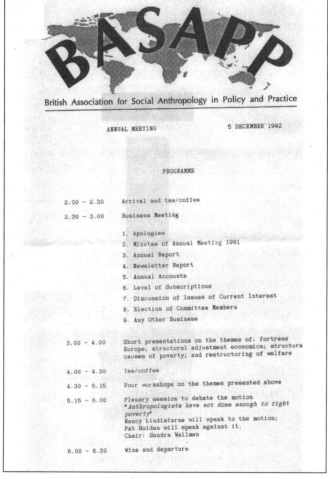

**Figure 1.1** BASAPP activities: agenda of the Annual meeting 1992

During the 1980s, several other small applied anthropology organisations had been set up in Britain. Lloyd's Social Anthropology and Social Work (SASCW), was convening meetings between researchers, students and social work professionals on social work practice, care for the elderly, and the transfer of patients from mental hospitals to community hostels. Brian Street and Oonagh O'Brien had set up Anthropology Training and Education (ATE) which was mainly concerned with anthropology teaching in schools and in access courses. A large and active British Medical Anthropology Society had been founded in 1976 and a smaller group on nursing was created in the 1980s. Lloyd had written to the ASA committee in 1986, suggesting that the ASA play a role in trying to bring these organisations together to consolidate and better disseminate their activities. This would also have had the benefit of reconnecting the academic and practising wings of the discipline. The ASA replied 'it would be unwise for the ASA to be seen as taking over above the heads of other organisations' (Mills personal communication). Stirling, Lloyd and I then made a successful application to the Wenner-Gren Foundation for a grant to create an umbrella organisation for applied anthropology in Britain (Lloyd 1988). Each group would retain its own identity and programme of activities but we would share a part-time administrator to streamline membership administration and publish a joint journal. GAPP, SASCW and ATE agreed to combine into the British Association for Social Anthropology in Policy and Practice (BASAPP) which was renamed, as soon as possible, Anthropology in Action (AinA) – still avoiding the term 'applied'. BASAPP was launched at the LSE on 3 December 1988 with mini case studies to engage participants in anthropological takes on issues of current policy interest (*BASAPP News* 1989) (Figure 1.1).

Each subsequent annual meeting was organised as a small conference reflecting on current policy issues. There was a smooth transition to new convenors, from myself as first convenor to Jean Collins in 1990, Oonagh O'Brien in 1992 and J.J. O'Connor in 1994. AinA moved to a base in Hull under the auspices of Allison James in 1997, with first herself, and then in 1998, Simone Abrams (Swansea) as convenor.

GAPP's cyclostyled newsletter, which had been produced 3–4 times a year since 1981, was transformed into *BASAPP News*, which kept the readability and 'feel' of a newsletter combined with reports on events and academic articles on a particular theme (Figure 1.2).

**Figure 1.2** BASAPP Newsletter: booklet format with reports of events and short articles (1988–1993)

Lloyd was the first editor, followed by Cris Shore (Goldsmiths) (1991–1994) who ran a competition leading to the new name, Anthropology in Action, and who raised the standard from that of a newsletter to an academic journal.[12] The journal was a means of communicating among the membership, a teaching resource for lecturers and a source of research ideas and contacts for students.

Meanwhile, as Convenor of GAPP, my first step was to write an article with Stirling (1988) reviewing the reasons why GAPP had emerged and defining its three aims:

1. Networking among anthropologists working in policy and practice, and linking them to the next generation of students.
2. Linking practising and academic anthropologists and creating a 'feed-back' loop from practising to academic anthropology by identifying issues arising from work in policy and practice which had a

bearing on central theoretical concerns of the discipline and were ripe for research.

3. Identifying the skills anthropologists have, and the additional ones they need, to work in policy and practice; holding workshops for staff and students to discuss aspects of undergraduate education; running training courses for research students to equip them to work in policy and practice.

The next step was to ensure there was an annual programme of activities which reflected those three aims.

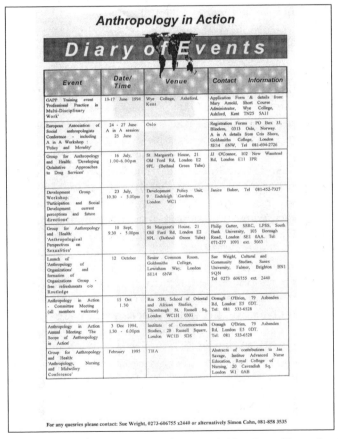

Figure 1.3 Anthropology in Action's activities, June–December 1994

## Networking

In 1984 GAPP had held a series of evening talks for students by practising anthropologists on such topics as 'anthropology and the media' and 'anthropology of large corporations'. Each anthropologist described the work they did, how her or his career had developed, the use they made of their anthropology, and the other skills they needed in their work. This proved a valuable way for students to gain insight into a field of work, and to gain a contact with practitioners. Nici Nelson (Goldsmiths College) revived this idea as GAPP Talks. The first, by an anthropologist who trained VSO volunteers, in November 1987, was followed by a vast array of anthropologists working in business and management, in international development, in international agencies, in all aspects of the welfare state, in conflict resolution, therapy, the media and film. Nelson organised monthly GAPP Talks through term time in London, continuously for approximately the next ten years.[13]

Other events brought together people who worked in the same field and addressed new or emerging policy issues. Nelson and Baker's (ITDG) workshops examined the burgeoning ideas and techniques about 'participation' in international development. Workshops organised by Mark O'Sullivan (civil servant) and I explored the use of 'culture' in organisational management. Oonagh O'Brien, Angie Hart, and Phil Gatter held a conference 'HIV and AIDS in Europe – The Challenge for Anthropology', followed by further events on drug treatment and on sexualities. Later, attention was given to forms of anthropological representation in newspapers and books, using the internet, photography and other art forms: indeed the 1996 annual meeting was called 'Poetry 'n Performance'.

Wherever possible, GAPP held sessions at anthropology conferences. At the SfAA conference which came to York in 1990, British anthropologists organised a 'shop window' of current activities, with eight sessions on ethnicity in schooling, indigenous rights, planned organisational change, community care of the elderly, social work, tourism, communication of anthropological knowledge, and training for applied anthropology (*BASAPP News* 1990). A whole day of sessions on 'Anthropological knowledge in policy and practice' attracted large audiences at the ASA Decennial Conference at Oxford in 1993. At the 1994 EASA conference at Oslo, a session 'Policy and morality' held a packed audience and resulted in a book in the EASA series (see below).

## Conferences and Publications

As well as producing issues of the journal on the above themes, it became clear that on some current policy issues, practitioners and researchers were generating information and insights that opened up a new field of anthropological interest or could make a contribution to core concerns of the discipline. On these issues GAPP organised academic-style conferences with the aim of producing edited volumes for an intended audience of lecturers and students in 'mainstream' anthropology programmes, as well as practitioners and researchers.

The first conference was organised by Tom Selwyn (Roehampton Institute) on the Anthropology of Tourism (Selwyn 1988). Concerned with commodification of culture, heritage, nationalism, sex tourism and third world tourism, it brought together academic anthropologists, non-government agencies concerned with the effects of tourism, and policy makers. This conference resulted in a new MA in anthropology of tourism at Roehampton. In 1990, David Marsden, O'Sullivan and I organised a conference, 'Anthropology of Organisations' at the University of Swansea, which resulted in the book *Anthropology of Organizations* (Wright 1994). The 1992 conference, 'Power and Participatory Development' attracted 200 practitioners, policy makers and researchers and resulted in a book with the same title (Nelson and Wright 1995). The session at the 1994 Oslo EASA conference resulted in *Anthropology of Policy* (Shore and Wright 1997). SASCW's work on anthropology and social work inspired further volumes (e.g. Edgar and Russell 1998).

## Training

GAPP revived the ESRC-funded, week-long Vocational Practice Course in 1989 and appointed Mascarenhas-Keyes as Course Director (Lowe 1989). She has run the annual GAPP training course ever since, moving it under the umbrella of the ASA when GAPP eventually came to an end.[14] The courses cater for 20–30 students and continue to use an experiential learning approach, based on new case studies each year addressing current policy issues. They continue to be designed and facilitated by a practising anthropologist, with non-anthropologists from relevant agencies invited to receive and respond to the students' presentations. Some years the course has been interdisciplinary or focused on methodology; and always it covers team working, professional responsibility, and organisational analysis. It has therefore been sustaining the agenda identified by the early GAPP courses, and highlighted by the Grillo report.

GAPP courses were intended to become redundant as departments picked up ideas from them, responded to the Grillo agenda, and developed their own competence in teaching policy and professional practice. To this end, practising anthropologists who had developed case studies for the GAPP course, or for the modules on organisational analysis, methodology, or professional practice contributed to the GAPP Training Manual (Mascarenhas-Keyes 1997). Although departments began to offer courses with more systematic approaches to research design and methods, due to ESRC requirements, continuing student demand for the GAPP course, and their response to it, indicated that most university departments were still providing a very 'academic' training. For those students interested in employment outside the academy, the course often provided their only experience of using their anthropology in practical contexts, or was an important supplement to their research training.

GAPP also ran occasional courses funded by the Overseas Development Agency (ODA, later DfID). The social dimensions of development gained increasing recognition in ODA in the late 1980s, the number of social advisers grew apace and, for a time, social analysis began slightly to unsettle the hegemonic hold of economic paradigms in ODA. ODA had its own network of consultants, but also funded GAPP to bring together practitioners and researchers who could reflect critically on their 'inside' experience of developing or implementing the new approaches or methods of project management. In 'Tools of the Trade' in 1992, experienced anthropology consultants and academics used case studies based on ODA projects to generate an accurate yet succinct language for ODA to describe anthropological approaches and methods. Nelson organised Training Workshops in 1992 on 'Participatory Research Techniques', in 1995 on 'Skills for Professional Practice' concerning 'poverty assessments' and 'logical frameworks' and in 1997–8 on 'Gender Issues in Development Practice'.

A third strand of educational activity was to open up debates about undergraduate teaching. A workshop 'The Practical Relevance of Undergraduate Anthropology' in 1989 attended by academics and recent graduates pursuing careers in advertising, youth work, mental health and primary school teaching, discussed whether undergraduates should be encouraged to engage in critical enquiry about current social issues, for example through projects (Sharma and Wright 1989). Ingold (1989) counter-posed that undergraduates should concentrate on theories and ethnographic texts as the principal 'means by which we come to know [the real world]' – undergraduates should not engage in experiential learning and fieldwork should be reserved for postgraduates. This set up a debate (Sharma 1989, 1991, Hanley 1989) and further events were held at Bristol, exchanging new ideas in undergraduate teaching (Thorne and Wright 1990, *BASAPP News* 1991). In particular Richard Thorne (UWE) demonstrated the kind of critical inquiry generated by teaching undergraduates via the use of visual and audio technologies. It was clear through these workshops that a small number of lecturers were exploring how to encourage undergraduates to use anthropology in critical analysis of social issues, and were questioning their teaching practices and the ideas and values underpinning them. This was at a time when higher education policy was itself the subject of debate and reform in the UK. Ultimately reflexive, we found ourselves doing an anthropology of our practice and of the changing policy context for university teaching. I obtained DfES funding to do a review of undergraduate anthropology teaching in the UK, with Mascarenhas-Keyes as researcher (Mascarenhas-Keyes with Wright 1995). This generated ideas for a National Network for Teaching and Learning Anthropology, a consortium of all U.K. anthropology departments, and a development programme which funded projects in ten departments one year and funded visits between departments to exchange ideas the next. Again, the aim was to create networks of practitioners and mechanisms for debating and exchanging ideas about our practice.[15]

## Conclusion

Through the late 1980s and 1990s anthropology, such a small discipline, supported three organisations. The RAI and AinA kept quite separate but there was a good working relationship. The RAI often gave GAPP small grants for events, and the two journals, *Anthropology Today* and *AinA*, both improved in quality without friction (Figure 1.4).

There was more tension in relations with the ASA. Lloyd's suggestion that the ASA, as the professional association, should try to bring the aca-

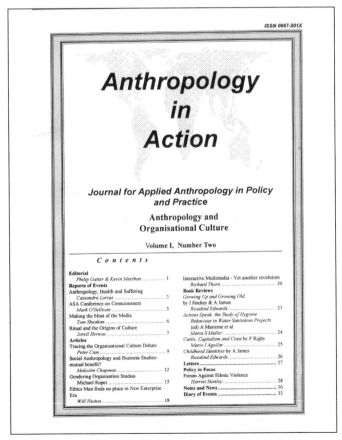

**Figure 1.4** *Anthropology in Action:* journal format with themed articles (1994–present)

demic and practising wings of the discipline together under its auspices, was rejected outright. This heralded a period when the ASA, crisis over, returned to a narrow definition of academic anthropology. The Research Assessment Exercise, whose results largely determined each department's income, focused academics' attention on 'mainstream' research. Although some people who had been active in GAPP gained academic posts in the late 1980s and carried GAPP's concerns and experience into their teaching and research, for the most part, GAPP's agenda was an unwelcome distraction from departments' core concern. GAPP's focus on postgraduate training coincided with the ESRC's training guidelines which, while echoing many of the recommendation in the Grillo Report, were often regarded as an imposition. GAPP's discussion of undergraduate teaching unfortunately coincided with the Quality Assurance Agency's (QAA) focussing academics' attention on an onerous and exhausting audit system. Each year, the AinA convenor made a report to the ASA/RAI Heads of Depart-

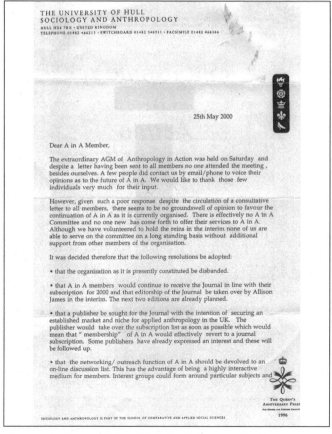

**Figure 1.5a** Letter disbanding AinA as a membership organisation with a programme of activities, May 2000 (p. 1)

ments meeting which was published in the Annals. Reminders of the existence of GAPP and AinA were met mainly with indifference, and occasionally outright hostility.[16] When I was invited onto the ASA committee (1990–4) to make closer links between the two organisations, it was at a stage when, despite a number of pressing policy issues, the ASA was quite inactive. The Heads of Departments stopped the annual meetings and set up an email network. It was the QAA's decision in 1988 not to include anthropology in its list of 42 disciplines but to subsume it within Sociology that prompted the anthropology organisations to form a Coordinating Committee (QAA 1998).[17] For two years we worked closely together to deal with this and four other major policy issues and consultations that affected the future of the discipline. However, by then AinA had ceased itself to have an active programme of events and AinA was disbanded as a membership organisation in 2000 (James et al. 2000) (Figure 1.5).

conferences , workshops organised by members. The on-line list would also ensure a  broader  and more  up to date circulation of events and activities of interest to anthropologists both within and outwith the  academy.   Denise Argent  has volunteered to set this up and to  manage the list. All A in A members should send their  email addresses to Denise if they wish to participate in this group (denise.argent@dtn.ntl.com)

• the Journal would have a regular reporting section on any interesting developments from the on-line discussion list.

• that  the suggestion made by Pat Caplan for closer links  with the ASA be followed up, possibly with the journal editor/ on -line list manager  being regarded as representative for ASA  of applied anthropology  in the UK.

•that until such time as the membership subscription  is taken over by a publisher that a new part-time administrator  be employed  to keep the data base up to date.

• that  A in A finances be managed in the interim by  Oriana de Suza  - a previous treasurer - who has kindly offered  to step into the breach.

These plans seem to be the only viable way to maintain the interest of applied anthropology in the UK  for those  inside and outside the academy, given that there appear to be no willing volunteers to  continue with A in A as it has been organised to date. This letter, therefore, is by way of a final consultation with A in A members and we  will proceed with the steps outlined above unless there is a groundswell of opinion to do otherwise.

With best wishes

Allison James (Acting Editor )  A.James@cas.hull.ac.uk)
Mark Johnson ( j.m.johnson@cas.hull.ac.uk)
Sally McNamee (s.a.mcnamee@cas.hull.ac.uk)
Denise Argent ( denise.argent@dtn.ntl.com)

**Figure 1.5b** Letter disbanding AinA as a membership organisation with a programme of activities, May 2000 (p. 2)

During the period when AinA was very active, with networks and events on international development, organisations, tourism, health and social services, there was very little contact with academic anthropologists who were not themselves AinA activists. AinA networked amongst practitioners and researchers in areas of policy and practice and linked them to students (aim 1, above); AinA also did a great deal to help students identify and express the skills that anthropology gave them, and acquire the additional ones they needed to work in policy and practice (aim 3); but AinA was not able to develop 'feedback loops' from practising to academic anthropology to maximum effect (aim 2). The conceptualisation of the discipline as 'pure' and 'applied' remained dominant. According to this way of thinking, pure anthropology would remain unchanged if graduates added a few skills to their repertoire and departed into applied work and were 'no longer' anthropologists. Instead of 'pure' anthropology bounding itself against the 'pollution' of practice, the alternative vision held by graduates at the 1983 ASA Decennial and by GAPP was of two wings of the discipline benefiting from each other. In particular, practising anthropologists' insights into changes in contemporary society, that they gained from their work in policy and practice, were a valuable resource for academic anthropologists to use in their research and teaching. In their daily work, practising anthropologists were encountering contestations over discourses and metaphors of sociality in the U.K. – individual versus community, market versus society, enterprise versus public service. How could practitioners (me included)[18] use our anthropology to understand these new concepts of governance and forms of power: not understanding the terms in use made us feel unsure about what agendas we were feeding into when writing policy recommendations. What was meant by the much vaunted 'empowerment'? For example, if residents of a council estate were invited to become self-managing tenants, or if marginalised poor people were invited to participate in international development projects, how did new liberal forms of power work in practice? What ideas could be drawn from anthropology to understand these forms of social organisation in relation to a changing constitution of the state? (Wright 1995a, Shore and Wright 1995, 1996, 1997b). These were core issues in anthropology – language, symbolism and power. Practising anthropologists were not only seeking to draw on theory to apply in practice but their practice was a site for generating anthropological problems that needed research and theoretical elaboration. If the pure and applied agendas had been better integrated, students might have been better able to engage critically with social issues 'on their doorstep' in the process of developing anthropological knowledge and imagination, instead of trying to work out how to 'apply' anthropology at the end of their degree. But, with a very few exceptions, university departments seemed not to develop ways of sustaining relationships with alumni, or build up relationships with anthropologists in their region who were working in policy and practice, such that they could engage in discussions over research, contribute to teaching, provide placements, or link students into networks through which to find employment opportunities.

If these weaknesses existed at the height of GAPP's and AinA's activity, what now? Are the paths that GAPP cut into the jungle growing over again? When students now get jobs in policy or practice, do they disappear from view? How do they find the previous generation of anthropologists who made inroads into different areas of employment and could help and advise them? How do practising anthropologists who are working in similar fields network with each other to exchange ideas and experiences? Do they have opportunities to explore with each other and with academic colleagues the questions that, as anthropologists, they ask of their everyday locations within changing systems of economic organisation and governance? How do anthropologists use their critical analysis of social and power relations in the more commercial environment in which many are working? In the 1980s anthropology graduates found 'safe' spaces in the public sector where they could analyse embedded systems of inequality and contribute critically and effectively through policy processes. The last 20 years has seen a major transformation of the state. Many functions have been privatised or reformed to run on a quasi-commercial basis. Some service sectors, creative industries, and marketing agencies seek employees who will critique their organisation's social constructions and representations and their own operations, and propose new ideas – but within limits that do not question basic rationalities of governance. How do courses in anthropology and other critical disciplines (O'Shea 2004) equip graduates to be 'critical citizens' in such a corporate world?

The establishment in 2004 of a practising anthropologists network under the auspices of the ASA is good news indeed. This is surely the best institutional location. It promises to be an important forum for practising anthropologists and a means for students to gain insights into anthropology in action in different sectors. But for ASA and other anthropology organisations to make practising anthropology fully a wing of the discipline (a wing in the sense that it is an indispensable part, without which it would fly round in circles – rather than an arm, which can be kept out on a limb and can wither again in time) it is equally important for practising anthropologists to be involved in their local departments, and for their insights into changes in contemporary societies to be drawn upon in debates about teaching  and incorporated into research. From GAPP's experience, the biggest challenge will be to overcome the vestiges of the pure/applied divide, and encourage both wings of the discipline to engage in analysis of contemporary social change, using insights from academic debate and from policy and practice to mutual benefit.

# Notes

1. I use this term in its complimentary meaning of a progressive force within an organisation (*Collins Concise English Dictionary* 1992: 1575).
2. David Mills has very kindly shown me the results of his research on the ASA archives during this period.
3. Some informants say Grillo drafted the submission to the Rothschild Commission. The ASA Annals attribute the successful portrayal of anthropology in the Rothschild Report to the evidence of Leach (ASA Annals 1983: 4).
4. Stirling set up SA4 with three other partners (Oxford-based anthropologists Jane Khatib Chahidi and Soraya Tremayne, and development consultant Michael Gillibrand).
5. The original name was also rejected because its acronym, AAG! sounds like a cry of despair or demise.
6. Academics on the GAPP committee were Stirling (Kent), Wallman (LSE), Eric Hanley (Edinburgh). Practising anthropologists were Sarah Ladbury a training consultant, Conlin, by now working for ODA, and Gill Shepherd, an overseas development consultant. They took on the regular tasks: Stirling was Chair, Wallman was Treasurer, Conlin set up a two-monthly newsletter and Hanley compiled a register of members with their experience and interests.
7. Details about the programme and speakers for this and all subsequent events have been compiled from Stirling's and Wright's archives and are in progress for publication on the ASA Applied Anthropology Network website at http://www.theasa.org/applications/index.htm, accessed 31 August 2004.
8. The first GAPP training event, on 29 October 1983 at SOAS was attended by 50 students, 6 departmental representatives, 4 representatives of agencies, and 6 GAPP facilitators (Conlin and Mascarenhas-Keyes 1983). Further events were held later in 1983 at Manchester, 17 March 1984 at Goldsmiths, 10 November 1984 at Cardiff, and 9 February 1985 at Goldsmiths and with each event, the method was refined and the repertoire of case studies extended.
9. The membership of the final working party consisted of the four original members of the Action Committee, nominees of ASA, RAI and GAPP, and coopted experts. Its personnel was Anne Akeroyd (York), Raymond Apthorpe (ISS, The Hague), Lorraine Baric (Salford), Sean Conlin (ODA), David Butcher (ODA), Yvonne Dhooge (Health Education Council), Ralph Grillo (Sussex), Eric Hanley (Edinburgh), Margaret Hardiman (LSE and RAI nominee), Sarah Ladbury (Adult Education), Carol MacCormack (Ross Institute), Gillian Shepherd (Consultant, ASA representative), and Sandra Wallman (LSE).
10. I did this as a member of the ESRC Training Board (1994–6) and Chair of the ESRC's Advanced Courses Recognition Panel for Anthropology.
11. The next editor, Delphine Houlton (journalist and Sussex graduate) sustained the standard of an academic journal. In 1998 she handed on the editorship to Sally McNamee in Hull, and in 2001 the current editor, Jonathan Skinner (Belfast) took over.
12. From time to time, GAPP members in the north of England and Scotland set up regional networks to link together practitioners and students. In 1988 Sarah Southwold (Manchester) launched a short-lived Northern GAPP with a conference 'Ethnography of the Northwest', a directory with members interests, and a report (Southwold 1988) and Ken Hahlo organised events in 1989. A decade later, Edinburgh became a focus for regional networking when Joan Stead and Robert Gibb organised a conference 'Anthropologists in Action: Public Image and Personal Experience'.
13. Each year, the ESRC application was successful, but only with great effort and uncertainty until the last minute. Eventually I persuaded the ESRC to include the Vocational Practice Course in its list of annual training courses, so that a £10,000 budget was available each year.
14. The National Network's participatory methodology and discipline-specific approach to educational development became the basis for a bid for the national Subject Centre for Learning and Teaching in Sociology, Anthropology and Politics (C-SAP) which I directed (2000–2003).

15. For example, at the ASA's 1989 annual conference, in his after dinner speech the chair, Peter Riviere, gave a long exposition of the Trio concept of *hata* which means 'so what! I don't care, they're responsible for themselves, it's up to them'. He recounted how one man hung some bananas over another man's hammock. When the latter returned, he found the bananas had rotted and were dripping into his hammock. He remonstrated with the owner of the bananas who said 'bananas-hata' – I'm not responsible for what bananas chose to do, it's up to them. This lead Riviere to the climax of his speech which was to pronounce 'GAPP-hata'.

16. By this time there were five anthropology organisations: ASA, RAI, AinA, SCHAD (Standing Conference of Heads of Anthropology Departments), NNTLA (National Network for Teaching and Learning Anthropology) and physical anthropology.

17. For example in 1991 I was seconded from Sussex University for 12 months to a local authority to make an ethnographic evaluation of their corporate anti-poverty and empowerment strategy.

# References

Akeroyd, A. 1983. 'Applied Anthropology Training Programmes in the United States'. *Annals of the Association of Social Anthropologists of the Commonwealth, 4* (also in Stirling archive).

ASA (Association of Social Anthropologists). 1983. *Annals of the Association of Social Anthropologists of the Commonwealth, 4.*

*BASAPP News.* 1989. 'The Launch – Workshop Reports', 2: 2–6.

———. 1990. 'Reports of Events at SfAA Annual Meeting', 6 (summer): 1–11.

———. 1991. 'One Day Conference on Projects/Placements', 10 (autumn): 19.

Conlin, S. and S. Mascarenhas-Keyes. 1983. 'Report on GAPP Workshop to ASA Heads of Departments Meetings', 11 November (Stirling archive).

Eades, J. 1981. 'Society for Applied Anthropology, 41st Annual Meeting, "Rethinking Applied Anthropology"'. *Royal Anthropological Institute News,* 44 (June): 10–11.

Edgar, I. and A. Russell. 1998. *The Anthropology of Welfare.* London: Routledge.

Gowler, D. and G. Clarke. 1982. 'The Employment and Training of British Social Anthropologists', Report for the Social Science Research Council. Oxford: Oxford Centre for Management Studies (Stirling archive).

Grillo, R. 1984. 'Working Party Report on Training for Applied Anthropology', Association of Social Anthropologists of the Commonwealth.

Hanley, E. 1989. 'Undergraduate Anthropology Projects at Edinburgh'. *BASAPP News,* 3 (summer): 4.

Ingold, T. 1989. 'Fieldwork in Undergraduate Anthropology: an Opposing View'. *BASAPP News* 3 (summer): 2–3.

James, A., M. Johnson, S. McNamee, and D. Argent. 2000. Letter to members of AinA, 25 May (Wright archive).

Lloyd, P. 1988. 'Birth of BASAPP'. *BASAPP News,* 1: 1.

Lowe, R. 1989. 'Vocational Practice in Anthropology'. *BASAPP News,* 2 (spring): 10–11.

Mascarenhas-Keyes, S. 1983. 'The Employment of Social Anthropologists. Report on Proceedings of a One Day Forum, 22 January'. Report to Nuffield Foundation (Stirling archive).

———. 1989. 'GAPP Vocational Training for Anthropologists'. *BASAPP News,* 2: 8–9.

———. 1997. *Professional Practice in Anthropology: a Resource Manual for University Teachers. (The GAPP manual).* National Network for Teaching and Learning.

——— with S. Wright. 1995. *Report on Teaching and Learning Social Anthropology in the United Kingdom.* National Network for Teaching and Learning Anthropology.

Mills, D. 2003. 'Quantifying the Discipline: Some Anthropology Statistics from the UK'. *Anthropology Today,* 19(3): 19–22.

Morris, L. and P. Stirling. 1982. 'People, Trouble and the State', Report for the SSRC's Social Anthropology Committee (Stirling archive).

Nelson, N. and S. Wright. (eds). 1995. *Power and Participatory Development: Theory and Practice.* London: Intermediate Technology.

O'Shea, A. 2004. 'Teaching "Critical Citizenship" in an Age of Hedonistic Vocationalism'. *LATISS – Learning and Teaching in the Social Sciences,* 1(2): 95–106.

QAA (Quality Assurance Agency). 1998. 'An Agenda for Quality'. *Higher Quality,* 1(3): 22 (Annex 8).

*RAIN (Royal Anthropological Institute Newsletter).* 1981. 'AAG', 44 (June): 15.

———. 1980. 'The Training and Employment of Social Anthropologists', 41 (December): 5–7.

Selwyn, T. 1988. 'Anthropology of Tourism: Conference Report'. *BASAPP News,* 1: 9–10.

Sharma, U. 1989. 'Fieldwork in Undergraduate Anthropology: its Merits'. *BASAPP News,* 3 (summer): 3–4.

———. 1991. 'Field Research in the Undergraduate Curriculum'. *BASAPP News,* 10 (autumn): 8–11.

——— and S. Wright. 1989. 'Practical Relevance of Undergraduate Courses'. *BASAPP News,* 2 (spring): 7–8.

Shore, C. and S. Wright. 1995. 'Towards an Anthropology of Policy: Morality, Power and the Art of Government'. *Anthropology in Action,* 2(2): 27–31.

——— and S. Wright. 1996. 'British Anthropology in Policy and Practice: a Review of Current Work'. *Human Organization,* 55(4): 475–481.

——— and S. Wright. 1997. 'Colonial Gaze to Critique of Policy: British Anthropology in Policy and Practice', in M. Baba and C. Hill (eds) *The Global Practice of Anthropology.* Williamsberg VA: College of William and Mary Press.

——— and S. Wright. 1997. *Anthropology of Policy: Critical Perspectives on Governance and Power.* EASA Series, London: Routledge.

Southwold, S. 1988. 'Ethnography of the North West: Anthropology in Policy and Practice'. Report of conference held at Manchester, 16 January (Wright archive).

Stirling, P. 1981. 'The AAG, Social Reality and Getting What Things Done?' 23 October (Wright archive).

——— and S. Wright. 1988. 'Past, Present and Future. Group for Anthropology in Policy and Practice'. *BASAPP News,* 1: 2–5.

Thorn, R. and S. Wright. 1990. 'Projects and Placements in Undergraduate Anthropology'. *BASAPP News,* 7 (autumn): 4–5.

Wright, S. 1982. 'Impressions of a Simulated Consultancy Workshop'. *GAPP News,* 3: 1.

———. 1984. 'Rural Communities and Decision Makers'. *Royal Anthropological Institute News,* 63: 9–13.

———. 1988. 'Group for Anthropology in Policy and Practice'. *BASAPP Newsletter,* 1: 2–5.

——— (ed.). 1994. *Anthropology of Organizations.* London: Routledge.

———. 1995. 'Anthropology: Still the "Uncomfortable" Discipline?', in C. Shore and A. Ahmed (eds) *The Future of Anthropology: Its Relevance to the Contemporary World:* pp. 65–93. London: Athlone Press.

———. 1995. 'Future Goals for Anthropology in Action'. *Anthropology in Action,* 2(1): 27–28.

*Chapter 2*

# DINNER AT CLARIDGES?
Anthropology and the 'Captains of Industry', 1947–1955

*David Mills*

## Introduction

The brief love affair between social anthropology and the 'captains' (all-male) of British industry in the years after the Second World War is one of the more glamorous chapters in the history of the discipline's application. Black tie soirees at Claridges are not an obvious anthropological haunt, but in what follows I tell the story of the prandial relationship between the Royal Anthropological Institute (RAI), Israel Sieff (co-founder of Marks and Spencer) and his friends. Sieff spent a great deal of time in the early 1950s wooing both academics and his business colleagues with his vision of anthropology's potential contributions to solving industrial welfare and personnel 'problems'. Misapprehensions about what the discipline could offer abounded, both amongst industrialists and anthropologists themselves. Ultimately little came of Sieff's efforts, save a number of grand repasts.

By the 1950s the nascent academic discipline of social anthropology had proved itself adept at gaining funding, both from independent foundations (such as the Rockefeller and Carnegie foundations) and the British Colonial Office. However, commercially sponsored research was of a different order, and anthropologists were suspicious about the motives of the companies concerned. In seeking to work with the RAI, Sieff challenged the professional 'comfort zone' that academic anthropologists, through the creation of the Association of Social Anthropologists in 1946, had established around the discipline. The new association was intended to represent the professional interests of academic social anthropologists, as opposed to the broader constituency of gentleman scholars, administrators, and enthusiastic amateurs that made up the Royal Anthropological

Institute. Sieff's vision for the RAI challenged the narrower scientific conception of the discipline espoused by Evans-Pritchard, Radcliffe-Brown and their colleagues.

## 'Plus ça change'?

Twenty years ago, the Association of Social Anthropologists held a decennial with the title 'Anthropology in the 1980s', of which one section was entitled 'Anthropology and Policy'. It had three sessions on 'The Politics of Anthropological Advice', Social Factors in Agricultural and Rural Policy', and 'Social Anthropologists as Policy Professionals'. This applied focus had partly been at the prompting of Sean Conlin, who worked with the ODA (Overseas Development Administration), and had proposed a few years earlier that future conferences 'take into account the particular problems and needs of those members working outside the academic sphere'. Raymond Firth, by then the grand old man of anthropology, was asked to comment on the proceedings. His conclusion? 'Déjà vu, deja connu, deja conçu' (Grillo 1985).

What did he mean? Had nothing changed over the 60 years in which Raymond Firth had been working as an anthropologist? To what extent does this book revisit a debate over the applications of the discipline that was thoroughly aired, if not hung out to dry, in the 1980s, or even the 1950s? On the contrary, I suggest that the relationship between theory and practice only makes sense within a particular institutional context. It is a debate one has to keep returning to. Looking historically at the changing relationship between the production and application of disciplinary knowledge reveals pivotal moments in the professionalisation of anthropology within British universities. By revisiting the debate, one best understands anthropology's contemporary relevance.

British anthropology's attitude towards its application can be characterised as one of serial ambivalence. There have been a number of attempts at different periods over the last 80 years to position the discipline as practically relevant, whether in the context of solving colonial 'social problems', or addressing late modern 'user needs'. Yet such strategies, at least since the war, have usually marched in consort with an affirmation of anthropology as primarily an academic and university-based project. Anthropology both depends on, and denies its utility. Part of the dynamic driving this strategic equivocation between 'pure and 'applied' has been the disciplinary aspiration to both gain funding for its students and their research projects, but also to ensure that the 'best' students are socialised as academic anthropologists and gain posts within U.K. universities.

The first part of the twentieth century saw repeated attempts by anthropologists and the Royal Anthropological Institute to convince the Imperial government that anthropology served a useful purpose and deserved funding. One could also argue that the relationship of anthropologists to colonial authorities can be analysed as part of a more general history of the applications of disciplinary skills and knowledge. In more recent years, the discipline, like the other social sciences, has continued to show its flexibility in adapting to the changing rhetoric and funding priorities of the SSRC and, since 1983, the ESRC. Throughout the century anthropologists relied on state funding to secure the discipline's future. What were the debates – both public and private –within anthropology over the potentials, and risks, of making it into a useful science? And what were the limits to the sorts of funding and support that were acceptable? This history reveals how anthropologists have successfully asserted their academic autonomy in the use of these funds.

First though, 'application' too is a concept in need of some history. In the first quarter of the century, early proselytisers like Malinowski made the case for anthropology's relevance and applicability. 'Application' had a very different meaning and resonance once anthropology's position was secure within British universities after the Second World War. It was only at this point that application could be seen as secondary and derivative to theorising. The primary focus on academic knowledge creation allowed anthropologists to distance their practice from that of colonial administrators and curious travellers, creating a disciplinary 'comfort zone' around their work. As Pels and Salemink point out, 'it is important to question the distinction between academic anthropology and other ethnographic practices and thereby to unsettle the comfortable boundary of professionalism that this distinction maintains around the former' (1999:1). This case study provides insight into how that boundary was mobilised and disputed.

## Dinner at Claridges?

Israel Sieff, born in 1880, grew up in the same street as Simon Marks, the son of the founder of the retailer Marks and Spencer. After making a loan to Simon and joining him on the company's board in 1915, they worked closely for the next 50 years to build the company from its Manchester roots to its place as one of the UK's most powerful retailers. He used his position as a public figure to great effect. Soon after its founding in 1931, he became involved in Political and Economic Planning (PEP), an independent think-tank promoting the science of 'national planning' as a solution to the economic and political crises of the time. It brought together an informal network of politicians, economists and journalists in working groups to develop practical strategies for tackling economic decline and mounting unemployment. Sieff co-authored an influential report on industry in 1932. As he later modestly recalled, his influence was in ensuring that the reports kept 'on a practical level' for 'theoretical and abstract approaches have always been above me' (Sieff, 1970: 172). After the war, its activities greatly expanded, and at the request of Sieff, a new PEP study group was launched to study human relations in industry. Networking and coalition-building were familiar territory for him, and with his amateur interest in anthropology (he was already a member of the RAI) he sought to involve the RAI in this new initiative. Over more than five years, Sieff devoted himself to build links between anthropology and industry, a project which involved wooing academics as much as his business colleagues.

The romance had actually been initiated by William Fagg, RAI secretary. In 1947 he approached Sir Robert Hyde, and asked him to come to speak to the RAI about the potential for 'co-operation' with industry. Hyde, born in 1878, had begun his working life as an ordained priest and warden of a Hoxton boys hostel, and his experiences led him to set up the national Boys Welfare Association in 1918. Campaigning for better working relationships between managers and employers, and in particular for the provision of basic workplace amenities like lavatories, canteens and changing room, Hyde's hands-on style was highly influential. The organisation grew into what subsequently became known as the Industrial Society (and is now called 'The Work Foundation'). By the late 1940s he had had a considerable impact on British industry and commerce, and his habit of visiting and spending time on factory shop floors made him sympathetic to an anthropological approach. After speaking warmly about the potential role of anthropology, he was made a member of the RAI council in 1945. He subsequently became a Vice-President of the RAI for a number of years, authoring a number of reviews and chairing the British Ethnography Committee in the 1950s.

A couple of years later, a similar approach by Lord Raglan (then RAI president) to Hyde's friend Israel Sieff, had a more tangible outcome. Sieff invited the RAI officers to talk over lunch about the needs of the organisation. Listening carefully, their account was enough to galvanise Sieff into action. He decided to host an informal dinner, in November 1951, bringing together the officers of the RAI and several committee members, including Meyer Fortes (then Editor of *Man*) and a number of Israel Sieff's friends and business contacts. Little is recorded of that evening's conversation, but it must have been a successful occasion, for soon after Israel Sieff's secretary sent a number of cheques from Sainsburys Ltd, Thomas de la Rue, Unilever, and Lotus to the RAI. One was a £1000 cheque Sieff forwarded from George Harris, Chair of Rowntrees, who noted 'how impressed he was by what he had heard at dinner', and in particular 'by the long and interesting discussion he had with Meyer Fortes'. According to Sieff, Harris had felt 'it would be an excellent idea if Fortes visit York and tell his colleagues there something about the work the Institute is doing', and Sieff promised to write directly to Fortes to suggest this. Sieff noted in general that his colleagues 'were much impressed with the great potential value of this work in relation to the major problems we are facing'. [1]

Buoyed by this initial response Sieff discussed with Lord Raglan the potential for formalising the link, and proposed the creation of a body entitled the 'Friends of the RAI'. Soon after Raglan sent out a formal invitation to members of the RAI Council to meet Sir Robert Hyde over dinner at Sieff's flat, and to 'discuss a number of interesting aspects of the industrial problems today in this country, in which he feels that we may be of valuable assistance to Industry in general, both in this country and in their activities overseas'. Again, the response was warmly positive, and the 'Friends of the RAI' were formally recognised at the next council meeting. At the Council meeting the following summer, the RAI also formed a liaison committee to work with the 'Friends', made up of twelve members, including Hyde, Sieff, and Webster Plass as representatives of industry. Along with the RAI officers and President, Evans-Pritchard, Fortes, Forde and Leach were also members of this new liaison committee. The report in *Man* of the RAI Council for 1952 presented the initiative to its membership in glowing terms – 'a group of industrialists who recognise the great potential importance of the results of fundamental anthropological research in the future of this country, both at home and abroad'. Whilst acknowledging that the research would 'in no way be at the expense of existing methods and fields of research', the RAI council was of the view that the Institute's role was to ensure that 'fundamental research should keep pace with developments in the application of research in social affairs'. This was to be a new and provocative twist to the relationship between anthropological theory and practice.

The Friends of the RAI liaison committee drew up a document for use by Sieff in his discussions with Friends, and potential Friends. Its rosy presentation of the RAI's past achievements and panglossian potential for solving the problems of modernity deserves quoting at length:

> We firmly believe that the RAI, now hampered severely in its great work by a rise in operating costs out of all proportion to its income, deserves our immediate and effective assistance. The Institute has gained a high international reputation and sponsored anthropological research from all over the world. Its forthright defence of the need to integrate human studies has played a vitally important part in the cross-fertilisation of ideas between specialisms, which to the detriment of our understanding of human behaviour are growing steadily apart.

> We live in a changing world, and new conditions require new methods of approach as problems of human relationship increase in magnitude and complexity, the political advancement of colonial territories, the economic development of backward areas, the increasing integration of world trade... the growth of nationalised industries and vast industrial combines, new forms of labour org, a managerial class, all these are creating a new situation in human affairs about which we know very little and on which, relatively speaking, research expenditure is negligible. Many believe that the broad approach of the Institute, rooted as it is in empirical research, is becoming increasingly important to an understanding of the world, and especially industrial personnel problems.

## An Engineer in the Works

On the back of this Sieff planned another major dinner for the Friends of
the RAI in the summer of 1952. Again the guest list was illustrious, and
included the chairmen of ICI, GEC, Unilever and Metal Box and many
other major industrial companies. Whilst only five out of the 20 or so such
magnates attended, amongst these was Thomas Padmore, Under-Secre-
tary in the Treasury. A number of anthropologists attended, including
Edmund Leach. From a wealthy industrial family himself, and originally
trained in engineering, Leach was perhaps less awed by the company of
such magnates than some of his colleagues. He found himself 'dismayed'
at some of the extravagant promises that were made by some of the RAI
representatives over dinner, and in a characteristically long and colourful
letter to Sieff, told him so. It was 'very natural', Leach agreed, that some of
the financiers should ask 'Of what practical use is this anthropology to us?'
and it was inevitable that in the circumstances 'anthropologists should put
forward claims for the practicality of their subject and the comprehensive-
ness of the RAI as an institution'. He went on:

> Nevertheless, I feel this is a very bad basis on which to make claims for sup-
> port. All the serious anthropologists I know have a strictly scientific attitude
> to their subject; they are interested in the structural relations of human soci-
> ety in much the same detached kind of way as physicists are interested in the
> structural relations of the atomic nucleus. The fact is that the anthropologist
> really does not know whether or not his subject has any important practical
> applications, but when anyone holds out a financial carrot he tends to invent
> them. This is not fair either to the anthropologist or to the financier.

This was somewhat of a caricature, but an insightful one. A few years
earlier leading members of the discipline had repeatedly argued for the
potential relevance of anthropology for understanding colonial 'problems', and received a significant amount of funding for doing so. Many of
Malinowski's generation of anthropologists were undoubtedly 'do-good-
ers', as Audrey Richards (1977) put it, partly through force of circumstance, working as colonial administrators. Once a university career was
more or less guaranteed, as it was by Leach's time, it was easier to talk of
'serious' and 'strictly scientific' anthropology.

Leach went on to dismiss as 'nonsense' the idea that anthropologists
might act, as it were, as social planners, or that they could provide the data
that would 'solve the industrialists' problems'. As far as Leach was concerned, 'Anthropologists are people who have made a specialisation of
techniques for describing the behaviour and organisation of small groups,
especially those of 'primitive societies', but it is anthropological information, and it is most misleading to suggest that it can be readily utilised or
made available to anyone who is not an anthropologist'. Finally, Leach
pointed out that until very recently, 'research work relating to "modern

society" has been felt to be outside the Institute's province' such that 'the Institute is not now equipped to provide the background data for sociological studies'. Instead, he proposed, that these resources could be developed, and that the Institute should 'aim at being a focal point for all the fields of sociological study, not only the anthropologists but the sociologists and social psychologists as well'. But he felt that the priority was for the 'institute to occupy its own building and pay its staff without pinching and scraping', and the 'immediate need therefore is for money for general purposes and not for money for specific research into this or that detailed problem for which the anthropologist may be ill equipped to deal'.

Leach copied his letter to Fagg, who privately expressed the view to his co-officers that it was evidence that Leach 'and the LSE generally are trying to wreck the whole thing'. This was an exaggeration, for Leach did, in 1952, nominate Kenneth Little to Council, suggesting that the 'work going on under the sponsorship of Social Anthropology in Edinburgh is just the sort of thing that Mr Sieff and his friends might be interested in'.[2] With Leach's encouragement, Little, who had done one of the first studies of a black British community, also wrote to Fagg expressing his regret at having not been told about the committee earlier, given his interest 'in extending anthropological research amongst advanced societies', and noting that much of his department's research activity 'is being carried on in this field'. In turn, Little nominated Noel Stevenson as a member of the liaison committee, who had significant experience as a colonial administrator in applied anthropology. Fagg took up the offer, inviting Stevenson to liaise(!) between the liaison committee and the Friends, in order to pre-empt the early souring of a relationship that Fagg felt was only beginning to develop.

Stevenson immediately got involved, and prepared a memo detailing the RAI's financial outgoings, which Sieff was to include in a further circular to his business associates 'about the RAI and the way in which it – and anthropologists – might help industry'. The RAI treasurer was of the view that £6000 would be enough for the RAI to 'accomplish its functions', which he suggested, was only a matter of 'ten of our wealthy industrial friends' agreeing to covenant £400 each for seven years (the sum that Marks and Spencer had already committed) 'which they would not really miss in these days of high profit'.

As the momentum for the campaign developed, Sieff and the liaison committee prepared a new more explicit appeal for research funds. In a draft that he sent to Peter Rowntree, Sieff noted that 'many of the causes of unrest, misunderstanding and unhappiness in industry are to be found in the past, and have their roots not in present events, but in customs, traditions, and group loyalties which no longer hold. The growth of business concerns, the disappearance of old personal relationships, the emergence of a managerial class, the breaking down of operations, are creating new situations in human affairs. We believe that this rapidly changing social pattern demands fresh methods of study and approach if adjustments in relationships, stability and integration are to be realised'. A draft fund-raising document proposed a 'research fund' for research into human relations in industry, strengthening the resources of the Institute so that it could (a) establish an information service, (b) complete the reorganisation of its unique library, (c) undertake investigations into specific industrial problems, and (d) enlarge its publications on industrial research. Finally, the document proposed the establishment of a 'Museum of English Life and Industry', providing material evidence of the traditional way of life in England. This last proposal was included mainly at the behest of Sir Robert Hyde, a close friend of Israel Sieff. Hyde felt that 'if we can bring in those who gathered around Sieff's table on some practicable issue such as this, it might lead to the development we all desire'.

Social anthropologists on the liaison committee were far from happy with the shape this fund-raising proposal was taking, and Raymond Firth, new to the committee in 1952, decided to prepare an alternative draft. His document was more abstract, spending time seeking to define the discipline itself: 'The great importance of anthropology is in giving general clues to the understanding of human behaviour … but it may also give some help in the solution of practical questions, provided that adequate study has been made of the problems … this necessitates a great deal of basic research which, like such research in the natural sciences, is not by any means always linked to the solving of some practical problems'. Sensitive to the need both to protect the discipline's autonomy and to train a new cohort of students, his plan was to ask for general financial support for the RAI and to establish a 'Research Fellowship' scheme.

This time it was the industrialists' turn to express their frustration. Robert Hyde, perhaps aggrieved that no mention had been made of his museum idea, felt that Firth's letter was 'too vague, and focuses primarily on problems', and 'fails to relate the work of the anthropologist to actual conditions prevailing in rapidly changing circumstances or to the wider influences that affect that relationship'. 'In my time' he added, 'I must have read hundreds of documents addressed to employers and have found that when direct argument falters the writers fall back upon "problem" or "factor" as an easy way out. For Hyde the solution was 'a more direct approach … to the ordinary business man', ideally with a few extracts 'taken from the American journal of applied anthropology showing in what direct and practical ways anthropology could be of service to industry'. Indeed, Hyde even proposed that the case for Applied Anthropology should be set out in a clear six-point structure:

1. Study of basic human relationships and loyalties.
2. Interpret traditional anthropological method to modern industrial practice.
3. Fields of application in industry.

4. Examples of successful applications.
5. Results to be expected.
6. Cost and return to industry.

The following year Peter Rowntree, one of the Friends of the RAI, expressed similar misgivings about a memo prepared by Professor Forde. Writing to Sieff, he explained that having 'read this with interest several times, some parts of it I must confess I am unable to understand. Basically I think there is a difficulty of communication. It would seem that there is considerable difference between the nomenclature in general use in anthropological circles and in the business world'. For Rowntree, the solution was to try and 'translate what the anthropologist has got to say into language which the businessmen will be able to understand'.

Increasingly, as further appeals and fund-raising dinners were planned, and the contact list of sympathetic 'prominent industrialists' reached almost 100, the Friends sought to define the relationship in their own way. Yet another fund-raising document written for them by Robert Hyde, provided practical examples of the use of applied anthropology, detailing how a 'pioneer study under the direction of Elton Mayo in a Western Electrical plant near Chicago demonstrated most forcibly that practical measures for improvements with regard to such matters as output, absenteeism, the understanding and acceptance of new instructions, depended in large measure on their adjustment to social necessities, both within the working unit and in the wider community from which managers and workers are drawn'. In his lecture to the RAI on the Application of Anthropological Knowledge to Industrial Society', Hyde pointed to the potential for anthropology to 'detect weaknesses in the industrial system which encourage discord rather than promoting harmony' (Hyde 1955), but also insisted that awareness of its utility was currently limited to America. Citing with approval the foundation of the U.S. Society for Applied Anthropology in 1921 and the journal *Human Organisation*, he was laying down an implicit challenge to anthropological practice in the U.K. The irony here was that of an industrialist recommending literature to the academics.

Rowntree repeated his concern to 'bridge the gap' between the academic and industrialist view in a further letter to Sieff in April 1954 after another 'very excellent dinner and representative list of guests'. This time, he was not just concerned with anthropologists' use of language, but also about the need for a 'really practicable proposition as opposed to generalities'. He also felt that it needed to be shown 'why the contribution of the anthropologist can be useful and in what way his training and experience differs from that of the psychologist'. Ominously he went further still, suggesting that 'the biggest stumbling block to getting ready acceptance of the ideas which are so important is the use of the word 'anthropology' feeling that it was 'a word which immediately conjures up into the mind a detailed study of foreign and primitive races, with particular reference to the study of physical attributes and trivial habits'. 'I believe', he ended, 'that when the time comes to collect money and to give publicity to the activities it will not be found that this can be done successfully for "Anthropology" or "anthropologists"'.

Peter Rowntree and Robert Hyde were not the only 'Friends' who felt that the onus increasingly lay on anthropologists to demonstrate their interest in this potential new research field. Minutes of a Friends meeting in June 1954 record one Sir Frank Shires pointing out 'that it was not only the industrialists who must be convinced of the value of Anthropology, but also the anthropologists who must be shown that one of the most fruitful fields of study lay in industrial organisations. A research project, supported by the fund, might achieve both these aims'. The Friends suggested lobbying the new Department for Scientific and Industrial Research (DSIR) to include anthropological studies. Its private secretary had already expressed the DSIR's interest in anthropological approaches (Stansfield 1953), and speaking at a liaison meeting about the prospects of DSIR support for anthropology, felt that 'there were already a certain number of studies that might be considered as anthropological in nature'.

At this point, however, apart from work carried out by Fernando Henriques and Noel Stevenson, and projects being initiated by Gluckman in Manchester and Little in Edinburgh, there was very little anthropological research into industrial issues. The first report of the joint DSIR/MRC committee on human relations in industry is silent on anthropological contributions. Firth's response to the Friends' criticisms of the lack of anthropological involvement in this joint committee was that the DSIR specifically stated that the work must increase productivity and that anthropology was not in a position to agree to such demands.

## With Friends like These ...

Dissent within the liaison committee kept growing through 1954. Despite Sieff's success at gaining donations from Friends, there was a tension about how the funds should be used, particularly in relation to 'commissioning research into industrial problems'. Once again, anthropology was put on the defensive. At a meeting in July, Sieff felt that there was still need for practical evidence of anthropology's potential contribution, whilst others asked why funds raised for sending anthropologists overseas were never used to send them into industry, and what anthropology offered that psychology had not already offered. Fortes sought to defend the discipline as a 'young science', asking for a five-year experimental period to develop 'a new side to the old tradition of devoted work with a high purpose', whilst Firth felt that the anthropological method of 'going to a society as a member and living like its people might be difficult to put into practice in industry ... by going into an organisation within his own community a man would most likely to be "taped" in accordance with the class from which he comes, and so cut off from his fellow workers'. For Firth, anthropology needed a chance to 'experiment' in industry, and not to be judged on a narrow burden of proof.

Gradually Sieff realised the limitations of the task he had set himself, especially in the face of a slow-moving RAI and the gap between the more utilitarian concerns of his fellow business leaders, and the scientific values espoused by the anthropologists. The strain was revealed in a letter that Firth sent to Sieff in 1954 about the most recent meeting. 'It was rather a wearing occasion, but I think it was worth it' he wrote. 'You sounded a little disappointed at the end. It seemed to me however that this was perhaps as much as we could have hoped for in realistic terms', adding that 'Wilson, our treasurer, told me that one of the Scottish distillers has promised £500 under covenant'. Firth went on to comment that another of the industrialists had initially been 'entirely sceptical, but in the end admitted that the anthropological case did make some sense ... he might be willing to put our case to the English Electricity board'.[3]

By 1955 the liaison committee was replaced by a new RAI 'Committee on Anthropology in Industry'. The aim of the new committee was to help the Institute to work more closely with the Friends and plan a potential programme of research. Yet the last thing that business representatives wanted was to be dominated by academic research concerns or the lumbering RAI bureaucracy in this way. Barnes wrote to Raymond Firth in May 1955 to record his 'slight progress' with the Friends of the RAI. He had been mandated by the new committee to draw up a draft letter of appeal, referring to the positive findings of such anthropological studies in industry as had already been carried out'. As he later recalled, 'This I did, and circulated it to other members. Castle liked the draft, Rowntree thought it was hopeless and should be completely rewritten. I heard nothing from Sieff'.[4]

The Friends' last initiative, in response to Firth's attempt at redrafting, was to prepare yet another. This latest riposte proposed a semi-autonomous 'Industrial Relations Research Group' in order 'to avoid involvement in the internal business of the Institute', and to 'make a greater appeal to industry'. The draft letter from this new group to employers made its case in terms of blunt commercial self-interest:

> As a modern employer of labour, you will know that full employment, high wages, and the provision of first-class amenities and working conditions have not been the complete answer to restlessness, dissatisfaction, high labour turnover or poor standards of work. Within your own factory you may have had these difficulties to face, and the incidence of unofficial strikes are sufficient indication that these are deep-seated problems. Our purpose in writing to you is to enlist your support for a method of scientific investigation and enquiry which, in our view, can help employers to find out root causes for labour stresses and strains within their organisation, not explica-

ble by the ordinary criteria of wage levels and conditions of work which have been principal yardsticks hitherto.

The letter went on to extol the resources of the RAI 'which is the recognised and long-established society for promoting the study of man himself in tribes, social groups and modern industry'. Such a straightforward promise of the benefits that anthropology might offer was not received well within the RAI, and there were extensive disagreements over this latest blunt proposal. At one committee meeting the President himself felt obliged to reiterate 'that all anthropologists depend upon the Institute, and that the main purpose of the appeal must continue to be the strengthening of the general purposes of the Institute'. This was unanimously agreed, but left Sieff, Rowntree, Castle, and the others more isolated.

Caught in the middle, the RAI too found itself unable to manage the growing rift between the worlds of academia and business. When Fagg circulated a draft Annual General Report of the RAI declaring that the creation of the committee on Anthropology in Industry was 'an earnest indicator of your Council's intention to encourage by all means in its power the anthropological study of British industrial communities', many senior anthropologists reacted with disquiet. Meyer Fortes was of the view that 'some reference to the traditional interests of the Institute should go into every report', whilst Forde felt that it 'may give the wrong impression' and 'hamper the collaboration in prospect'. John Barnes felt it important to tone down such a statement to one simply 'encouraging anthropologists to take an interest in the study of contemporary industrial society' lest it 'raise false hopes'. He added wryly that 'it is not lack of funds that has prevented sufficient attention being paid to this in the past, it is merely that most people, quite rightly, think that the Bongo Bongo are more attractive than Mancunians'. The mood hardened. When Barnes wrote to Raglan at the end of 1955 asking if the committee on Anthropology in Industry was likely to play an active role in future, the response was frank: 'as long as we have any hope of money from Marks and Spencer or any other industrial concern we must keep the Committee for Anthropology in Industry, otherwise they cannot legally give us any money. Whether we can still hope for such money is quite another matter'.[5]

At this point Sieff lost patience, and turned his energies to other projects. There were to be no further soirees at his Kensington flat or dinners at Claridges. Writing to Lord Raglan in January 1956 he apologised for having not been able to continue with his work of strengthening the Friends, and noted instead that 'the situation with regard to the economic problems of the State of Israel has compelled me to devote practically the whole of my leisure time to the work of the various Zionist organisations and funds for the Jewish Agency and world Jewish congress here and abroad'. He had become Chaim Weizmann's personal secretary; was spending a great deal of time in Israel, and was also still actively involved with PEP.

Sieff attended one final RAI reception in June 1956 with 18 other industrialists, and Firth and Forde, to celebrate the completion of an ethnographic study of Selfridges, carried out by an anthropologist (but never published). The occasion was used by Firth to articulate once again the singularity of the anthropological approach. Unlike industrial psychology, he insisted, it was not based on the interviewing of people, 'but preferred to be among them as they worked, seeing how they behaved, and from that, building up its patterns'. For Firth, it was an 'observational science' that 'functioned on a long-range planning basis; it did not promise quick solutions of industrial problems but sought rather an understanding of what led to the existence of such problems'. In welcoming the report, Sieff agreed too that it 'would have been quite impossible for a sociologist or an industrial psychologist to have made a similar study', and that 'social anthropology could go further afield in this country'. However, Sieff was clear that social anthropology 'should be used by industry, not in place of, but in addition to, industrial psychology as both skills had their different contributions to make'. Sieff was probably a better judge of this than Firth, as he had continued to be highly active in PEP, involved in publishing reports on industrial relations, the Press, and the film industry. After the event Sieff sent out a final letter and further appeal for funds; this was to be his last. Sieff also resigned from his role as Vice President of the RAI in 1957, ending a 30-year association with the Institute.

Without Sieff's energetic leadership, the Committee on Anthropology and Industry rarely met after 1956. Marion Smith, appointed RAI secretary from 1955 to 1961, tried hard to reinvigorate the committee, writing to Sieff to persuade him to reconsider his resignation. She used her contacts to invite Dr Margaret Mead to come and talk to a meeting of the Friends. Mead was advertised in the circular letters as being 'in close touch with recent developments in anthropology in America which have proved useful to businessmen both in management and in their overseas contacts', and she talked on the importance of cross-cultural awareness within business. Whilst the Report of the RAI Council in 1956 again emphasised the number of lectures and publications now focusing on the anthropology of Britain, demonstrating the 'ever enlarging scope and significance of anthropology', the momentum had been lost. Further efforts by both Marion Smith and her successor Anthony Christie at organising events came to little. Marion Smith attempted to follow up links with DSIR. Meyer sent her a letter with a note about two BP directors who might be interested in a closer relationship with the RAI – though noting that Sieff had 'had a crack' at ICI, with little success.

If little came of the original ambitions of the Friends, a good deal of money was raised for the RAI, and a £1000 annual covenant from Marks and Spencer for seven years helped the Institute through a difficult financial period. Through his contacts and support, Sieff also secured the extensive library of Sir Richard Burton for the institute. Apart from the study of Selfridges, only one company is ever recorded as having approached the

RAI for advice over industrial welfare issues. Booker Bros McConnell and Co. Ltd. approached Firth to see if research could be carried out into the 'lack of communication between management and workers and other difficulties, despite liberal loan provision for workers to buy their houses' and 'the general problem of skilled labour'. Firth characteristically replied that such research 'would be of a fundamental kind without necessarily yielding any results which could be analysed by industry', and suggested a five-year time span for such research. They also discussed a potential anthropological study of the labour situation in Ankole, Uganda, where a large sugar estate was planned. One Mr Caine from the company attended a couple of RAI seminars, and Firth had lent him Oscar Lewis's book on 'Group Dynamics in a North Indian village', which he returned, with a polite note saying that it had provided 'another insight into the methods and purposes of anthropological research'. There is no record of further communication.

## Conclusion

The Friends of the RAI episode is intriguing for the gaping misrepresentations of what anthropology could offer to the study of industrial society, given its history and fields of expertise. Misapprehensions abounded about what anthropology could offer, both amongst the industrialists and anthropologists themselves. Ultimately, little came of Sieff's efforts, something of which he was perhaps aware. In his own memoirs, Sieff devotes twelve pages to his involvement with PEP, noting that it was one of the things in his life he was most proud of (Sieff 1970). He makes no mention of anthropology.

What relevance does a set of black-tie dinners in the 1950s have on anthropology's relationship to its application today? The case is one of the first and only times that social anthropologists have turned down financial patronage, refusing to adopt the rhetoric and priorities of potential funders. That this occurred in relation to commercial sponsors is no surprise. But perhaps it should also be read as a salutary tale of anthropologists seeking to maintain their independence in the face of a very specific set of ideological and practical agendas. The initiative threatened the academic professionalism that academic anthropologists, through the creation of the Association of Social Anthropologists, had begun to nurture/practise. They had only just been able to distance themselves from the RAI and that group of administrative ethnographers, missionaries, travellers and amateurs that had for the previous 50 years defined anthropology. In the 1940s anthropologists had accepted the funding and prestige that Colonial Office patronage offered. By the 1950s there were a growing number of academic posts and research fellowships available, and the discipline now no longer needed to sell itself to the highest bidder.

The tale of institutional bureaucracy within academia has lessons for similar bureaucratic duplications and divisions existing today. At the post-war moment, the RAI was no longer able to speak for or represent anthropologists, and academic anthropologists had no wish to see the former dictate the shape of academic research. The division between the RAI and the ASA made it ever harder for anthropologists to speak with a singule voice. This would seem to be confirmed by a similar history of initiatives around training and employment in the 1980s. The case conveys some of the misunderstandings, and different styles of organisational working, that continue to bedevil close collaboration, not only between business and universities, but even within the discipline.

Academic anthropology's relationship to its application continues to be an ambivalent one, for anthropology both depends on and denies its utility. This dialectic of practical engagement and theoretical 'purification' continues to invigorate the discipline. Practical problems and topics repeatedly become topics for theoretical debate. Despite the invocation of a 'pure' and 'applied' hierarchy, the social sciences continue to reinvent themselves through the incorporation of new 'applied' fields of study, most recently in the fields of development, medicine and social welfare. The history of anthropology's 'practical' uses thus remains integral to its theoretical development. This becomes a problem when this dynamic is one-way. For as long as academic promotion structures and career paths are structured to reward primarily theoretical 'outputs', narrowly defined, the connections between theory and practice will always be difficult to maintain. Sieff's attempt to promote anthropology's use beyond the university setting offers an important case through which to understand the rhetoric of academic purity and the risks of practical engagement.

## Acknowledgements

I would like to thank Sarah Walpole, the RAI archivist, for all her help in providing access to the house archives of the Royal Anthropological Institute, on which this article is primarily based. I also acknowledge the support of the Leverhulme Trust and the British Academy in carrying out this work.

## Notes

1. Unless otherwise noted, this and subsequent references draw on the RAI's House Archives A57 'Friends of the RAI'.
2. RAI Archives A95/31/11.
3. Raymond Firth's personal correspondence, in Firth A9, LSE archives.
4. ibid.
5. RAI Archive A95/39/13.

## References

Grillo, R. 1985. 'Applied Anthropology in the 1980s: Retrospect and Prospect', in R. Grillo and A. Rew (eds) *Anthropology and Policy*. London: Tavistock.

Hyde, S. R. 1955. 'The Application of Anthropological Knowledge to Our Industrial Sector'. *Man*, August 1955: 122.

Pels, P. and O. Salemink. 1999. *Colonial Subjects: Essays on the Practical History of Anthropology*. Ann Arbor: University of Michigan Press.

Richards A. 1977. 'The Colonial Office and the Organisation of Social Research'. *Anthropological Forum* 4: 168–189.

Sieff, I. 1970. *Memoirs*. London: Weidenfeld and Nicolson.

Stansfield, S.M. 1953. 'Report on the Work of the DSIR/MRC Committee on Human Relations in Industry'. *Nature*, Spring.

# PART II

# ANTHROPOLOGY AND INDUSTRY

*Chapter 3*

# THE PURE AND THE IMPURE?

Reflections on Applying Anthropology
and Doing Ethnography

———— ✺ ————

*Simon Roberts*


## Introduction

Writing in 1981, Raymond Firth complained that 'much has been written of what anthropology can do, little has been shown of what anthropology has done'. Uncertainty as to the applicability of anthropology as a practical discipline is not new. This volume, and the efforts of which it is a part, marks a re-engagement with a critical question confronting organised anthropology in the U.K., namely, what is the present and future of anthropology outside the academy? From this question spring others, including how the subject is taught and its contribution to, and voice in, wider society. This chapter is an account of what one person, and his small company, do with anthropology, and a look at some of the issues that this practice throws up for the discipline.

When I was writing up my thesis I was regularly asked what I planned to do next. My stock answer became the following bold assertion: 'I'll do anthropology but I'll be paid for it'. Some contemporaries would have said that, as a student with a comparatively generous grant from the ESRC,[1] this was already the case. However, I knew that when I had finished my thesis I would not continue doing the sort of anthropology in which I was then engaged. I also knew that I wanted to do something 'anthropological'. The following is a personal look at what I have ended up doing; of the work in which I am involved and the contexts in which this work takes place. I examine the relationship of this work to the discipline of anthropology.

———————

Notes for this chapter begin on page 88.

I would suggest that there are three key contexts in which the work that I undertake is currently situated. The first is the rise of anthropology (and more specifically ethnography) as a 'brand' (Suchman 2000). The second is the growing interest in ethnography as a research method in a wide variety of settings. The third, a renewed airing of familiar questions about the use and applicability of anthropology outside the academy.

As has been suggested by Lucy Suchman (2000), through a process of 'discovery' and subsequent use, anthropology has been constructed as a 'commercially consumable' discipline. She refers specifically to its utilisation by commercial research and development teams in industrial and product design fields, and she notes too the rising use of anthropology (as a perspective and methodology) to inform marketing and communications requirements for these, and other firms. Quoting a range of articles from American publications, from broadsheet newspapers to business magazines, she outlines the variety of benefits that its practitioners and advocates recount in favour of their use of, or conversion to, anthropology and anthropologists. One such advocate, John Seely Brown, then head of Xerox PARC (a renowned R&D facility where Suchman herself once worked), praises anthropology and anthropologists who 'let you view behaviour through a new set of eyeglasses' (in Deutsch 1991).

These genuflections to anthropology are building a public face or 'brand' for the discipline as it exists outside traditional academic environments. This is a brand that makes it easier to consume or talk about anthropology, particularly for those with limited knowledge in the area. If this nascent 'brand' makes the discipline more comprehensible, or at the least visible, it also acts to mask significant differences within the discipline, differences which are now openly debated. In particular there are clear differences of opinion about what actually constitutes applied anthropology, what practising it actually entails, and who does (or can do) anthropology. The rise of anthropology as a brand is a reflection of the growth in its use (and its enduring appeal to business journalists). The questions that this increased accessibility and use of anthropology throw up reflect both boundary maintenance from certain quarters of academic anthropology, and equally valid questions that are central to the present and future of the discipline, both within and outside the academy. This series of questions and tensions is one of the three contexts in which my use of anthropology is situated.

The rise, and rise, of ethnography is one crucial component of the 'anthropology as brand' idea. As Gellner and Hirsch point out, there is 'ethnography of the classroom, ethnography of television audiences, ethnography of medical students, and ethnography of the police' (2001: 1). However, this list is merely indicative and is confined to samples of recent academic work undertaken by trained anthropologists and it barely scratches the surface of a much larger phenomenon, in which ethnography is becoming the vogue, if not exactly predominant, methodology in commercial, public sector and organisational research. From industrial design and product development, to programmes of consumer 'closeness' or 'intimacy', ethnography is a label increasingly applied to other method-ologies, or is used as a methodology in its own right. By the reckoning of one practitioner there are 130 companies offering ethnography in the U.K. and U.S.A.[2]. If, as Suchman suggests, anthropology has become a brand, then ethnography is at the heart of this brand and how many people unfa-miliar with anthropology itself come into contact with the discipline.

As I suggested above, the simplicity of this idea of brand conceals deep running debate and division. A brand, just like a symbol, can have many meanings to different parties. Here is not the place to enter into the ques-tion of the definitions of ethnography that are thrown up by the ethnog-raphy practised by these companies and individuals and the debate that this engenders. I shall have more to say on this towards the end of this chapter. However, it is worth noting at this point as evidence of the lure and appeal of ethnography that little connection to anthropology (or other social sciences) is either implied or claimed by many practitioners of ethnographic techniques. As I discuss below ethnography has become a convenient way of describing a mix of methods, a label for a range of qualitative techniques which are based on 'being there', or which claim what I would call a 'methodological propensity' that brings them close to ethnography. Overall, as I would be the first to admit, the ethnography that I conduct, and which I describe below, is distantly related to what anthropologists in the academy would understand by the term.

Skirting the questions of definition and meaning for the time being, it will be valuable to further locate Ideas Bazaar's own practice of ethno-graphic research in a little bit more detail. Our activity sits within a broadly defined social and market research industry. Within this field, ethnography is 'on the up', sometimes as sensibility, sometimes as vacu-ous 'brand', sometimes as methodology. In this world, the rise of ethnog-raphy is a result of new business challenges (i.e., changes in focus from products to services), a thirst for new methods and techniques, and a new focus on how research findings and ideas are actually communicated to those who are to use them in their work. It also tracks a more general interpretative turn and a move from 'words' (focus groups) to 'action' (participant observation), best documented by Gordon and Valentine (2000). Overall, the rise of ethnography indexes an appreciation of the importance of understanding cultural context, situated action, and of cul-tural processes and meaning.

So outside the academy, anthropology (and ethnography's) defining interest in context, culture and meaning are responsible for its rise as research 'brand' and practice at the hands of both anthropologists and others. This rising interest in anthropology and ethnography occurs at a time when the academy appears to be asking related questions. One is about the applicability to, and application of anthropology, 'outside'. Another is how the discipline should therefore teach and train under- and postgraduate students. No less important are issues about the primacy of methods, and ultimately questions of definitions (what makes or breaks an anthropologist, what is ethnography?) and professional identity.

This particular contribution to the discussion does not set out to either address or answer all these questions. However, these issues do have very practical implications which is why I feel they need to be addressed. They are likely to inform the way students are taught, and prepared for their futures, and shape the nature of professional associations and identities. They contribute to the relationship between anthropology in the academy and outside it. They determine, ultimately, what part anthropology and anthropologists can play in public conversations in the U.K. (and beyond).

These then are the three main contexts which I regard as having most direct impact on my work and experience as a practising anthropologist. To summarise, these are the rise of the anthropology brand, the growth in interest in, and practice of, ethnography, and renewed engagement with the issues of application and applicability within academic anthropology. In the next section I outline in more detail how what I do sits within these three contexts. First, I describe what Ideas Bazaar actually does, and what motivated me to experiment with an anthropology company in the first place. Secondly, I examine the motivations or interests of our research project stakeholders and their understanding of ethnography.

## Story of a Beginning

One understanding of myth is that it acts as charter for the present, and the future. Like many myths, this myth changes each time I tell it. At the core of the story is my sense that there was a way of continuing to do anthropology which did not involve a typical academic career path. I was convinced of the ability of anthropology, if not my own abilities with it, to be useful. At this early stage I was vague about the utility, but I knew that my enjoyment of the subject might allow others to enjoy it, and use it.

More pragmatically, I was also bored by the time I reached the end of my Ph.D. research and wanted to explore interests in others areas. At the time I completed my thesis it was late 1999 and all the talk was of technology, new media and an online world. Despite some initial scepticism I saw a fair degree of fit between some of the theoretical and practical interests of my thesis (understanding technology and communication change in socio-cultural context) and the opportunity to actively research this emerging and exciting world. I was also attracted to the idea of shorter projects which had endings in the foreseeable, not distant, future. I imagine that longing is frequently felt by disenchanted graduate students.

Perhaps most idealistically, and contentiously, the creation of my own research company was part of a belief that some sort of applied anthropology can sit comfortably between the market and the state, the worlds of policy and business and the academy. I sensed that this would be valuable and fun to do and of practical utility and benefit for those commissioning the sort of work I had in mind. Moreover, I thought that by answering my own questions about the applicability of anthropology, something to which I had committed eight years of study, I could feed into wider debates about its applications.

So much for the dreams and the idealism. The reality is a small research company called Ideas Bazaar that currently employs four people full time, and a host of freelance researchers, many graduates or postgraduates of anthropology. Our work to date has focused on three principal areas, some by design, some by accident: Print and Broadcast Media, Technology and Communications, and Organisations and Change. The projects we undertake are very varied, ranging from audience research and programme idea development for the BBC, and more open-ended investigations of mobile phone use; from studies of late night television viewing to those of readers of local and regional newspapers.

Additionally, I and other Ideas Bazaar associates are involved with the iSociety research project at the London-based not-for-profit think-tank and consultancy, The Work Foundation (formerly the Industrial Society). The iSociety research programme investigates the impact of information and communication technologies (ICT) in the U.K., with special emphasis on technology in everyday life, at home, in communities and at work. Ideas Bazaar associates help design and plan individual research projects and I have co-authored reports on technology such as broadband, mobiles phones and technology in U.K. workplaces (Crabtree and Roberts 2003a; Crabtree et al. 2003; Nathan et al. 2003). Perhaps uniquely for a think-tank, most iSociety projects use ethnographic research as a first choice methodology.[3]

Our work is very varied, both in terms of what we do and how we set out to meet our objectives on projects. One way we describe the way we work is as being methodologically neutral. We are not restricted to any one methodology, though we regard ethnography as a speciality. A project might involve interviewing, focus group discussions (a more multi-faceted and useful method than their reputation might suggest), workshops and photography. Occasionally, as a means of communicating findings at a later date, we use video cameras.

Earlier I set out some of the reasons why clients are curious about, if not demanding of, a broadly ethnographic approach. It might help to explain more about what they need or want from the work we do for them. All projects are different and it would be invidious to contend otherwise. Their needs and objectives are also varied. However, broadly speaking we help our clients understand the worlds in which they operate, from their audiences' perspectives, and then we assist them in acting upon this understanding. Our job, as we see it, is to give to them a new understanding of a familiar environment. In a language more familiar to anthropologists, we render the familiar strange and the strange familiar. Our job, as we describe it to them (and by so doing contributing in our own way to the development, or distortion, of the anthropology brand), is to help them see things differently. Our aim is to try to introduce a fresh language, and with it fresh perspectives, to things they take for granted; things which are invisible to them due to their overt, everyday visibility.

Our work might sometimes be a self-standing project or enquiry, at other times it might feed into other streams of investigation or projects. In the former project type, an ethnographic approach is usually supplemented with other techniques, particularly group discussions or workshops. In the latter, the role of a stand-alone ethnographic method is to be slightly more provocative or breathe some fresh air into a tired research outlook. Importantly, as this suggests, those who subscribe to some of our (and other's) promises about ethnographic approaches view them as capable of shaking up familiar perspectives and reframing commonly held beliefs and opinions. This is what they are increasingly demanding or expecting of ethnography.

In describing what we do, and what it can do, we refer to anthropology's ability to produce 'closeness' and 'revolution'. One imperative of our clients, and one demand from the research they commission, is that it helps them understand the world outside their door. In this context, ethnography is valued because it is seen to provide closeness. It can offer an appreciation of real lives in context, not of life in the laboratory-like environment of a focus group viewing facility. It situates actions in context and understands the difference between accounts of action and action itself. All of our projects entail a duty to return to the client with a sense of what 'being there' is actually like. This plays naturally to the ontological priority or bias of the discipline of anthropology and the ethnographic method.

Our clients' other requirement, at least as we see it, is the revolution of the everyday. We regard the demand for ethnography, and in our case research undertaken by people with training in anthropology, to be due to its ability (or their belief in its ability) to turn their perspectives or everyday understandings on their head. In part, our just 'being there' provides the reason for belief, since it is so methodologically different from other approaches they use. But ethnography is not simply about spending time with people. I would argue, and I expand on this below, that it is a method and a mindset. As a mindset it is informed by a broad canon of research and literature centred around, but reaching beyond, social and cultural anthropology. I would like to think that clients like our work because of our ability to bring this background to bear on our ethnography (or even our focus group discussions). In reality, I suspect, they care more about where we 'get them to' and much less how we get them there.

## From Theory to Practice: Ethnography in Suburbia, Anthropology in the Boardroom

So much for the background of what we do, and the interests and imperatives of those for whom we undertake research. This section sets out an account of the research in order to provide a clearer illustration of what it actually involves. Specifically, it is an account of a more ethnographically focused project which is constructed by merging a mixture of projects to give a composite and fictional account, but one which I hope is nonetheless instructive.

One feature of this fictional account is that it deploys some of the standard literary devices of anthropology – the arrival and tales of the fieldwork encounter – in order to portray a *verité* to the methods employed. I do this with an awareness that I could be accused of 'passing off' our work as something that it is not. That is not the intention. On the one hand, a 'fictional' account helps skirt issues of client confidentiality. On the other, it retains something of the narrative quality of an ethnography which I feel is central to what our clients like about work that uses ethnographic methods.

This account therefore sets the scene for a discussion of various elements of our fieldwork that are noteworthy, in practical or theoretical terms. The surface commentary I offer undoubtedly raises more questions than it answers. However, I hope it sets the scene for later examination.

All projects begin with a process of briefing by a client, and a response in the form of a proposal. In the client's research brief, objectives and issues are laid out, to be interrogated through dialogue and responded to in the proposal. The brief for the research I describe, in its broadest terms, was to inject stimulating ideas, perhaps a degree of controversy and suggest new ways of looking at a familiar problem. The stakeholders for the research came from across the business. The methodology chosen is sometimes a matter of keen interest to the client; sometimes they expect the researchers to recommend the best approach for the task in hand. In this illustrative project, the client came with ethnography in mind as her chosen approach. In addition to a number of household studies, we also recommended two audience workshops – interactive group discussions – to follow the preliminary household investigations and build on some of the insights to which this stage of research will have given rise.

Despite the enthusiasm and support of the client in this project, within her business and beyond, there are a good number of professional sceptics who question how such a small study can be representative. They ask how its findings can provide the support they need to make decisions. Such doubts are rarely quelled completely by our explanations or assurances: probably we are talking a different language. However, these doubters illustrate to us what business needs the research must satisfy, and how evidence is understood and used in some quarters of the organisation.

These doubters also indicate that there is a lack of understanding between purveyors and buyers of ethnographic approaches. This misunderstanding is not easily explained away, since it exists at the levels of methodology, analysis, representation of finding and the subsequent use of evidence in supporting decision making. What we are learning to do over time is to explain our approach, and its pleasures and limitations. The sceptics need to be engaged and encouraged to see the merits of not only a different methodology but a different interpretative approach. Over time we are finding ways to represent the ethnographic method and the anthropological approach in ways that are both captivating, comforting and challenging. This is best done by example, and as our stock of examples grows, we are learning how to talk about the applicability of ethnographic research. However, ultimately those with a predilection for numbers will make judgements based on other criteria and a rather different view of how to represent and interpret the world. If nothing else we always aim to get this particular tribe of doubters to look anew at our method and its results.

In closing the meeting, having agreed timings and costs, the client reminded us that much rested on the project. Others in her department and beyond have heard that she has commissioned an ethnographic study, and levels of curiosity are running high. This is ethnography as brand again, giving 'just another piece of research' some vitality, resonance, perhaps even excitement. A sense of novelty and the unknown is at the heart of the emerging ethnography brand.

We have been commissioned to undertake ten household studies in and around London, the Midlands and the Manchester area. The studies will be completed over the course of about a month. Our first priority is to locate households willing to participate in the study. We are often asked where such households are found. Companies specialising in the recruitment of participants for such studies exist across the UK. They manage vast networks of recruiters. The recruiters are primarily female and know, and are known to, their local neighbourhood. Given an oral brief that describes the 'type' of households we are looking for, or a more formal questionnaire that acts as a 'screener', they phone households and then escalate their search by snowballing the request across a wide social network. These recruiters act as our gatekeepers, locating families who are defined as suitable and, most importantly, willing informants.

It should be clear from this then that far from relying on serendipitous discovery and 'opportunistic' recruitment of informants during a longer period of fieldwork, we find households beforehand and co-opt them into a tightly defined time period of research. This short-term involvement is based on an economic transaction: households receive between £100 and £200 for their participation over three days. This sum is known as an 'incentive' or 'gift'. This is clearly a significant departure from 'typical' ethnographic fieldwork in which chance encounters mature from contacts, to informants and then friends or even brothers (Kumar 1992) over a much longer period of time. The economic dimension is clearly not unimportant either. If in some sense this economic encounter complicates matters, in many ways it makes transparent the nature of the encounter. It also makes explicit one understated (or even hidden) element of traditional participant observation: an economic dimension to the relationship between researcher and researched.

These households are picked on the basis of criteria such as 'life stage' and social class. Often selection is made, at the insistence of clients, on the basis of categorisations derived from earlier (usually quantitative) research. Typically these are 'attitudinal segmentations'. Such segmentations, the meat and drink of modern commercial marketing, almost invariably turn out to be unhelpful, one-dimensional and essentialist constructions of 'target consumers'. If nothing else, they provide a first point of entry for interrogating a company's assumptions about its audience, and a way into a more thoroughgoing critique of their outlook.

Within just over a week, ten households have been selected. Introductory phone calls have been made by the fieldworkers who will be visiting them, to introduce themselves, answer any questions and explain how the research will work in practical terms. At present we use a team of researchers with different experiences and backgrounds drawn primarily, but not exclusively, from anthropology, to undertake the primary research. This wider team and the diversity of perspectives it brings are crucial in shaping the research. The fieldworkers enter the household with what we refer to as an 'ethnographic script'. This script is the product of collaboration between all members of the research team.

The ethnographic script is a framework for guiding the research encounters, the exact focus of which is open to fieldworkers to explore. It contains a series of prompts and cues for the fieldworker to be aware of, and a loose set of guidelines that aid in the contextualisation of the action observed: look out for this, be aware of this and explore this. As a document it is not dissimilar from that laid out by Spradley (1980: 78). The script binds the team around a core set of objectives and focuses them on the cultural and social arenas on which we are focusing our attention. However, it also gives them the latitude to investigate as their own encounter demands. The script could be seen, in its most directed form, as a set of hypotheses, though we try to reign in that tendency. It is designed more to stimulate the researcher to explore. As a document it raises questions and provides suggestions, rather than hypothetical statements to compare against the social action encountered.

Importantly, I think the collaboration involved in the production of this script, as well as the research itself, are examples of multi-person fieldwork. This may not in itself be very new where anthropologists and other researchers are 'embedded' within organisations and work collaboratively on projects, or in the academy (Marcus 1995). However, the methodological implications for this are important and team-based anthropology is certainly a significant direction for a discipline which has tended towards a model of fieldwork that is, as Geertz put it, 'person-specific': 'this ethnographer, in this place, with these informants, these commitments, and these experiences, a representative of a particular culture, a member of a certain class' (1988: 6). Yet even a team-based approach to fieldwork and all that offers in creating a shared basis for encounters, and later analysis, is still based on a person-specific model of doing the fieldwork. One person, in one place, at one time undertaking fieldwork with one household.

I arrive at an address in a village just outside Oldham.[4] Through the window I can see two children in front of the TV watching Nickelodeon. Denise, their mother, answers the door. I was last with the family earlier on in the summer, during iSociety research on mobile phones. As a result, I am familiar with the family set up, some of their everyday concerns and outlooks, and the initial stages of the encounter is to some extent about re-familiarising ourselves, rather than starting from scratch. At that time, Ben had been expecting his GCSE results, and the family was preparing for a holiday in France. Mike was anxiously awaiting news of work and Denise's job was supporting the household. Months later, the home-made wine they had been preparing is ready to drink and Mike pours me a glass as we catch up on what's been going on in each other's lives since we first met.

It is fortunate that the project in hand concerns TV viewing, since my arrival coincides with the denouement of a storyline in Coronation Street that has been building for several months. The family settles down to watch, except Ben, who later texts from the pub kitchen where he works to ask someone to record the episodes. Later we eat in front of the television and the children are despatched to bed. Conversation continues until late.

I leave them for the night, returning to my hotel to finish writing up notes and return the following evening. The picture is much the same, though the evening goes differently as I begin to develop a little more focus to the study by introducing the household to some of the specific areas of interest. In addition to participant observation, guided by the ethnographic script, I give the family a media use diary and a disposable camera with which to record specific activities and attendant moods and thoughts, during the following week. These 'cultural probes' (cf. Gaver *et al.* 1999) have several uses. The diary is more a prompted notebook format than a chronologically ordered document. It allows the family to record information about events and occurrences and to record television viewing experiences and patterns. The diary resultantly brings informants closer to the subjects at the heart of the research and acts to enhance their involvement in the study. It also provides the researcher with material that can be discussed and interpreted by both parties at a later point in the study. Crucially, the diary and camera gradually sensitises them to the research process turning co-opted families into more involved research partners.

The following day, in another part of Greater Manchester, I travel to another household and begin another encounter that will follow a broadly similar shape. Those unfamiliar with the simultaneously directed and directionless nature of participant observation ask what we 'do' exactly. The answer of course is that we both observe social action and participate in it. We note actions and contexts, we listen, we look for cues and hints, and we collect fragments which might be pieced together to create an understanding. The ethnographic script prevents overload and encourages focus, and it also provides welcome steer when, as it inevitably does, the feeling that nothing is 'happening' arises. Those familiar with such fieldwork endeavours will appreciate that it is sometimes uneventful and unspectacular.

Unsurprisingly households often ask a similar question at the outset of the encounter: 'What would you like us to do?' My answer to them, which never quite seems adequate given the artificiality of the encounter, at least at the outset, is 'forget I'm here'. But it is worth being honest about the extent to which these encounters are artificial. It is also important to understand that for those who commission the work, these encounters mark a significant move away from the artificiality of focus group discussions or more decontextualised telephone interviews.

Returning to Manchester the following week, I revisit the households adopting a similar, but slightly more directed, research pose. Time is not a luxury enjoyed in this model of research. An average encounter spans over a three-day period. Again, whilst it is important to be clear that these encounters are mere moments when compared to the time periods that dominant ethnography is understood to involve, it is a significant advance on even shorter modes of enquiry. The brief encounter is drawn to a close through a semi-structured interview in which the researcher not only pursues lines of enquiry that have been laid out in the ethnographic script, but also shares and discusses with informants their interpretations of what has been observed.

Time is, it seems, the *sine qua non* of traditional ethnographic studies. It might be, for many, the single defining feature of ethnography. It is certainly the basis on which our ethnography is criticised by purists. The hours and minutes of our studies are dwarfed by the weeks, months and years of fieldwork within academic boundaries. And quite apart from any need to learn a language and the additional time that this requires, time is rightly regarded as the essential resource required of detailed ethnographic studies. Time allows researchers the ability to explore areas of interest from a wide variety of perspectives and from the perspective of different social actors. Time will tell them that their original sense of what was going on and what it meant was partially or barely 'correct'. Time is the ingredient that contributes to one of the hallmarks of anthropological enquiry and analysis: a recognition of the complexity and multi-faceted nature of social realities and the attendant importance that cultural accounts display a resistance to simplifying and simplistic accounts and explanations. If time is at the heart of what ethnography is then our practice certainly subverts the practice.

Elsewhere across Britain, a similar process has taken place in the other eight households by the primary research team. We gather later in the month to spend a day going through our materials, sharing portraits of the households and working through encounters with an eye on the ethnographic script. Fieldnotes are exposed to the collective gaze of all the fieldworkers, subject to none of the secretive handling of notebooks that anthropologists typically rely on or expect. As with the fieldwork itself, so with this so-called 'download' session, we attempt to generate as wide a possible set of perspectives and interpretations before the core team sit down to synthesise the work of the other researchers.

The way we communicate findings to the client often depends on what is really driving the project. The key difference from a more academic study is that stakeholders in the research do not expect to receive a tome. The findings are expected to continue the 'closeness' that lies at the heart of the whole research exercise and are expected to enthuse the client team. Clients do not expect to have to wade through a mountain of words. In this respect, the pictures from the cameras and any video footage that has been shot are invaluable.

The communication of findings can range from a one-off debrief to a much longer series of meetings that act as seminars in which the research is poured over by stakeholders with different outlooks, objectives and expectations. In this way, over time, the research findings start to become appropriated by the client organisation. A project of conversion begins in which the analysis, the language and analogies start to transfer to the teams who will act upon it. My own feeling is that the drive of anthropology to problematise everyday understandings is what gives this ethnographic research the ability to become appropriated culturally by the organisation. Put another way, we regard a successful project as such when old ways of looking at things are replaced by new ways of thinking over which there is debate amongst the client teams. The appeal of ethnographic and anthropological techniques in the arenas we use them is that they provide highly transferable or translatable insights and ideas. In short I believe that ethnography, because it brings lives to life, is a powerful way to connect people with ideas. Story telling, vignettes and the recounting of episodes that have shaped the way the research has developed give the research a vitality that makes its findings (and implications) more real and urgent.

## Unbounded Anthropology, Undoing Ethnography?

The imperative at this juncture is to ask what these activities mean for anthropology, if anything, and to explore their present and potential relationship with the discipline in the future. To facilitate the discussion, I preceded my account of research with an outline of some of the contexts that frame our work, and have characterised two normative modes of anthropology and ethnography.

These modes are to a large extent caricatures of opposing positions, that tend to obscure undeniable differences in approach and opinions within each position. On the one hand, I painted a picture of bounded, 'traditional', academic anthropology. In this setting, ethnography means long-term studies and analysis enlivened by debates framed at theoretical and regional levels. Here, practitioners of ethnography are primarily, but far from exclusively, anthropologists and other social scientists. On the other, a unbounded, 'rougher', applied anthropology. This entails a more impure ethnography: shorter, more focused studies that borrow from anthropology, but also draw techniques from elsewhere (market research, industrial and product design) and are probably less rigorous in the reading of literature that traverse areas of interest. (This is not to say that practitioners are disengaged from past and current writing, or afraid to engage with it in their analysis). It is worth stressing again that these caricatures are not designed to account for clear real world positions, but to provide a way of characterising the debate.

However, while there is this distinction between pure and impure caricatures, the work of Wright (this volume) appears to suggest that it is a tension, and a vocabulary, that has animated professional anthropology in the U.K. (if not elsewhere) during the twentieth century. She suggests that elder statesmen of the discipline saw the purity of anthropology being sacrificed through its application in the 'real' world. Mills (this volume) refers to the 'serial ambivalence' of the anthropology establishment to the very idea of an applied anthropology. It is clear to me that this distinction between pure and impure is a feature both of the past, and to some extent, the present. It is also one with which it is worth grappling. So my concern in the final section is to understand where anthropology and ethnography, within and outside the academy, are going and what those on both sides of the debate can learn for the future. I think it is particularly important to raise questions about methodology and training, and of occupational or disciplinary identity.

From the portrait of the research process presented in the previous section some elements of the research will appear familiar to academic anthropologists. However, some will be anathema: paid informants, the very short period of time spent with the households and a narrow focus of vision on the part of the research team (a 'narrow fieldwork funnel'). This reaction will neither surprise nor offend. Neither will it stop people commissioning such work nor stop postgraduates of anthropology contacting us, and others like us, with enquiries about work opportunities. In a sense the message of this paper is an uncompromising one. This process, one of the appropriation or application of anthropology, depending on your viewpoint, has begun. It is worth engaging in and learning from.

I would suggest that this style of ethnography, this way of applying anthropology, is worth discussing and constructively engaging with because it actually creates the possibility for a new way of 'doing anthropology'. And new ways of doing anthropology will lead in ever more fruitful directions. Whatever the deficiencies of the methods discussed, and their distance from the more traditional ethnography of academic practitioners, it is a tenable way of conducting useful research, that is found to be practically applicable. It is a form of research that is increasingly finding a willing audience in diverse 'real world' arenas. It is 'good enough' research. If people can use its findings and work with it, that is often enough.

There is an obvious danger here, which is that the terms of this debate act to essentialise ethnography. It is not a closely defined methodology, even as practised within academic contexts. It is, within this context too, a brand of research which encompasses a wide variety of techniques and one that resists formal and practically orientated explication. The training of ethnographic methods is often vague. Some perhaps would wonder if 'it' can be taught at all. Some participants at the conference at Loughborough (2003) had mixed reactions to the assertions that it was taught. Many saw a disciplinary assumption that ethnographic skills were transferred from supervisor to student through osmosis. As with training, so with its general development, in practical and theoretical terms, the idea and practice of ethnography has never been static or stable. The activities I have described above are simply one of a large variety of ways of doing it that are currently emerging.

This unboundedness is most obvious in talking with people from other disciplines, such as Human Factors, HCI, industrial and product design.[5] They too all speak of 'doing ethnography'. They mix methods; incorporating encounters such as I described with probes, workshops, projective techniques, diaries and photography. They too debate what ethnography is, and what counts as 'it' and what does not. They tend not to regard an education in anthropology as a prerequisite for doing ethnography, but there is certainly a keen discriminatory eye cast over claims made about ethnography.

This returns us to the idea of anthropology, and specifically ethnography as brand. What unites people who disagree about specific definitions is the notion that ethnography is a meaningful umbrella term for a wide range of research practices. Consider the following list of research approaches being offered within commercial and social research:

accompanied interviews; accompanied shops; accompanied shopping; accompanied trips; active observation; anthronomics; anthropological research; applied anthropology; applied ethnography; at-home ethnography; attitudinal data collection; beeper studies; behavioural observation; commando ethnography; commercial ethnography; consumer ethnography; consumer immersion groups; consumer-oriented ethnography; consumer observation video evaluation research; context-based research; contextual inquiry; conversation analysis; conversational interviews; co-operative inquiry; cultural analysis; cultural inventorying; customer experience research; customer-intercept; customer narratives; customer observation; customer research; customer visits; daily routine shadowing; day-in-the-life; deep dives; deep hanging out; depth interviews; design ethnography; direct interaction research; direct observational research; empathic design; ethnographic interview; ethnographic customer research; ethnography studies; experience audit; experience modelling; experience research; face-to-face interview; field research fieldwork; friendship pairs; group immersion experiences; guerilla ethnography; human ethnography; immersion; immersion days; immersive research; *in situ* interview; in-context research; in-depth interviews; in-depth research; in-environment; in-field data collection; in-home research; in-home interviews; in-person observation; in-store interviews; individual depth interviews; insight gathering; intercepts; interpreting; interviewing; introspection; language context analysis; lifestyle research; living the life; longitudinal studies; man-on-the street research; motivational research; naked behaviour research; narrative analysis; natural environment research; naturalistic inquiry; naturalistic observation; need states thinking; non-traditional research; observed shopper interviews; observation; on-site intercepts; on-site interviews; one-on-one interviews; open-ended research; out and about; participant observation; participative inquiry; participatory inquiry; people research; people-centred research; photo-documentary studies; photo ethnography; product anthropology; pubbing; rapid ethnography; real world research; recording life histories; retail aisle observation; retail ethnography; remote research; ritual analysis; shadow days; shadowing; shop-alongs; shopnography; site visits; site-based studies; social inquiry; social network observation; sociological ethnography; stakeouts; store walks; street research; street-level research; surrogate observation; systematic observation; talking heads; task analysis; target market immersion; team-based ethnography; time-lapse observation; triangulation; unconventional research; unobtrusive observation; unstructured observation; user research; user safaris; video ethnography; visual data analysis; visual ethnography.[6]

Quite apart from the obvious questions, such as what is 'commando ethnography', what does 'unobtrusive observation' look like and what sort of training does one require to undertake a 'shopnography', this terrifyingly diverse list of activities underscores how wide a range of methodologies are considered to fit within a broadly ethnographic space. Anthropology and ethnography are being imagined and implemented in very broad ways. It just so happens that some of the researchers using these techniques have postgraduate qualifications in anthropology. However, many, probably most, do not.[7]

This list suggests another way of approaching the issue of the relationship between anthropology and ethnography, within and outside the academy. What this list makes explicit is a focus on technologies of method above technologies of analysis. It reveals more about methods, than it does about interpretative outlooks or approaches. Perhaps practitioners of these methods regard it as unnecessary to make explicit, or be specific about, their interpretative frameworks. If this is the case, it suggests that we should ask if it is the methodology, the method of analysis, or a mindset, that defines anthropology or the anthropological approach.

Certainly most of these methods, with their explicit or implied affinity to ethnography, are grounded in a contextual understanding of people (or in this case consumers). This is, as I argued above, part of the allure of the brand of ethnography. It is the claims of proximity, of 'being there', that give these methods much of their appeal. In this sense the method becomes practically an end in itself. I would argue that this not only short changes anthropology but also provides it, as a discipline, with a great opportunity. I would argue that anthropology's contribution to unbound ethnography should be its analytical sensibilities and the uniquely broad intellectual tradition in which these are located. Anthropology is about much more than simply a way of doing research.

Lambert and McKevitt make a similar point in their discussion of the use of ethnographic research in health care settings. They refer to the 'misguided separation of method from theory, of techniques from their conceptual underpinnings', adding that qualitative research 'is in danger of being reduced to a limited set of methods that requires little theoretical expertise, no discipline-based qualifications, and little training' (2002: 210). The tendency is for ethnography to become simply an adjectival prefix to qualify any form of research that goes beyond the focus group environment, survey or interview.

Their call is for anthropology to be written or theorised back into such practice. This represents a challenge, but also an opportunity for the discipline. There is much to be lost if this opportunity is not grasped because the tendency of unbound ethnography is to neutralise anthropology, to obscure it from view or even actively shut it out of the conversation. There is also much to be gained. A reassertion of the benefits and pleasures of an anthropological perspective, and a confident statement about the importance of theory, can enhance an understanding of the relationships between anthropology and ethnography.

This restatement of a relationship might have several positive effects. One, it reasserts the right of anthropology to a seat at the table of unbound ethnographers. It gets it back into a dialogue, as a discipline, with those outside the academy who are practising a form of research over which it has a uniquely strong claim of guardianship, but from which it can appear quite disconnected. Secondly, it might also act to allow anthropology to draw on the interest in ethnographic research to further its own agendas (or begin to redraw what these agendas are). Specifically, the popularity and allure of ethnography currently affords anthropology a strong opportunity to assert its place in public conversations about a huge range of issues in which ethnographic research is being conducted. Thirdly, and most practically, restating the relationship forces a revaluation of the training of anthropologists. This is either in respect of undergraduate courses and their vocational propensity, or postgraduate research and the need to refresh the training agenda for students about to embark on fieldwork.

It should be clear from the above that I am, in the words of Mills, an anthropological missionary and not a mandarin. No doubt there will be some who view the type of ethnographic research I have outlined above to be a rather impure practice. Such detractors are likely to be mandarins. However, I believe the growth of unbound ethnography raises more opportunities than it does threats. Ethnography has taken on a life of its own away from its traditional masters in the academy and is being widely employed in 'real world' contexts. Anthropology can learn from these practitioners and their techniques. In turn, future students of anthropology can understand better how the discipline, or elements of it are being put to use. Conversely, ethnographers have much to learn from the discipline of anthropology. The discipline can act to ensure that the academy speaks back to those practising ethnography. I think both sides will benefit from this dialogue. Practitioners of academic anthropology can extend their influence in applied settings. Practitioners of unbounded ethnography will learn that anthropology, as a source discipline for their activities, has much to offer them and can inform and enrich their work.

## Notes

1. My doctoral study at The University of Edinburgh and fieldwork in India was supported by an ESRC grant, R00429524285 (1995–2000).
2. Clynton Taylor, personal communication, Gestalt Research (www.clyntontaylor.com, accessed 19 July 2004).
3. I am happy to report that the use of ethnography by think-tanks is becoming more common and, at the time of writing, Ideas Bazaar are working with Demos.
4. All names are pseudonyms.
5. This discussion is drawn from conversations with the U.K. based Ethnography in Design Forum.
6. I am indebted to Clynton Taylor of Gestalt Research who compiled this long list of research descriptors from his on-going research into commercial research firms and who allowed me to use it here. (www.clyntontaylor.com, accessed 19 July 2004).
7. A recent advertisement for an ethnographer at General Mills read as follows: 'Full Time Ethnographer Needed – General Mills is looking for an ethnographer to join their staff as a full-time employee at their corporate headquarters in Minneapolis. An opportunity exists to conduct divisional ethnographic research to aid in advertising, positioning, new product and product improvement guidance. Position allows for a high degree of

creativity, team collaboration, facilitation, and close consumer interaction. Applicants must possess a Bachelors Degree and ideally, the following: MMR, MBA in Marketing or MA in Psychology, Mathematics or Economics; 3–5 yrs business experience with Consumer Research; Understanding Ethnographic and/or qualitative research experience'. Posted to the anthrodesign discussion mailing list: http://groups.yahoo.com/group/anthrodesign/, accessed 19 July 2004.

# References

Crabtree, J. and S. Roberts. 2003. *Fat Pipes, Connected People: Rethinking Broadband Britain.* London: Work Foundation/iSociety.

—— and M. Nathan. 2003. *MobileUK: Mobile Phones and Everyday Life.* London: Work Foundation/iSociety.

Deutsch, C. 1991. *Coping with Cultural Polyglots.* New York Times, *24 February.*

Firth, R. 1981. 'Engagement and Detachment: Reflections on Applying Social Anthropology to Social Affairs', *Human Organisation,* 40(3): 193–201.

Gaver, W.W., A. Dunne and E. Pacenti. 1999. 'Cultural Probes', in *Interactions* vi(1): 21–29.

Geertz, C. 1988. *Works and Lives: The Anthropologist as Author.* Stanford: Stanford University Press.

Gellner, D. and E. Hirsch (eds). 2001. *Inside Organizations: Anthropologists at Work.* Oxford: Berg.

Gordon, W. and V. Valentine. 2000. *The 21st Century Consumer – A New Model of Thinking.* MRS Annual Conference.

Kumar, N. 1992. *Friends, Brothers and Informants: Fieldwork Memoirs of Banaras.* Berkeley: University of California Press.

Lambert, H. and C. McKevitt. 2002. 'Anthropology in Health Research: From Qualitative Methods to Multidisciplinarity'. *British Medical Journal,* 325: 210–213.

Marcus, G. 1995. 'Ethnography in/of the World System: The Emergence of Multi-Sited Ethnography'. *Annual Review of Anthropology,* 24: 95–117.

Nathan, M., G. Carpenter, and S. Roberts. 2003. *Getting By, Not Getting On: Technology in U.K. workplaces.* London: Work Foundation/iSociety.

Roberts, S. 2000. *'Another Member of the Family': Aspects of Television Culture and Social Change in Varanasi, North India.* Unpublished Ph.D. thesis, The University of Edinburgh.

Spradley, J. 1980. *Participant Observation.* New York: Holt, Rinehart & Winston.

Suchman, L. 2000. *'Anthropology as 'Brand'*: Reflections on Corporate Anthropology', published by the Department of Sociology, Lancaster University at: http://www.comp.lancs.ac.uk/sociology/soc058ls.html.

*Chapter 4*

# THE NEED TO ENGAGE WITH NON-ETHNOGRAPHIC RESEARCH METHODS
## A Personal View

## *Adam Drazin*

Some anthropologists would consider themselves to be fundamentally different from market researchers, and see market researchers as similar rather to marketing executives. The author's personal experience, however, is that many market researchers would see themselves as similar to anthropologists, united by an interest in doing research. This chapter argues the case for anthropologists to engage with a wider 'research industry' which is large enough to incorporate many professions. A handful of different kinds of research methodologies from the author's experience are examined briefly, in terms of their appropriateness for different contexts and questions. On any particular project, ethnography may be best used to complement other methodologies, not as a stand-alone alternative, even if it produces alternative research perspectives. Applied anthropologists then need to work alongside other research professionals, and with very un-anthropological perspectives, if they are to further the interests of anthropology as a profession.

Central considerations for this argument are the definition of anthropology, and the perceived threat of the dissolution of the core discipline outside wholly anthropological institutions. I do not address these issues by asking what defines anthropology, but rather who defines it. The definition of anthropology results from constructive and critical exchanges, both among anthropologists and with non-anthropologists. In short, non-anthropological researchers are also defining us. In many applied contexts, a research product appears anthropological due to its generally striking, unquestionable difference from other researchers' products, not because it appears similar to other anthropologists' research. I can testify that my research appears both highly distinctive and recognisably anthropological in multidisciplinary environments, but find it hard to highlight exactly which aspects of my training and experience as an anthropologist have made it so. Thus the immediately apparent danger is of the lone anthropological worker losing touch with anthropology itself if they are not careful, but the actual danger would be a failure to realise what distinguishes the borders of anthropology as a whole. Among the suggestions of this paper is that anthropologists work not so much towards definitional terms for the discipline, but engage representational terms suited to the explication of sameness and difference alongside other researchers and research products, and I attempt to identify particular areas from experience where this is the case. Overall, the chapter aims to stimulate debate around these issues more than assert final conclusions.

I have often found personal, confessional accounts of research to be more useful than scholarly analyses, and this paper is written wearing my applied anthropologist's hat, rather than my mortarboard. I proceed by discussing this idea of engagement with a broadly-defined research industry: my own experience, the history of ethnography in industry, and certain advantages to engagement. There then follows a discussion of several possible research contexts for an applied anthropologist, based on my own search for locations from which to apply anthropological methods effectively. By anthropological methods, I mean principally those approaches defined as 'ethnographic', but I also mean a fluid reserve of approaches to research data in general, which develop and proliferate in the literature. Lastly, I discuss four representations of the role of the applied anthropologist and what he or she does.

## Anthropology and Research

The cover of a recent edition of *Research*, journal of the Market Research Society (MRS), sports a portrait of a child with the caption 'when I grow up, I want to be a researcher' (May 2003). The MRS and organisations like it are in the habit of frequently mentioning the 'Research Industry'. Representing research not only as an activity or a commodity, but as an industry, is one way in which the Society is able to promote market research as a profession, with its own diplomas, qualifications and career grades.

In between my first anthropology degree and my Ph.D., I worked for several years in this industry of market research and opinion polling. During this experience, I was struck by how the idea of 'research' is at the heart of what it means to be a 'market researcher', and is often much more important than the 'market' part of the appellation. Many market researchers I know would very frequently identify with academic anthropologists in the sense that both are interested in research first. There are dissenters, of course, but it is well known that the best market researchers are people who are simply dying to get on to the next piece of research and find something out. Like anthropologists, many try very hard to conquer their pre-existing presumptions when conducting a project. When organisations such as the MRS, or employers, exhort researchers to be 'client-oriented', it is because there are unfortunately still researchers who take the money because they enjoy doing the research, while ideally they would put the client's money foremost. The stereotypical marketing executive, with narrow interests in profits and sales, and lack of respect for the timing and details of research, is often represented as being on the outside of this world. Stereotypical academic researchers, although their idea of research is sometimes seen as a little pedestrian or unpragmatic, do nonetheless count as researchers and are frequently welcomed for their open minds and for simply being involved in the research process, from the conception of the research, through fieldwork to the analytical or interpretive phase and writing up.

Imagine my amazement when I began my anthropology Ph.D., and rediscovered how lecturers and students seemed to have the idea that market researchers are a form of marketing executive. At this stage of my anthropological career, although I was initially less well-read than some other doctoral students, I found myself relatively well prepared as a fieldworker for conducting ethnography in Romania. Hundreds of market research projects, chains of focus groups, and training involving tramping the streets of Essex towns knocking on doors with a clipboard, had equipped me fairly well for participant observation and data collection, if not for academic seminars. In early seminars at university, I found myself tremendously frustrated by the way a speaker would begin with a literary overview, when what I wished to hear and come to grips with was Who did the researcher speak to? Where? When? and How? I found it hard to convince myself to trust presentations of research without these politic methodological niceties.

The research environment outside of academia thus does not share the same intellectual stance to research, but is involved in a comparable research process. Although these two sets of researchers do not think the same, in many ways they do the same. Not every applied anthropologist will welcome the idea of applied anthropology as existing within a research industry, but it is a worthwhile endeavour to conceive of what this might involve, and examine the possible implications.

Anthropology has been involved to some extent in commercial research from its inception, especially through the employment of ethnography, yet rarely in the mainstream of research. The first structured market research methodologies were quantitative. Qualitative methodologies grew especially from the 1950s, and witnessed the victory of methods inspired by psychology over those developed by the social sciences. Mike

Imms (1999) has outlined how Ernest Dichter brought Viennese psycho-analytical methods to the U.S.A. and applied them in market research. In 1959, Bill Schlackman introduced these methods into the U.K. During this period, the value of depth interviews and discussion groups, conducted by researchers with psychological training, lay in gaining information beyond the immediately obvious. By divining the unspoken and the unconscious, researchers could outline information about people's motivations which other methods could not.

Imms suggests that in the present day the research industry is experiencing a form of crisis of qualitative methodology. In the 1980s to 1990s, discussion groups held by trained psychologists turned into focus groups convened by researchers with on-the-job training, not necessarily experienced in producing psychological models which dig deeper behind the research data. In addition, the psychological model of the mind as the wellspring of motivation is increasingly recognised as insufficient to explain the whole picture. Qualitative research is still required however to 'divine' – that is, to identify and describe – that which is not immediately apparent, and herein lies its value. In this respect, ethnography is one methodology to which potential research clients turn. The conception of people and consumers as existing within a social context, or within relationships, provides an alternative reservoir of unspoken or unconscious data to gain a perspective on their problems.

Seeing research as an industry first (as opposed to, for example, a craft or a profession) has a number of implications. Dictionary definitions of industry focus on the idea of a product, while the alternatives would imply research is a type of training, or a skill:

| | |
|---|---|
| **Craft** | an occupation or trade requiring special skill. |
| **Industry** | a branch of commercial enterprise concerned with the output of a specified product: *the steel industry*. |
| **Profession** | an occupation requiring special training in the liberal arts or sciences. |

*(Collins Concise Dictionary)*

Among the pragmatic implications of involvement with a research industry is thus a focus on the *product* of applied anthropology, in order to establish its position alongside other research professions. I shall develop this theme later in the chapter. Other potential advantages, which I shall discuss now, include the idea of good and poor quality in research, the way that an anthropologist is perceived by informants, and recognition of anthropology by those who would benefit from its research methods.

In June 2003, the cover of *Research* carried a provocative statement, half-obscured with a censor's pen marks: 'Researchers are lazy, expensive and downright unskilled – Inside: clients speak out uncensored, unplugged & uninterrupted.' The issue is quality. There is a continual sense of soul-searching over quality among the commercial research community, at least at a collective level. Article after article, and conference after conference, exhort individual researchers and companies to produce research of a better quality for clients. Implied in such exhortations is the tacit admission that some research is conducted which is simply not up to scratch, and it is the responsibility of the industry as a whole to improve it. In some cases, companies emerge which conduct activities outside the code of practice of the industry (for example, some types of indiscriminate data-gathering on people, or certain kinds of mystery shopping) and in this case the research industry strives to distance itself entirely from the activities concerned, sometimes saying they comprise wholly different industries. Anthropology generally takes the latter approach, but not the former. Often, poorly-conducted research is just not admitted to be anthropology. Some anthropology is good anthropology, but bad anthropology is much more likely to be exiled to the category 'not anthropology at all'.

Admitting of membership within a research industry has some potential advantages for conducting research. This is more the case in certain research contexts, or certain countries, than others. We should not presume in conducting research that 'anthropologist' is the only paradigm within which we are commonly understood. In the U.K., for example, many informants have a much better established conception of researchers than of anthropologists. Given this, faced with the person of the researcher, it is common for people to assume a role of advocacy. Lury (1994) observes in his research conducting focus groups in the U.K. how during the 1980s group participants began to see themselves as 'consumers'. Given understanding of a new role, they responded accordingly to being researched. In much applied anthropology, such considerations can be very useful in the pragmatic everyday mechanics of research, since traditional explanations (such as 'I'm writing a book') do not necessarily apply.

In most cases, a commercial client does not buy anthropology. They buy research in order to address problems. Much commercial research begins with a problem. This is true of all kinds of clients – not only companies and manufacturers, but charities, public bodies and policymakers. Clients however go first to research companies in order to solve these problems, for some of which anthropologists or ethnographic methods are useful, and not for others. If anthropology does not engage with the wider research industry, then we are leaving it to other commercial researchers, psychologists, economists and non-anthropological professions, to decide when to call on anthropology. Only by wider engagement can anthropologists encounter at an early stage the problems which we have the tools to address. The alternative is to find ourselves trying to fit ethnography to inappropriate issues, or else sniping away at the peripheral left-over difficulties of companies and clients, which no profession could address with satisfaction.

'Anthropology' describes what we do as applied anthropologists much better than 'research' does. Yet the two terms are not mutually exclusive. It is simply that we need to find ways to help people understand better what the first term involves. The label of research has a pragmatic value for us. It is the label that other people put upon us as anthropologists with some degree of understanding. If these clients, with half an awareness of anthropology, are to be assisted in understanding whether we can help them with certain issues and not with others, then inclusion within a research industry is important. This inclusion would help to give diverse client institutions access to applied anthropological methods and inter-·pretations.

## The Search for the Ideal Career

The pursuit of the perfect job is not the preserve of anthropologists. The last few years of my own career have involved working, often as a free-lancer, in a mixed bag of several fields of research in which an anthropological training has been useful. The general thrust of my experience, given my interests, is that working in the field of design anthropology has proved most successful. Anthropological fieldwork is more useful at an early, more conceptual stage of a project, rather than later on; and as with any anthropological project close attention must be paid to relationships, with informants and with the people I have termed clients. It is difficult to position oneself with respect to each of these groups, but the anthropological literature really only discusses how to position oneself with regard to the former. I have rarely conducted research alongside other anthropologists, but more usually with researchers from other professions – jobs are simply unlikely to be found in which we have the luxury of working with other anthropologists. Multidisciplinarity, however, is often an advantage, since in very many cases strictly anthropological research methods are not the most appropriate to address a particular problem.

### *Quantitative Social Trends Analysis*

Market research is continually making forays into the idea of culture, developing research methodologies which investigate in different ways the underlying social trends in society. There are a few such models on the market in the U.K. The methodologies often involve certain ways of sampling, or patented questions, which can be analysed in such a way as to produce a usable diagram which models sociocultural phenomena. A large, demographically representative sample of people across Great Britain may be interviewed periodically, producing a cluster-diagram of their social attitudes. The close correlation between certain attitudes means that attitudes can be grouped, each group comprising distinctive social perspectives. Such diagrams are produced using multivariate and cluster analysis, resembling the methods employed by Bourdieu (1984) in *Distinction* to model consumption tastes in France. Some companies, and some research products, may represent these clusters as groups of people, while others may represent them as groups of cultural perspectives. Part of the value of these research products is that models can be produced across different countries in Europe and further afield, giving them a clear capacity for cross-cultural comparison. The people who administer them additionally need to be fairly highly-trained, and able to provide a high degree of consultancy in interpreting the findings of projects.

Once a sociocultural model has been produced by research of a sufficiently large and statistically reliable sample, it can be put to a variety of research purposes. Depth interviews can be conducted in which the individuals are seen to represent social groups or perspectives identified in the larger model. Thus this approach seeks to present material which, while conducted with individuals, and in a commercially efficient fashion, is not socially isolated but in some sense contextualised. While nationwide surveys to build a model may be conducted by a nationwide field force of market research interviewers, research on specific projects may be conducted by individual researchers with training in different professions, such as anthropology, and integrated into the bigger picture. Many market research companies have a certain number of highly educated researchers, especially for qualitative research. Material on specific projects can be highly detailed and evocative of their everyday lives, involving depth interviews, ethnography, photographs and video.

This type of research product, modelling culture, communicates itself very well. Smart, attractive diagrams are produced which can be passed from desk to desk within an organisation, such that the research can fit into the institutional environment where it must have an impact. For full understanding, however, it nonetheless requires some explanation and consultancy. Presented in the right fashion, it can still encapsulate some of the valuable nitty gritty of people's everyday lives. Social diagrams need explanation, meaning that the researcher is able to speak with authority while preserving a degree of closeness to informants' points of view, and yet the number of ways one can represent informants is restricted within the terms of the model. At the same time, not every client finds the product useful. Some companies, and the businesses of some countries, operate with an idea of society or culture much more effectively. Other companies prefer to trust information which includes direct statements from individuals saying what they want. You are more likely to find a client who can use information about society in many European countries than in America, for example.

Such products should be taken account of by anthropologists. It would be very wrong to presume that anthropology is the only discipline which researches and models 'culture', because influential non-anthropologists in commerce are actively engaging with the idea of culture and modelling it. If we wish to be in tune with how culture is seen, defined and deployed within applied research, we need to engage critically and constructively with these methods. Cultural modelling may not be recommended by anthropology, nor even approaching culture through quantitative methods. Yet it is a valid question. If asked to advise on such a cultural model, an anthropologist should be able to advise on what questions might be better to ask.

## Consumer Consultancy

Consumer consultancy, in its assorted manifestations, is one of the fields in which there has been an increasing interest in ethnography and anthropology in recent years. Consultancy is a different business from market research in terms of its aims. Much consultancy aims at insights into what is happening in very general terms, insights which are communicated by individual experts whose personal interpretation is crucial to the value of the research. Individuals' skills sell the consultancy. In terms of the way consultancy addresses broad, underlying issues, it would seem to be a good area in which to apply anthropological approaches. Yet at the same time, consultancy does not require unspecified novel observations into consumption, but specifically insights which may be of use to companies, and which will sell. The specificity of ethnographic data is not always convincing in terms of communicating valid broader insights.

Consultancy work in which I have been involved has included adopting a networking approach to investigate domestic material culture and consumption. The remit can be quite specific, or else very openly-defined, exploring the assortment of associations which are made around consumed objects. Such research projects result in a number of immediate products. The research products are agreed on in advance, and are the prime objects of research contracts, and the measure of the fulfilment of the research objectives. Research products can include transcripts, photographs, video, summary reports or deeper analyses. I obtain written permission from people to use the information. I also change all personal and place names make information as anonymous as possible, and remove photographs of informants from the material. Research information is employed in different ways by different consultants. Dense, detailed information about people's lives is often welcome, but it is not always perceived as a unified product. Photographs in particular may make their way into different parts of consultancy literature and presentations.

Some of the value of research for consultancy hinges on information about brands and branding. Typically, these brands are pretty well formed, so possible interventions from research would be at a late stage, less likely to be relevant to the fundamentals of the branding project than more subtle adjustments. Unfortunately, branding and its subtleties are not necessarily of prime interest to informants in conversation. Left to tell their own stories, people do not necessarily talk about the functional use of the things they've bought, or the brands, but move swiftly on from the object to talking about their relationships and difficulties in everyday life. Some consumer consultants are equipped to draw conclusions from this type of data about trends in consumption, but not every consultant. The conception of the relationship between people and objects as comprising a 'consumer' evaluation of all available information, followed by a rational decision between clear choices, is highly prevalent. The 'consumer' format and understanding of the person is also the information format which consultancy clients find most useful.

One important lesson is to charge enough for the work of ethnography. A high enough price helps ensure that people pay attention to ethnography in meetings, and may return to the data to explore its themes; a lower price may mean the risk of not taking it seriously. Much ethnography needs an integrated, perhaps ongoing, analysis by an experienced ethnographer, preferably close to the field site, if it is to be made full use of. The pricing of research is a highly significant factor in attempting to develop an ongoing research project in which information can be returned to and explored in more depth. In many consultancies, salaries and timesheets are an obstacle to people spending substantial time doing ethnography themselves. A day out of the office is seen as too expensive. Outside consultants are paid by the day, which is difficult to calculate for ethnography, since good ethnography can involve a lot of hanging around waiting for the right opportunity. Developing an ongoing project, including analysis and consultancy, thus requires some skill.

## Laboratory Research and Usability Studies

Laboratory research and its techniques are highly influential and found to be useful in many research contexts and are not to be dismissed lightly. The laboratory has many manifestations and its techniques are not only employed in the physical sciences, but by psychologists. By extension, mainstream research techniques such as discussion groups owe a great deal to the tradition of attempting to establish laboratory conditions. When research is focused on particular issues, products or policies, the laboratory becomes an authoritative research tool.

In much product design work, lab-based research becomes especially significant for anthropologists in the field of usability and user studies. This field involves a wide variety of professions, including computer scientists, psychologists, designers, economists, sociologists, and the odd anthropologist. In design work, an anthropologist will typically find themselves working on the usability 'bit' of a project. Anthropologists are broadly well-equipped to assess contexts of use for new products and technologies, but by definition a new product will never be found in context, since it does not yet exist in everyday life. In order to produce focused results which they are able to analyse, usability experts often work in research laboratories, alongside scientists and engineers whose work requires the quantifiable data and the conviction which lab-based work provides. There is a need to produce research data which is comprehensible and authoritative to those people who are going to use it. Methodological considerations typically include an experimental design in which every participant experiences the same research process, and the use of a control group. Data varies, but could include questionnaires filled in by participants on their opinions, videos, and fluid discussions with them about their experience. Sometimes, pair-work can be used in order to introduce an element of verbalisation and interaction. There are manifold methods (see Dyers 1999).

Not every usability project is lab-based, many involve contextual observation, and there is often discussion and debate between team members over lab vs. context choices. The advantages of the lab include considerations of time and money, and the impracticality of taking new products or technologies outside the building. Prototype products can be highly commercially sensitive. They can be unique, unwieldy, flashy, expensive or embarrassingly cheap.

In my experience, the experimental set-up involves a few opportunities for the anthropologist to gain contextual information through which to draw conclusions. There are some opportunities during the search for willing participants who have an interest in the matter in hand, and in the process of introduction. So long as it is judged not to affect the results of the experiment, it is possible to chat with participants about their backgrounds, homes, their experiences and their motivations on key issues. This is thin data, but it is something, and in a multidisciplinary team it is the responsibility of the anthropologist to lever whatever sources are available for usable information. However, in lab contexts I consider anthropological observations and analyses can be more important than searching for specifically anthropological data sources. The kind of observations which an anthropologist makes are frequently different from other professions. The questions an anthropologist asks are distinctive. In product design, a device or technology has many other dimensions apart from its functionality, its capacity to inform, or its technical perfection. The object is also a way of relating to other people and building identity. Thus even in a piece of research which is not anthropological in design, the anthropologist can make valuable alternative analyses and observations.

## Design Anthropology

Design anthropology is a term which is becoming increasingly common, particularly in hi-tech firms. Think of a company in Silicon Valley and it is likely that nowadays they employ perhaps one or two anthropologists.

While ethnography has a long history in certain areas of design, such as Scandinavian design, recently contextual design and participatory design have been gathering steam within the design mainstream. In some instances a company has the resources to employ people exclusively as ethnographers, rather than having product designers do ethnography themselves. The most successful commercial applied anthropology projects in which I have been involved have been conducted in this field, and I have also taught ethnographic methods to designers. The exploration and inter-rogation of a context, or of broad themes and concepts, seems to have an affinity with the anthropological project although it is not an academic one. An example of the findings of such a project, conducted at and by Hewlett-Packard Laboratories, is published in more detail in Frohlich (2004).

Design anthropology in general varies a great deal in methodologies employed, but invariably means working in a multidisciplinary team, for example as the user studies expert. When a project is contextually-focused, however, the case for ethnographic techniques is strong, and the anthropologist is at an advantage in many situations. The kinds of methodological considerations which come into play are varied, and cov-ered in the extensive anthropological methodological literature. When it comes to working alongside other professions, however, it is not so much a question of how to engage with alternative methodologies, as of how to analyse and present anthropological data to a non-anthropological audi-ence. The anthropologist may, for a change, find themselves in the situa-tion not of being another team member, but addressing an issue about which they are themselves the authority, so the data has to stand up to scrutiny and address the problem. Even more than in an academic anthro-pological project, it is essential to find the right 'entry point' for ethnogra-phy, and ways of proceeding which will explore paths of relevance to the issues in hand, and relevant to the areas of expertise of the audience. There is also a need to consider the end-point of the research, since pro-jects have very definite deadlines and cut-off dates which strongly affect interactions with informants. Where the anthropologist works for a com-mercial company, gifts and incentives become expected, and pre-arranged interview/discussion situations the norm. Maintaining a contact in an acceptable fashion, and eventually terminating it in an acceptable fashion, is difficult. The process of interviewing and recording, with its implica-tions of commercialisation, is generally interpreted as a natural end-point in a relationship. Conducting ethnography for design is thus difficult, but often socially more acceptable than some other kinds of research. In con-trast to work on branding or consultancy, I have found informants very open to working with an anthropologist on issues of design. The progres-sive project of developing new technologies is one which has salient pur-pose for many informants, and which many people judge as dovetailing with their own interests. Some of the difficulties in relationships in design anthropology can derive from this perceived closeness, rather than from the effort to bridge a chasm which characterises many fields of applied ethnography.

## The Anthropologist Engaging with Non-anthropologists

In each of the examples given above, I have worked as an anthropologist alongside non-anthropologists, and found an unexpected phenomenon. Characteristics which I might have thought to be distinctive of my discipline are characteristics which other professionals use to represent theirs as well. Even the unlikely profession of market research presents itself in many respects as similar to anthropology. At the same time, my research contribution invariably distinguishes itself as anthropological. In general, no researcher from a different background and training seems to be capable of making a similar contribution. Thus the more one works with other fields, apparently in danger of losing one's anthropological expertise, the more the distinctiveness of anthropological approaches becomes evident. The question here is partly the definition of anthropology, but I wish to ask not 'what' is anthropology in these diverse, applied contexts, but more pertinently 'who' defines anthropology. The definition of anthropology can proceed internally, by anthropologists themselves stating what anthropology is about. Alternatively, it can proceed relationally by defining the borders of anthropology as against other professions and disciplines. To put it another way, both more rationalist and more empiricist approaches can be taken to anthropology's definition (see Moore 1999). The recent personal experience of the author has been that the two approaches are mutual, but that the latter may precede the former. That is, very many anthropologists must work in contexts where definitions of the nature of their own subject arise in a representational dialogue.

I would argue strongly that working alongside other professions, and engaging with non-anthropological methods, is of value to anthropology as a discipline. The more we do this, the more other researchers will familiarise themselves with the moments when anthropology and anthropologists will be useful. It is rare that a single methodology alone can provide all the answers which a research client requires. Based on my own experiences of research as an applied anthropologist, a few of which I have presented above, there are a number of ways in which the figure of the anthropologist can see him– or herself and the activity in which they are engaged. The hope is to clarify the self-identity of the applied anthropologist and his or her project, to illuminate the moment of the encounter with an informant or with a client.

## Challenging

Many applied anthropologists construct an analysis of their own situation which is essentially about power relationships. This analysis represents the anthropologist as a fighter, and anthropological research as a challenge. Most commonly, because the anthropologist almost invariably empathises more with their informants than with their clients, the way that they can best help the client is by allying with informants, and challenging the client to realign their misconceptions. I have heard a commercial research consultant with an anthropological training stress the prime importance of first challenging the given research brief. An anthropologist in the public sector meanwhile stated that the agenda of policy is dictated from above, prior to any research, so an aggressive stance is essential. Within design anthropology, some companies deliberately employ 'oddball' figures, who are supposed to provide abrasive alternative points of view which will stimulate creativity, like the grain of sand in the oyster; and this is the role in which anthropologists may find themselves. The challenging stance does not extend to customers or informants – both anthropologists and institutions are engaged in reaching out hands to them.

The idea of the anthropological research process as antagonistic is of course long-standing. Long ago, Emile Durkheim suggested that social facts are recognised through confrontations:

> A social fact is to be recognised by the power of external coercion which it exercises or is capable of exercising over individuals; and the presence of this power can be recognised in turn either by the existence of some definite sanction or by the resistance offered against every individual act that tends to contravene it. (Durkheim 1972: 64)

Ethnomethodological texts examine the matter in detail, but the role of direct critique has been a long-established way of pushing academic thinking forward.

There are, however, several limitations to the power analogy. To what extent can it help us to examine our relationship to our informants? Perhaps we can also communicate best with our informants by challenging them too; or perhaps we are somehow on their side, allied against the clients. Yet in either case, the analysis does not help particularly. A second issue is one of usefulness, or pragmatism. In what fashion is challenging useful? The idea of challenging does not indicate any particular approach to analysis, or modelling, on which it is possible to act or develop policy. Thirdly, and perhaps most importantly, there is the question of the role of challenger within a multidisciplinary team environment. It is unclear whether the anthropologist must always and invariably give the alternative perspective, about whatever and to whosoever.

## Providing

One of the most common complaints of applied anthropologists is that they do not have enough time. In this analysis, the anthropologist is seen as a producer, and their research as a trade-off between time and value. The complaint runs that either there is not enough time to do good field-work or else not enough to produce a satisfactory analysis. Many employers presume that one should spend time in the office, and that time spent outside is not productive. According to this perspective, the anthropologist is a figure whose role is to supply a particular creation, the prime value of which is the work he or she has put in to it. Following the dictionary definitions, this would place anthropology in the category of a 'craft'.

One of the main areas which it is necessary for applied anthropology to work on is justification of use of time, and demonstration of the value of time. It is not enough to say that we require more time. Rather, it is necessary to argue in specific terms what could be done with an extra day, or with an extra week, or month, or year. There will never be much hope for clients who would like to have ethnographic data tomorrow, or who have a fundamental misunderstanding of the value of ethnography. Yet the value/time balance needs to be spelled out quite explicitly for many potential beneficiaries of anthropological research.

## Analysing

Some applied anthropologists would see themselves as thinkers, and their research as a mode of analysis or inference. This analogy represents anthropology as a 'profession', requiring special training. The corpus of anthropological literature contains a number of characteristic approaches in which anthropologists are, or should be, trained. In my own experience, anthropological observations can be distinctive and valuable, even when non-ethnographic data is concerned. Even though we use different analyses in different situations, and shrink from the blanket imposition of any particular method, nonetheless an anthropological way of thinking, alongside non-anthropological approaches, generally stands out.

Yet it is not in fact clear to many of those who might benefit from anthropology just what the anthropological exercise is at an intellectual level. Clearly, anthropologists are never going to agree completely on a uniform definition of what we are about; but from the outside, many commonalities are apparent. The development and clarification of two areas might help in this respect: firstly, the way we represent modes of inference, to illuminate the exercise we are engaged in; and secondly the end aim of that exercise, what the topic of the anthropological exercise is. With regard to the inferences which we make, there are ways in which anthropologists can make the processes of their thinking more clear. A simple example is photography. A picture speaks volumes about context, and is largely self-justifying. Upon simple ways of communication such as this, more complex analyses can be communicated once the ice has been broken. There are certain keywords which, while they over-simplify the anthropological exercise on their own, recur over and over in anthropological presentations. If some such key terms were more widely understood than at present, the understanding of anthropological research as a whole would be advanced. Interpretation, reflexivity, perspective, contextualisation; these are the kind of terms which are found continuously in anthropological works, but whose anthropological usage is not commonly understood by other disciplines.

When it comes to the end aim of anthropological thinking, there are many people, even those familiar with using research of many kinds, who are completely mystified by anthropological representations. It is very clear to many research users that when psychologists present their research, they are talking about the individual mind. Psychologists rarely have to be explicit about this underlying creation, the presumption of a thing called the mind, which frames the usefulness of their research. Likewise, economists have created the commonly-understood idea of the economy. Anthropologists prefer terms such as culture, representation or interpretation. A better-developed understanding of the social object(s), in particular culture and society, towards which our methods and actions are directed would be of great benefit to applied anthropology. A business meeting or presentation is limited in time. The first ten minutes of a half-hour presentation is taken up with explaining anthropology, or that there is a thing called culture. We need not always lose this ten minutes, with a little propagation of terms such that the audience at least believes themselves to know the general topic in advance.

*Exchanging*

At the beginning of this chapter, I suggested that working within a wider research 'industry' implies seeing research in terms of its products. The self-conception of the applied anthropological role as an exchanger or trader between informants and clients, would mean consideration of the actual physical elements of research information, and ensuring that these are constructed in an appropriate fashion for the exchange. Marilyn Strathern (1987) has suggested that in her research in Melanesia, her informants proved interested in an ongoing interaction (comparable to a gift relationship), while in the U.K. they thought in terms of products and clear rights to products:

> In endlessly producing 'products' Western bourgeois culture is constructed
> as endlessly creative, a model that does not simply involve the permutations
> of products but the notion that production is also control, including control
> over the values given to things. What irritates the English villagers is not a

wish to gain what the anthropologist has but the way they see the arrogation of authorship. (Strathern 1987: 21)

As always, the spectre of an outdated gift/commodity contrast surfaces here in the contrast between two field sites, but the effort to define the research as a thing with particular exchange characteristics is nonetheless clear and valid. Let me give an example.

In my ethnographic work in Romania, it soon became evident that stylising research in too formal a fashion was inappropriate. While people agreed to my initial attempts to arrange 'interviews', I soon discovered that they would probably not be at home when I called at the prearranged time. Or, last-minute problems would mean they had to politely decline to meet. It was necessary for me to wait patiently for an invitation, which, it being a hospitable country, would come sooner or later. Likewise, asking people to sign consent forms for data would have appeared disrespectful; the closest parallel for this type of formal, official holding of data on individuals was the Communist secret police. The most significant and valued areas of social and economic life are largely based on domestic sharing, giving, and on ongoing exchanges. Most people would thus prefer an ongoing effort to interact, to make the effort to help with problems if possible, and when researching to check whatever is written with informants themselves. The data is constructed more in a stereotypical 'gift' form than as a commodity, although this may change over time. Meanwhile, in my first ethnographic research in the U.K., I found that informants preferred a commodity form of data. The request for an interview, the consent form by which they relinquish their rights to data, and the payment of an 'incentive', these are often taken as signs that the research is serious, and that consequently the researcher has their heart in the right place. When data is commoditised in the U.K., it is clear to informants that it is going to progress beyond the researcher, and thus have a wider impact. This is what makes it significant and valuable research in informants' eyes.

It is worth noting that the commodity form of data is also the most appropriate data form in many institutional contexts. Many firms go to extreme lengths to ensure that the data is commoditised to the utmost, that rights to it are highly transferable within the institution, and they are abnormally keen that payments are made to informants. The commodity form is the most appropriate form of research data for institutions because it must be fully transferable between different offices and meetings, and it would in a sense be immoral to possess data in other forms for these purposes. Thus the commodity stands at the apogee of institutional morality, and extreme efforts at commoditisation are often made.

There are interesting variations on this theme, which I can illustrate with reference to photographs in Romania and in the U.K. In Romania, photographs played a large part in my fieldwork. Taking photographs became my role at events such as birthdays, weddings and parties, and I would provide copies for many informants. Often, people insisted that they pay for these pictures. By contrast, in ethnography in the U.K., money changes hands around photographs much less often. Whether I provide photographs to informants, or whether they provide them for me as fieldworker, they are generally freely given. While in successive projects informants have seemed fairly keen to sign a consent form through which they transmit full rights to use recordings of their voices, to texts and comments, rights around photographs are much more variable and specific in the U.K. Informants prove happy to give copies of photographs, and even seem encouraged by the idea that they may be used elsewhere. In a sense, the more people see one's photographs the better. But the property rights over the photographs are a different issue, and are more contradictory and contested. They are in a sense like paintings, in which the photographer's name should be inalienably inscribed underneath. Sometimes, consent forms can wind up with a full renunciation of rights over audio and text information, but with parts of the document referring to photographs deleted; such informants still informally express a happiness for photographs to be circulated, want them circulated, it is just that they are their photographs. There can be contradictory expectations that voice and textual data should be anonymised, while photographic creations should be personalised. The different elements of data can thus require different treatment.

It is highly important to attempt to construct the products of research data in such a way that it is appropriate for the context of informants, and for clients. This exercise can mean a particularisation of different elements of the data, and consideration of how we specifically package the physical outputs and deliverables. Consent forms, the use of names and pseudonyms as appropriate, and the possible necessity of ongoing contact with informants, as they prefer, are all possible tools in this project of the appropriate research product.

## Conclusion

Applied anthropology is an imperfect exercise, and this chapter has been aimed more at pragmatism than perfection, and is open to contestation.
I have presented a personal viewpoint arguing for an open approach by anthropology to engagement with all kinds of research and with other professions' methods. I have attempted to present primarily the case for engagement with a research industry, and an approach to anthropology which considers not only core definitions, but the relationships in which we engage and the representational terms appropriate to these. Taken to extremes, approaching anthropology purely through core methods and modes of inquiry would lead inevitably to the conclusion 'unite or die'; while the lone anthropologist would seem always at greatest risk from the

perfidious snipers of other disciplines and intellectual traditions. Yet, of course, anthropology is well-equipped to learn about itself from peripheral figures and relationships with other professions.

This argument is not only a matter of the current fashion for multidisciplinary research – both in commerce and in academia, research money is increasingly contingent on working across disciplines – there are also research benefits. Non-anthropologists need to know more about anthropology and when to use it, and even in projects deploying non-anthropological methods, the involvement of an anthropologist can result in distinctive analyses. The question of how we conceive of applied anthropology is not only presentation, a matter of icing on the cake. There are also strategic implications on the ground for how an applied anthropologist behaves in the everyday face-to-face encounters of research. Conceiving of anthropology as a craft, as a profession, or within a research industry, results in different stances to the aims and value of the research project. The work of research, the analyses, the products, and the stance with respect to informants and beneficiaries of the research, are all implicated. A central concern is how to promote a wider understanding that the usefulness of much anthropological research hinges on multiple perspectives, while attempting to position oneself as more closely allied to communities of informants than to communities of clients. I hope this chapter has said enough to provoke some form of debate around these issues.

## Acknowledgements

The opinions expressed in this paper are wholly those of the author. Particular observations are not based on any single study, but a broad experience of working as an applied anthropologist in a variety of contexts.

## References

Bourdieu, P. 1984. *Distinction*. London: Routledge & Kegan Paul.
*Collins Concise Dictionary*. 1999. Glasgow: Harper Collins.
Durkheim, E. 1972. *Selected Writings* (ed. A. Giddens). Cambridge: Cambridge University Press.
Dyers, J. 1999. *A Practical Guide to Usability Testing*. Bristol: Intellect Books.
Frohlich, D. 2004. *Audiophotography: Bringing Photos to Life with Sounds*. London: Kluwer Academic Publishers.
Imms, M. 1999. 'A Re-assessment of the Roots and Theoretical Basis of Qualitative Market Research', in *Conference Papers of the MRS Conference*. London: the Market Research Society.

Lury, A. 1994. 'Advertising – Moving Beyond the Stereotypes', in R. Keat, N. Whiteley and N. Abercrombie (eds) *The Authority of the Consumer*. London: Routledge.

Moore, H. 1999. 'Anthropological Theory at the Turn of the Century', in H. Moore (ed.) *Anthropological Theory Today*. Oxford: Polity Press.

*Research*. 2003. May, June Nos. 444–5. London: Market Research Society.

Strathern, M. 1987. 'The Limits of Auto-Anthropology', in A. Jackson (ed.) *Anthropology at Home*. London: Tavistock Publications.

# PART III

# ANTHROPOLOGY AND THE PUBLIC SECTOR

Chapter 5

# INTERNATIONAL DEVELOPMENT, SOCIAL ANALYSIS, ... AND ANTHROPOLOGY?
Applying Anthropology in and to Development

*Maia Green*

## Introduction: Social Development and Anthropology

This chapter explores some aspects of the current place of social anthropology within the international development sector. It looks at the changing context and nature of anthropological input as approaches once associated with anthropology become subsumed within 'social development' as an emergent specialisation within an increasingly professionalised field. Social development methods and approaches have much in common with social anthropology, but there are substantial differences. Perhaps the most fundamental of these is the fact that what constitutes social development knowledge is determined by the need to meet policy priorities within what is defined as 'development' at a particular time rather than the pursuit of knowledge as an end in itself (Green 2002). The relation with policy frameworks and the need to produce instrumental knowledge that can be made to work, at least in the ideal, in serving a distinct policy agenda, means that social development knowledge is not so much concerned with the locally specific as with the production of models that can be applied in more than one setting. This is quite unlike anthropology which, being field-based, draws on 'an over determined setting for the discovery of difference' (Gupta and Ferguson 1997: 5).

Social development presents itself as a technical discipline, based on what are claimed to be core competencies in a development practice, which, whilst acknowledging the importance of process, remains essentially committed to an understanding of social analysis as a prerequisite for the management of social transformation. In this, social development

Notes for this chapter begin on page 126.

adopts the perspectives of social policy, and of a particular sociological tradition that has prioritised understanding society with a view to social improvement. This contrasts with the perspective predominant in social and cultural anthropology that has, since Durkheim, prioritised the analytical dissection of social and cultural forms rather than their manipulation (Rabinow 1995: 171).

The need to produce knowledge that can be operationalised within the particular institutional settings of development, constrained by budgets on the one hand, and, on the other, by expectations about what constitutes technical expertise, has consequences for social development methodologies. Like anthropological methods, these are people focused and based on qualitative techniques. Unlike anthropological methods, premised on extended fieldwork lasting up to several years, social development methodologies are designed to fit into dramatically shortened time frames. The social development adaptation of social research methods entails a dissembling into simplified components, which are then presented as 'tools' accessible to non-specialists, and which have been designed for use in short periods of time. Such methods have evident limitations. Notwithstanding the lack of depth to research produced so rapidly, the toolkit approach to social analysis tends to either predetermine the imputation of causality, or, as in 'stakeholder analysis' (a technique for exploring significant social relations in development) be reducible, ultimately, to a simple pictogram of mono-directional links between what are assumed to be significant social categories (Green 2002).

Conventional understandings of anthropologists working in development as translators of culture have been transcended in practice by a range of changes within the structure and practice of international development and within anthropology itself. As anthropology becomes increasingly aware, both of its potentialities and its limitations, its object of study is revealed as an increasingly self-conscious choice made by the anthropologist, and facilitated by the institutional context in which he or she works. Anthropology, like much of what it critiques, is explicitly political and anthropologists, in selecting topics for research, are making political choices, even if this fact is underplayed within the discipline (cf. Scheper-Hughes 1995).

Social development, as a framework for the knowledge used to support policy instruments or the choice between them in the drive to achieve development objectives, is also explicitly political. However, the institutional location of social development practice within development organisations, and within the institutions funded to produce their knowledge, means that social development knowledge has to appear less as politically determined than technical knowledge. Its proponents are less free than their anthropological counterparts to make explicit the political contingencies on which the production of such knowledge frameworks depend. Social development knowledge, like other kinds of knowledge, including anthropology, is produced and reiterated within institutional environments that both delimit what is recognised as knowledge, and the kinds of persons authorised to engage in its production (Douglas 1986; Watts 2001; Cooper and Packard 1997: 21).

Although I am a professional anthropologist, employed to teach and conduct research in anthropology within an academic department inside the formal university sector, I am at least partially recognised by some international development institutions as a social development professional, that is as a person able to practise social development. This positioning allows me a privileged insight into the applied versus academic anthropology divide[1] as one who practises both social development anthropology and academic anthropology as two distinct and largely unrelated fields of expertise.[2] It also allows me to turn the anthropological 'gaze' reflexively on my own practice within the development sector.

The representation of an 'applied' anthropology as what anthropologists do in development, distinct from academic or theoretical anthropology, is now largely an imagined construct of academic anthropologists, at least in the U.K. context. Within international development, people like myself with anthropology backgrounds, or who have jobs as anthropologists but who nevertheless work in social development, may apply anthropological insights and make use of knowledge gained through studying anthropology, but we work increasingly as planners and managers of processes of social and institutional transformation aligned with global policy templates (Cooper and Packard 1997: 24). These templates, through which development policy is globally effected, assume a universality of social architectures as either social facts, or as desirable outcomes of the development endeavour (Green 2003). Moreover, changes in the structure of international development and the ways in which development policy is thought to operate most effectively, have reduced the potential entry points for anthropology, even of the 'applied' sort, within the official frameworks of international development assistance. Where anthropology and other social science research probably contributes most to development is, as Escobar and others have shown, through closely observed accounts of what people do, which may challenge previously held truisms in development thinking, that is in the anthropology of development rather than development anthropology (Escobar 1997: 498).

## International Development: Delimiting the Field

The field of international development to which I refer in this chapter is the network of institutions and agencies engaged in the activities and transfers associated with international development assistance. These include multilateral agencies like the World Bank and the various United Nations bodies, as well as the bilateral agencies of national governments such as the United Kingdom's Department for International Development; national and international non-governmental organisations (NGOs) and those agencies in recipient countries which work in 'partnership' with donor institutions for the joint implementation of projects and programmes. Typical partner organisations include national governments, national NGOs and the lower tier community-based organisations (CBOs).

The institutional context of international development extends far beyond the formal institutions charged with implementing development oriented programmes. As ideas about development and cultural attitudes informed by development aspirations become increasingly entwined with popular cultures within so-called developed *and* developing country settings, development, as a social institution, transcends the limitations of what I have referred to elsewhere as 'project space' – the space of social action that formal sector development agencies strive to plan as the object of project management techniques (Green 2003). Rural communities in Nepal utilise the category of 'developed' (*bikas*) as a means of classifying people according to perceived class position and social networks (Pigg 1992; Shrestha 1995). Conversely, relatively wealthy individuals in the U.S.A. provide money for communities perceived as 'poor' via World Vision's child sponsorship scheme, which emphasises the absence of facilities within entire communities as epitomising the absence of the kind of exemplar of 'development' in the form of infrastructure that the anticipated resource transfers could provide, if only individuals were willing (Bornstein 2001).

While accounts of the interface between development agency and the agents of development reveal important truths about the social relations development brings into being, anthropological studies of development have generally focused on the processes of social transformation, both positive and negative, conventionally associated with development in the popular meaning of the term, as a transition towards directed change, towards modernisation, industrialisation, capitalisation and so on, whatever components are associated with the idea of progress at any particular time. More recent critiques of development as modernisation have exposed the culturally specific origins of this perspective, and the absence of a clear relationship between the attributes supposedly constitutive of 'development' and social transformation. They have also pointed to the scale of the asymmetries between developer and developee that characterises development interactions (Crewe and Harrison 1998) nationally, as when development becomes a new profession for a small, educated elite (Sampson 1996; Pigg 1992) and internationally, when rich countries and institutions determine the policy choices and levels of public services of those countries they aim to develop (Moore 2001).

Although the evolutionist concept of progress continues to inform paradigms within international development thought and practice in myriad ways, international development institutions today are not primarily concerned with effecting this kind of transition towards an assumed modernity, nor with the transition to global capitalism, despite what critics of international development attest. International development policy is more complex and more contested than a juggernaut imposition of global forces on poor nations. Many international development agencies are more concerned with protecting people from the full impacts of globalisation and market forces, than with wholesale integration; with the establishment of mechanisms for some level of social protection in poor countries, and with ensuring that social changes bring some benefits, at least to those at the bottom of the social hierarchy. It is not unusual for such agencies, even if they are government departments, to find themselves at odds with the priorities of other sections of their own governments over policies that prioritise interventions assumed to lead to economic growth, but are also likely to have negative impacts on the poor. Such differences of opinion frequently arise in relation to large-scale power projects, which may involve dams and population displacement, the sale of arms to poor countries, and the spending priorities of poor countries, which may prioritise growth at the expense of the vulnerable.

Human development is no longer assumed to be an automatic concomitant of economic development.[3] Development in practice must be defined not as an undefined set of outcomes around social and economic change, but in policy terms, as what the institutions charged with its implementation claim they are setting out to do (Green 2002). The project of development, and by extension development projects and the programmes within which they are embedded, is essentially concerned with achieving these policy objectives through the large-scale transfer of resources from donor agency to recipient institutions. As a transfer of resources, financial, human, and technical, oriented toward the achievement of specific outcomes, development as an institution is as much concerned with the practice of management as with the specialised kinds of knowledge that may or may not pertain to achieving development policy objectives (Green 2003). This relation between development and management has implications for the kinds of knowledge that development needs in order to operate. In the current institutional configuration of development practice, knowledge is perceived as a means of achieving policy objectives. Knowledge within the institutional context of development is then not merely a resource to be managed, as Mehta (2001) demonstrates in relation to the World Bank's bid to become the global source of development knowledge, but a management tool.

For much of the past decade the major Western agencies and multilateral organisations have interpreted development at its most basic in terms of the elimination of poverty. Poverty, defined in relation to the presence or absence of basic services and in income terms (less than one dollar a day), comes to be a proxy for the absence of development, and a justification for intervention. Development is thus defined in negative terms not so much as the presence of something, as the elimination of an unacceptable state. Poverty and development are measured by indicators and targets, some global, others national that become a highly politicised part of the international development framework (Apthorpe 1997). Institutional mechanisms for the measurement and assessment of poverty now form part of the international development architecture. More fundamentally, the equation of poverty with *un-development* and, by extension, the absence of material things with backwardness, informs the conceptualisations of the beneficiaries of development, the poor themselves, as lacking in the material wherewithal to participate in progress (Shrestha 1995; Pigg 1992; Green 2000). Representations of poverty shared by developer and developee as an attribute of particular social categories, most obviously women, children and indigenous peoples, and of the places in which they live, owe much to these kinds of representations (Jackson 1996).

As the elimination of poverty is the goal of the international development effort, so poverty must be measured and assessed as an index of development's functioning (Green *in press*). National poverty assessments and indicators are now standard devices for development implementation in poor countries. The focus on poverty does not necessarily imply that poor people are more involved in the development planning process than previously. The Participatory Poverty Assessment (PPA), a scaled-up version of the Participatory Rural Appraisal, with scaled-up limitations, as the institutional mechanism for listening to the poor on developers' terms, allows for the limited articulation of key concerns that conform to the policy priorities of development institutions. The poor, like Marx's peasants, 'cannot represent themselves, they must be represented' (Marx 1987: 332). The anthropologist David Mosse has shown how participatory research methodologies used in development may operate to exclude certain social categories from involvement in the research process at the same time as restricting the kinds of issues which the research can address (2001). Paradoxically, participatory research methods may actually obscure the exposition of social issues, the very issues which constitute poverty, not so much as the absolute condition characterised by international development, but as a social relation. If poverty assessments can be seen as a scaling-up of small-scale and micro-oriented approaches to development research, development interventions have undergone a parallel increase in scale. This is evidenced through the shift from projects to programmes and more recently to national strategies for poverty reduction (PRS) through which sector programmes,[4] national policy and other interventions are combined in a unified programme oriented towards a common goal. Both 'scaling-up' and participatory methodologies have consequences for the role of anthropology in development, and for social development practice.

## Anthropology in Development

If international development agencies define development practically in terms of their policy objectives, social anthropology has not necessarily shared this vision, tending to view development in the same kind of evolutionist terms as the processes it has set out to critique (Sahlins 1999: ii).[5] Suspicion of change, which could broach the integrity of cultures, has led anthropology in the U.K. and the U.S. to be sceptical of 'development' in general, and to operate in a heightened state of awareness of culture loss and culture change. The anthropologist Marshall Sahlins has argued that such assumptions rest on unfounded notions about history and culture, which, despite anthropological claims to having transcended the a-historicism of functionalism and the purported break between 'hot' and 'cold' societies, or West and Other, misses the essential point about the very cultures that anthropology has sought to describe and protect. Culture is not an arbitrary attribute which people 'have', but a project that people work to produce. As such, it is continually being changed by people as they make history. In a globalised world, this ongoing process of cultural construction is itself influenced by anthropological representations in the context of ethnic differentiation, and within discourses of heritage and authenticity (Sahlins 1999: x). In any case, change does not necessarily mean loss. It can mean gain or intensification. What change means is determined by the people whose societies and situations change, rather than by the judgements of anthropologist observers. For example, despite the claims of evolutionist influenced anthropology in the 1970s that hunters and gatherers would transform into wage labourers and lose their 'culture', a significant proportion of hunting communities continue to make their living through hunting. Further, they continue to culturally prioritise these modes of livelihood, not so much through isolation from the global economy, as integration within it.[6] In the case of Inuit peoples of North America, adoption of hunting technologies and modern forms of transport allow for the intensification of hunting, at the same time as integration into the national welfare state subsidises this mode of subsistence (Sahlins 1999: vi–ix). Equally, the mode of livelihood associated with Southern African hunter gatherer communities was, arguably, not an inherent expression of culture associated with a particular population so much as a response to wider economic and social transformation, contingent on integration into world markets, and the development of the cattle economies of communities like Herero (Wilmsen 1990).

If anthropology has conventionally been suspicious of unplanned changes, perhaps even of history, it has been particularly distrustful of directed change and of the international development project, which has had directed change as its objective (Escobar 1991). The ambivalent relationship between anthropology and development has its origins in the colonial administrative project of governance, and coterminous with this, the projects of social improvement which comprised the New Deal in the United States, and informed the emergence of what became the subdiscipline of applied anthropology (Gupta and Ferguson 1997: 22). While British anthropology under Malinowski strove to make anthropology useful to the 'practical men' of colonial administration, as the discipline consolidated itself in the 1930s through accessing public funds, its eventual institutionalisation led ultimately to the separation of applied and academic fields, paralleling a new division of labour in the colonial service between administrators as 'men of power' over colonial populations, and anthropologists as 'men of knowledge' about them (de L'Estoile 1997: 346).

Despite the protestations of Kuper (1973: 116) that anthropologists played a minimal role in the encounter between British colonialism and indigenous populations, anthropological knowledge was fundamental to the institutionalisation of ethnicities, on which indirect rule was premised. In this sense, 'the connection between the development of anthropological knowledge and the colonial venture was thus not accidental or external, but indeed structuring' (de L'Estoile 1997: 347). The relationship between anthropological knowledge and colonial governance was also strong in France, where van Gennep, amongst others, argued for the integration of the anthropological project into the colonial endeavour in the firm belief that, 'better science was the means to better colonial government' (Rabinow 1995: 165). This particular history of implication has contributed to the critical perspectives with which so-called applied anthropology has often been viewed within, and outside, the discipline, and to the suspicion with which anthropology is still viewed in many countries that have fairly recent histories of colonial domination.

The involvement of anthropology in development did not end with the dawning of the postcolonial era. Anthropological knowledge was, arguably, as central to the imagination of the new subjects of international development as it had been to the self-same subjects of colonial governance. Anthropology was not only intellectually enmeshed in the postcolonial project. Institutional incorporation followed. The formal inclusion of the discipline within the institutional structures of international development gathered pace from the late 1970s reaching an apex in the 1990s when a limited number of anthropological positions were institutionalised within a number of key bilateral and multilateral agencies, including the World Bank (Cernea 1995: 340–341). These positions should be differentiated from the employment of 'anthropologists' within such institutions. As Little and Painter make clear, the majority of those with anthropological training working within international development *do not work as anthropologists* and are not employed to do so, but as managers, civil servants and administrators of the large-scale resource transfers which comprise the development enterprise (1995: 603). As in the colonial context where, despite their discipline's contribution to the representations which gave colonial governance its specific character, the direct engagement of anthropologists in actual processes of governance was limited, the involvement of anthropologists within development institutions has tended to be muted, even marginal. Horowitz goes so far as to suggest that social science within development institutions, including anthropology, has tended to ghettoise itself, acceding power to the dominant economistic paradigms, which drive agency agendas (1996: 1–11).

This new role for anthropologists within development agencies in the 1980s and 1990s coincided with a new people-oriented discourse in international development, and a renewed consideration to issues of social exclusion and marginality. Cultural brokerage in the form of understanding the poor and the cultural dispositions which seemed to work against the goals of modernisation became central to the project of international assistance; a project which changed in emphasis as new insights were adopted from social research and from activist professionals such as Robert Chambers, whose combination of Freirean action, learning and social analysis lead to the promotion of 'bottom up' perspectives and what have come to be known as 'participatory approaches' to development (Green 2000). But anthropologists working in such agencies remained largely concerned with cultural issues, interpreting practices around areas difficult for others to access and which seemed mystifying for those without detailed comparative knowledge of social organisation. Common themes included gender, kinship, transhumance, and common property resources. Anthropological input was confined to restricted points in a project cycle, at the initial appraisal stage, and at the end, analysing why planned outcomes had not transpired.

Alongside this expansion in the international sector, what was now called 'applied anthropology' was growing within the United States as a specialisation that used cultural knowledge to inform the planning of public interventions for groups whose needs were perceived to be somehow culturally opaque – at least to the White American policy maker. Anthropology in the U.S. and in South America was associated with cultural brokerage between indigenous groups and national governments, and between indigenous groups and private companies, often those associated with natural resource extraction. The 'anthropologist as advocate' position continues to characterise much applied anthropology in Papua New Guinea and Australia to this day. Such positionalities not only raise ethical dilemmas and point to contestations about what counts as knowledge, and the obligations of anthropologists (as recent Australian court cases demonstrate) (Mardiros 1997; Brutti 2001; Strathern and Stewart 2001), but contribute to the perpetuation of a perception that when anthropologists work in 'development,' or with 'local' people, what they are doing is brokerage, advocacy or cultural translation work. It also contributes to the essentialisation of what anthropologists think anthropologists do, can, or should do, which seems to hinge on an obligation to represent the interests of fieldwork populations, as if these were unitary and unproblematic.

Arguments within the discipline about the roles and obligations of anthropologists conducting so-called applied work, hinge on an assumption that doing anthropology or being an anthropologist are clearly delimited fields of activity, with coterminous moral sensibilities that seemingly oblige the anthropologist to adopt certain positions (Scheper-Hughes 1995; Gow 1993).

These views depend on an unrealistic notion that one can delimit anthropology, as a practice, and as a profession, and conflict with claims made within the discipline that fieldwork-based research must generate knowledge that is based on research findings, rather than on predetermined obligations to represent certain kinds of truths for certain social categories of persons (Mardiros 1997). In practice, neither position is tenable. Accepted critiques within the social sciences, and within anthropology have exposed the fallacy of seeking, and trying to represent objective truth and the false promise of scientism, while explicit alliance with certain political positions equally compromises any claims to, if not truth, an honest presentation of research findings. In actuality, anthropology has neither more nor less moral credibility than the other social sciences, with which it must struggle for survival in an increasingly interdisciplinary universe. Its boundaries are permeable and weak. In a discipline which has minimal presence outside the ivory towers of established universities, the majority of those identified as anthropologists or who identify themselves as such, are part of a tiny group of academics employed within an elite university sector. Such individuals continue to practise what those established in the profession recognise as `anthropology'; occasional, if extended, periods of field-based research and the production of articles and books oriented towards a community of specialists pursuing questions of theoretical interest to anthropologists. These questions mostly hinge on issues of cultural comparison and translation. However, not all anthropologists confine themselves to this kind of anthropology. These same individuals also do other kinds of social research work, and for different audiences. Whether this is 'anthropology' or not is less significant than the fact that different kinds of social research and analysis work can be done by people with a similar background, whether or not they are 'anthropologists'.

## Changing Contexts of Anthropological Input

Anthropologists today do highly diversified kinds of work for governments, international agencies and the private sector, and the work they do is changing. Just as the field of anthropological inquiry has changed within the academic sector, and what constitutes anthropological knowledge has broadened, it is now accepted that what anthropologists can do in other sectors, extends beyond the project of cultural translation. That very project, dependent as it is on a particular kind of relationship between subject and translator, is now open to question. This is not only within a more self-aware anthropology sensitive to post-colonial critiques, but within the new institutional frameworks of doing development that create the possibility of allowing, albeit formally, the subaltern to speak.[7] By the 1990s the old role of anthropology as cultural brokerage was beginning to change, in the international development sector at least, where participatory approaches institutionalised through PRA (Participatory Rural Appraisal) and RRA (Rapid Rural Appraisal) had become expected, if not the norm. Specialist social researchers and consultants certified in these fields facilitated the kinds of studies that anthropologists may have been commissioned to undertake previously. Such surveys became not merely opportunities for the generation of knowledge, but fora where critical understandings about relations between so-called beneficiaries and policy makers could be negotiated (Mosse 2001). At the same time, a new cadre of professional social researchers from within developing countries was beginning to emerge. The 'local' consultant, assumed to have more intimate access to local populations, as well as local knowledge and expertise, came to be a required part of project appraisals and scoping studies; in the process assuming the mediating role of translator between recipient community and donor agency.[8] Participatory approaches to development and the utilisation of local experts where possible have limitations, but do, to an extent, obviate the need for an outside 'expert' to explain the Other when the new frameworks allow the others to begin to explain themselves.

The modalities for international development assistance were also changing. While development had always been concerned with resource transfers on a massive scale, through financial aid and direct government to government loans and transfers, this less visible aspect of development has always received less attention in anthropology than small-scale projects and programmes, despite the fact that the former has always accounted for the bulk of development spending. Structural adjustment and the conditionalities associated with financial aid attracted much negative attention from activists and academics concerned about the negative impact on the poor, as governments forced to control spending, cut back on social sectors. Previously protected prices and subsidies for certain interest groups were eroded. Development agencies in the orbit of the World Bank began to rethink the delivery of aid and to refine the instruments they used to implement development policy. The result, worked out during the 1990s, was an attempt to make the delivery of aid more effective and efficient, reducing the fragmentation of numerous projects, and striving to ensure that a greater proportion of the benefits brought about through resource transfer would benefit the poor as the ultimate targets of development policy. Moves to promote efficiency-oriented reforms in government services in poor countries aimed to compensate for public spending cuts by making services work better. New management techniques, user participation, and cost sharing were widely promoted as common strands in a reform template implemented from Antigua to Zambia, and which is still in process.

The World Bank itself recognised the complex environments in which development policy was supposed to operate and had failed. A modified policy discourse spoke of the need to include local populations in development planning, of the potential role of civil society, of the importance of local social networks, and of partnerships as the defining attribute of relationships between donor organisations and their poor country counterparts (World Bank 1999).

Effective policies and programmes were not merely concerned with impact as the great unknown of the international development effort. Another side of effectiveness was efficiency, reducing the inputs of money and personnel required to achieve outputs. This was to be attained through scaling up, reducing the costs of the development transaction by applying the same effort to fewer larger initiatives, and through working more closely with other donors, thereby allowing efforts to be concentrated in a unified way on particular areas of activity. Sector programmes paved the way for an additional tier in macro management in the form of the national poverty eradication strategies, initially as a UNDP initiative which became globally significant as the key instrument of the Highly Indebted Poor Countries (HIPC) programme of debt relief in return for country anti-poverty strategies. National poverty reduction strategy papers (PRSPs) created through collaborative negotiations with government, donors and various interest groups (including national and international NGOs) currently form the basis of the country assistance strategies which legitimate and prioritise donor focus and spend in the countries in which they operate, as well as, in theory, the policies and priorities of national governments.

## Applying Anthropology to Development

These modalities for the management and institutionalisation of development assistance and the political influence that accompanies it are fairly recent. Not much is known about the extent to which such mechanisms represent a real opportunity for governments and donors to work on effective strategies for reducing poverty or achieving development objectives in particular countries, nor even what it would mean, and for whom to eradicate poverty, in countries like Tanzania or Nepal. The bulk of research examining the PRSP process or poverty as a development category is conducted well within the borders of the development federation, the informal alliance of agencies, universities and research institutes supported by and working within international development that help shape what is recognised as development research and development knowledge (Goldman 2001: 205). Those outside this federation have limited access to these processes and within affected countries, few remain outside it for long as academics and consultants quickly get drawn into the new and lucrative institutional relationships around the poverty reduction process.

Whatever the longer-term impacts of the new anti-poverty architecture on poverty, politics, and the countries where such mechanisms are implemented, the shift in international development towards scaling upwards and institutional reform has altered the entry points for anthropology and transformed the nature of social development itself. Previously the category of the social had referred in practice to particular social categories as the targets of development. Social development expertise in this context was oriented towards accessing these targets, hence the consolidation of knowledge about social categories such as the poor, women, children, indigenous peoples, and those with disabilities. In the new perspective, what constitutes the social in development is shifting from the specific to the general, from the minority to the majority, and from a focus on specific groups to efforts to address poverty as a state, in which substantial proportions of populations in so-called developing countries live. This perspective fits in with the scaling-up ideology. Projects previously aimed at social groups are superseded by programmes that aim to address poverty as an absolute condition by raising incomes or improving access to services. A *social proportion* rather than a *social category* becomes the target of development assistance and, under the poverty reduction strategy framework, of the activities of national governments. This shift has consequences for the kinds of knowledge about the social that development requires. Whereas the social was previously perceived as a category of development activity and expertise in much the same way as the health or natural resource sectors, as separable domains of specialisation, the new approach allows the social to be foregrounded in every aspect of development activity. This is obviously important but as the social becomes generalised so too does the expertise required to address it. In DfID for example, the U.K. agency for international development assistance, the social development division is in the process of being downsized, as staff are moved into general development management, and policy positions. Requests for social development specialists with expertise in participation, gender, or poverty have been superseded by requests for specialists in the new processes of PPA (participatory poverty assessment), engaging civil society and the preparation of PRSPs. A recent list of required competencies for social development specialists within DfID highlighted the latter attributes above skills in social analysis, knowledge of so-called developing countries, or sociological, or anthropological knowledge.

This background of a dynamic development sector requiring limited competencies, which it defines, frames the kind of work which I have done in international development. Although it was work done by an anthropologist, it cannot really be described as applied anthropology, and was not intended to be. I was not asked to conduct the work because I was an anthropologist, but because I was seen to have some of the 'competencies' that would allow the work to be completed successfully. These 'competencies' in practice centre on an understanding of the policy process, and the ways in which programme documents can be used to further its objectives. My work has entailed producing programme documentation to meet policy purposes and the production of the analytical frameworks that will justify or amend policy determined interventions. This is not simply a matter of producing documents to policy guidelines. It necessitates a kind of social analysis of the situations, which the proposed intervention will be designed to address. But, unlike academic analysis, the parameters of the analysis, the issues to consider, are constrained by the policy environment in which the proposed intervention is to occur. This is not merely a matter of perspective or field of vision, the limitations as it were of the social development 'gaze'. Such a position is explicitly set out in the design of the social analytical input at the point of contracting knowledge via the terms of reference (TORs), which define and delimit the parameters of the work, and which explicitly situate the 'outputs' of the analysis (report, conclusions, findings) within the interlocking spirals of the policy cascade. The analysis must contribute to the identification of the workable limits within which an intervention can be expected to operate in a particular social setting, so that policy objectives can be achieved. This operates at two levels, firstly that of fitting activities into the framework of policy acceptability regarding such issues as legitimate beneficiaries, the kinds of organisations with whom it is acceptable to work, and whether the intervention will reduce 'poverty' as defined in the current indicators and targets towards which both government and donors are working. Second, the analysis must also operate at the level of reality, asking basic questions regarding viability and practicality; whether indeed the problem as represented by policy presents itself in such a way, if at all, as to be potentially addressed through the kinds of interventions currently deemed to be effective. Such parameters necessarily constrain the kind and scope of knowledge generated through such efforts, as well as reiterating the kinds of activities and content that counts as authoritative knowledge (Goldman 2001).

From an anthropological perspective, this kind of work is essentially one of representation, of matching two representations of reality together in such a way that one might be influenced by an input of something else, cash, people, or structures. This is not to suggest that social development works solely with abstractions or with creating representations of reality. As anthropologists have shown since the beginnings of the discipline, cultural representations, the classificatory systems through which the social imagination is possible, constitute the domains of social action through the structuring of social institutions and of social order (Durkheim and Mauss 1963; Douglas 1966). In Geertz's memorable phrase, such representations are both a 'model of' and a 'model for' reality (1973: 93). Cultural representations are not abstract models, but structure social practice and make it meaningful (Bourdieu 1977). Development representations through project documentation and the social analyses that are fed into projects and programmes, are similarly concrete in their implications. This is because the role of reporting within the development framework is constituted within a matrix of social and institutional relations in which projects become social institutions; a matrix not merely of purported cause and effect relations between inputs and outputs, but of the totality of social relations each project brings into being (Green 2003).

Unlike an anthropology predisposed to emphasise the locally specific and the uniqueness of situations, social representation in development needs to work with the generalisable, where possible making local specificities adapt to the generalisable models of global policy templates. This does not mean overriding difference, but rather trying to find viable entry points for policy within particular settings. This need to generalise is the key weakness of representing the social in development, in that it becomes all too easy to lose track of what is historically specific and local about a particular context. In my work to date this has not been a problem. Most of the work I have done has been in areas I know well, and where I have some linguistic competence. I am able to differentiate between the local and the general, between the reality of the context into which policy will engage and the model of reality invoked by policy. These differences may matter less to non-anthropologists and to those who are not area specialists. It is not uncommon for people who do this kind of work to operate across several continents. Indeed, as competency is viewed by agencies in terms of process it transcends locality. It is thus not unusual for those working as consultants to get targeted information about work or invitations to bid for opportunities in countries where they have no prior expertise, and minimal knowledge, but where they may have previously worked on what are deemed to be identical policy processes, for example PRSPs or local government reform. Of course, from an anthropological viewpoint, such processes could not be viewed as similar if taking place in completely disparate social settings.

That the anthropological perspective would opt for comparison rather than equivalence, brings us to the ultimate incommensurability of the two ways of working, and of seeing, unless of course one takes a more interdisciplinary and fluid perspective on the applications of knowledge than is espoused, within some quarters of anthropology at least. Indeed, it is an anthropological perspective that allows me as a social development practitioner to see that the boundaries between the two fields are socially imposed categories, and refer less to real differences in the content of knowledge than to the parameters each discipline imposes. This perspective allows me to apply my own knowledge gained from anthropology to social development practice and to development institutions. While the work I do 'in' rather than 'on' development would not necessarily be recognised as `anthropology' by my colleagues working in university anthropology departments, it is informed by anthropological knowledge about local institutions, cultural practices and social relations, by research skills gained through fieldwork and library study, as well as by professional practices honed within the pedagogic settings of academic anthropology. The latter skills allow me to work effectively to the tight deadlines of days or weeks demanded within development settings. The former enable me to imagine the kinds of consequences that various policy visions could have in particular settings, and to interpret policy intentions in relation to local contexts with a view, in my case I hope, to trying to ensure that it is the intended beneficiaries who derive some benefit from the development spend.

## Conclusions: Applying Anthropology to Development

My own practice as both anthropologist-ethnographer and social development professional demonstrates that being an anthropologist does not constrain in what other fields I apply my knowledge or acquire new competencies. As an anthropologist I can perceive the limitations of both anthropology and of social development, and comprehend the institutional structures and discourses within which each is located and the points of contact and separation. What I do in both is consciously thought out and self-aware. Indeed, while some from the anthropology community will doubtless criticise my engagement in development as working for governments, or making knowledge instrumental, as anthropologists we must also acknowledge that there is no anthropology outside politicised institutional settings, and that what we do as ethnographers and as anthropologists is always part of some sort of political agenda, even if this rather uncomfortable fact is often unacknowledged within anthropology, as within the social sciences more generally.[9] Michel de Certeau states this position explicitly: *'The Bororos of Brazil sink slowly into their collective death, and Levi-Strauss takes his seat in the French Academy. Even if this injustice disturbs him, the facts remain unchanged. This story is ours as much as his. In this one respect (which is an index of others that are more important), the intellectuals are still borne on the backs of the common people'* (1984: 25). There is no doubt that this injustice did disturb Levi-Strauss, whose *Tristes Tropiques*, an account of the tragedy of what would now be called the developing world, makes his feelings plain (1973), but it drove him in a direction away from instrumental knowledge, towards an anthropology of abstract symbolic structures and representations (Ferguson 1997: 156). This was not an escape into pure knowledge. The kinds of cultural anthropology that privileges symbolic logic over socially determined practice itself, contributed to pervasive representations about the Other as the object of Orientalist fallacies, traditional, lacking historical agency, and preoccupied with the irrational as the antithesis of progress (Fabian 1983; Said 1978).

Anthropology has since moved onwards. By shifting the object of study, 'scaling up' in development speak, anthropology has come to apply its own insights to the institutional context of its production. The new anthropology, and the ethnography which informs it is changing understandings of how social processes happen and of the constitution of agency in different settings. It is also increasingly oriented towards an understanding of the historical production of specific forms of 'Western' knowledge. [10] Studies of development are increasingly viewing development as a historically determined social institution, as opposed to the inevitable outcome of unilinear historical trajectories of globalisation. The field of knowledge, in anthropology of development (Escobar 1991), is growing at the same time as development anthropology, for reasons outlined above, is shrinking. Although development anthropologists had argued for more engagement in policy as the means to influence in development (Gow 1993: 392; Cernea 1995: 348), the transformation of development into a policy machine leaves less scope for a (development) anthropology still focused on traditional anthropological issues and approaches. [11] This is not to say there is no clear future for anthropology in development, just that as anthropology, it is more likely to be as a perspective informing practice rather than as applied to development objectives. [12]

## Acknowledgements

Thanks to David Hulme and Rosalind Eyben for their comments on this chapter.

## Notes

1. For an overview of the applied versus mainstream anthropology debate, see Ferguson (1997). See also Escobar (1991; 1997), Cernea (1995) and Little and Painter (1995).
2. The bulk of my academic output concerns the anthropology of religion.
3. This is explicit in the Human Development Reports produced annually by the United Nations Development Programme, which differentiates between economic growth and a series of human rights and social entitlements to inform a liberally inspired scale of progress. Social evolutionism is still present in this line of thinking, but it is less as a judgement on those at the lower end of the scale than as the representation of a state to aspire to, where even less wealthy states can seek some sort of balance between economic and social justice.
4. Also known as Sector Wide Approaches (SWaPs).
5. For example, Escobar (1997) writes, 'Let us define development, for now, as it was understood in the early post World War II period: the process to pave the way for the replication in most of Asia, Africa and Latin America, of the conditions that we supposed to characterize the more economically advanced nations of the world-industrialization, high degrees of urbanization and education, technification of agriculture and widespread adoption of the values and principles of modernity, including particular forms of order, rationality and individual orientation' (1997: 497).

6. Sahlins drily remarks that, despite the predictions of evolutionist thinking: 'One of the surprises of later capitalism, for example, is that hunters and gatherers live – many of them – by hunting and gathering'(1999: vi).

7. The subaltern is defined through his or her position as occupying a subject position from which they are unable to articulate themselves, not so much in actuality as in the representations made by others about them which obliterate or appropriate their agency (Prakash 1994). Whether or not participatory approaches in development really alter this position is, of course, open to question. I have shown elsewhere how such methodologies may achieve the opposite through denial of the agency of the subjects of development to achieve change on terms other than those of the developer (Green 2000). However, PPAs do claim to provide a space for the voices of the poor, albeit on agency terms.

8. 'Local' consultants do have considerable knowledge and are highly competent, but like any outsider, cannot automatically be assumed to have uninhibited access to local populations. Factors such as class, gender and experience all impact on an individual's ability to conduct social research. These factors apply to both 'local' and 'international' (a euphemism for expatriates usually from developed countries) consultants and researchers.

9. Nancy Scheper-Hughes is a notable exception, but the response to her (1995) article advocating a politically engaged anthropology demonstrate the depth of feeling on this issue within the profession, most of which is at worst hostile and at best suspicious..

10. Examples include Rabinow (1995), Nader (1996).

11. Escobar (1991) argues that development anthropology in the 1990s remained preoccupied with the conventional approaches associated with the anthropology of the 1960s, unreflexive, evolutionist and uncritical of development or modernism. He points out that development anthropology's position *vis à vis* these issues, and its commitment to objectivism, widened the gap between it and critical anthropology during the 1980s and 1990s. Escobar underlines the paradox of development anthropology's objectivism and belief in science when the rest of the discipline had accepted the tenets of postmodernism and the social construction of knowledge, including Western science.

12. These problems are acknowledged within the applied anthropology profession, although their analysis of the causes are different from mine. Both Scudder (1999) and Hackenberg (1999), for example, view the lack of relevance for anthropology in development as due to institutional exclusion and lack of influence rather than as a failure to 'scale up' or out in the right places.

# References

Apthorpe, R. 1997. 'Human Development Reporting and Social Anthropology'. *Social Anthropology*, 5(1): 21–34.

Bornstein, E. 2001. 'Child Sponsorship, Evangelism, and Belonging in the Work of World Vision Zimbabwe'. *American Ethnologist*, 28(3): 595–622.

Bourdieu, P. 1977. *Outline of a Theory of Practice*. Cambridge: Cambridge University Press.

Brutti, L. 2001. 'Where Anthropologists Fear to Tread: Notes and Queries on Anthropology and Consultancy, Inspired by a Fieldwork Experience'. *Social Analysis*, 45(2): 94–107.

Cernea, M. 1995. 'Social Organisation and Development Anthropology'. *Human Organisation*, 54 (3): 340–352.

Cooper, F. and R. Packard (eds). 1997. *International Development and the Social Sciences. Essays on the History and Politics of Knowledge*. Berkeley: University of California Press, pp. 1–41.

Crewe, E. and E. Harrison. 1998. *Whose Development? An Ethnography of Aid*. London: Zed.

De Certeau, M. 1984. *The Practice of Everyday Life*. Berkeley: University of California Press.

De L'Estoile, B. 1997. 'The Natural Preserve of Anthropologists: Social, Scientific Planning and Development'. *Social Science Information*, 36(2): 343–376.

Douglas, M. 1986. *How Institutions Think*. New York: Syracuse University Press.

———. 1966. *Purity and Danger*. London: Routledge.

Durkheim, E. and M. Mauss. 1963. *Primitive Classification*. Chicago: University of Chicago Press.

Escobar, A. 1991. 'Anthropology and the Development Encounter: The Making and Marketing of Development Anthropology'. *American Ethnologist*, 18(4): 658–682.

———. 1997. 'Anthropology and Development'. *International Social Science Journal*, 154: 497–515.

Fabian, J. 1983. *Time and the Other. How Anthropology Makes its Object*. New York: Columbia University Press.

Ferguson, J. 1997. 'Anthropology and Its Evil Twin. "Development" in The Constitution of a discipline', in F. Cooper and R. Packard (eds) *International Development and the Social Sciences. Essays on the History and Politics of Knowledge*. Berkeley: University of California Press, pp. 150–175.

Geertz, C. 1973. 'Religion as a cultural system', in C. Geertz, *The Interpretation of Cultures*. New York: Basic Books.

Goldman, M. 2001. 'The Birth of a Discipline. Producing Authoritative Green Knowledge, World Bank Style'. *Ethnography*, 2(2): 191–217.

Gow, D. 1993. 'Doubly Dammed: Dealing with Power and Praxis in development Anthropology'. *Human Organisation*, 52(4): 380–397.

Green, M. 2000. 'Participatory Development and the Appropriation of Agency in Southern Tanzania'. *Critique of Anthropology*, 20(1): 67–89.

———. 2002. 'Social Development: Issues and Approaches', in U. Kothari, and M. Minogue (eds) *Development Theory and Practice. Critical Perspectives*. Basingstoke: Palgrave, pp. 52–70.

———. 2003. 'Globalizing Development in Tanzania: Policy Franchising through Participatory Project Management'. *Critique of Anthropology*, 23(2): 123–143.

———. (in press) 'Presenting Poverty, Attacking Representations. Anthropological Perspectives on Poverty in Development'. *Journal of Development Studies*, forthcoming.

Gupta, A. and J. Ferguson. 1997. 'Discipline and Practice: The "Field" as Site, Method and Location in Anthropology', in A. Gupta and J. Ferguson (eds) *Anthropological Locations. Boundaries and Grounds of a Field Science*. Berkeley: University of California Press.

Hackenberg, R. 1999. 'Advancing Applied Anthropology. Strategies and Game Plans'. *Human Organization*, 58(1): 105–107.

Horowitz, M. 1996. 'On Not Offending the Borrower: (Self?)-ghettoization of Anthropology at the World Bank'. *Development Anthropologist* 14(1&2): 1–12.

Jackson, C. 1996. 'Rescuing Gender from the Poverty Trap'. *World Development*, 24(3): 489–504.

Kuper, A. 1973. *Anthropology and Anthropologists. The Modern British School*. London: Routledge (revised edition).

Levi-Strauss, C. 1973. *Tristes Tropiques*. London: Cape.

Little, P. and M. Painter. 1995. 'Discourse, Politics, and the Development Process: Reflections on Escobar's "Anthropology and the Development Encounter"'. *American Ethnologist*, 22(3): 602–616.

Mardiros, D. 1997. 'Whose Side Are You On? Aboriginal Land, Resource Development and Applied Anthropology in Western Australia'. *Global Practice of Anthropology*, 58: 25–46.

Marx, K. 1987. 'Peasantry as a Class', in T. Shanin, (ed.) *Peasants and Peasant Societies* Oxford: Basil Blackwell (2nd edition).

Mehta, L. 2001. 'The World Bank and its Emerging Knowledge Empire'. *Human Organization*, 60(2): 189–196.

Moore, S.F. 2001. 'The International Production of Authoritative Knowledge. The Case of Drought Stricken West Africa'. *Ethnography*, 2(2): 161–189.

Mosse, D. 2001. 'Social Research in Rural Development Projects', in D. Gellner and E. Hirsch (eds) *Inside Organizations. Anthropologists at Work*. Oxford: Berg.

Nader, L. (eds). 1996. *Naked Science: Anthropological Inquiry into Boundaries, Power, and Knowledge*. New York: Routledge.

Pigg, S.L. 1992. 'Inventing Social Categories Through Place: Social Representations and Development in Nepal'. *Comparative Studies in Society and History*, 34(3): 491–513.

Prakash, G. 1994. 'Subaltern Studies as Postcolonial Criticism'. *American Historical Review*, 99(5): 1475–1490.

Rabinow, P. 1995. *French Modern. Norms and Forms of the Social Environment*. Chicago: Chicago University Press.

Sahlins, M. 1999. 'What is Anthropological Enlightenment? Some Lessons of the Twentieth Century'. *Annual Review of Anthropology*, 28: i–xxiii.

Said, E. 1978. *Orientalism*, New York: Pantheon.

Sampson, S. 1996. 'The Social Life of Projects. Importing Civil Society to Albania', in C. Hann and E. Dunn (eds) *Civil Society: Challenging Western Models*. London: Routledge, pp. 121–142.

Scheper-Hughes, N. 1995. 'The Primacy of the Ethical. Propositions for a Militant Anthropology'. *Current Anthropology*, 36(3): 409–420.

Scudder, T. 1999. 'The Emerging Global Crisis and Development Anthropology: Can We Have an Impact?' *Human Organization*, 58(4): 351–364.

Shrestha, N. 1995. 'Becoming a Development Category' in J. Crush' *et al.* (ed.) *Power of Development*. London: Routledge.

Strathern, A. and P. Stewart. 2001. 'Introduction: Anthropology and Consultancy: Ethnographic Dilemmas and Opportunities'. *Social Analysis*, 45(2): 3–22.

Watts, M. 2001. 'Development Ethnographies'. *Ethnography*, 2(2): 283–300.

Wilmsen, E. 1990. *Land Filled with Flies. A Political Economy of the Kalahari*. Chicago: University of Chicago Press.

World Bank 1999. *World Development Report 1999/2000: Entering the 21st Century*. Washington, DC: World Bank.

*Chapter 6*

# ANTHROPOLOGY AT THE CENTRE:
Reflections on Research, Policy Guidance and
Decision Support.

*Mils Hills*

## Introduction

This chapter offers something of an insight into the application of anthropology in government in terms of its contribution to research, and wider
uses in the development of policy, doctrine, strategy, and decision support
within and without the context of crises. I hope this contributes something
distinctive to the range and breadth of writing in this book.[1]

I joined the Civil Service via the U.K. Ministry of Defence (MoD's)
research agency DERA (the Defence Evaluation and Research Agency) in
1998. This followed the completion of my Ph.D. at the University of St
Andrews. More recently, I have been seconded from DERA's successor
organisation[2] to the U.K. Cabinet Office. I was therefore the first social
anthropologist to join the MoD and, more recently, the first to work in the
U.K. Cabinet Office.

This idiosyncratic career trajectory could be diverting – although not
massively interesting – merely because my formal qualifications are in
social anthropology.[3] As the reader may appreciate, not that many civil servants in defence and security research nor in the centre of government are
drawn from any – let alone this – wing of social science. However, as well
as holding my two degrees as formal evidence of my anthropological credentials, I have consciously and consistently drawn on social anthropological concepts and principles in my work. I prefer not to spell out exactly
how this has been achieved in practice. I opt to do this, not least because my
progress has tended mainly to be the result of tiresome and incremental
demonstrations of value rather than any customer or stakeholder assuming

that my approaches would inevitably add value![4] The reader will appreciate, however, that my strategy has centred on not restricting my opportunities by, for example, only focusing on the conduct and assessment of standard anthropological and field research. I have followed interesting research and challenging problems rather than searching out how and where anthropology *per se* could be applied. One might say that in building our anthropological brand, we have nothing to lose but our specialisms.

This brief chapter comprises a sort of manifesto or call to arms for those who may consider the options for career development outside those seemingly established 'tracks' for anthropologists, namely teaching and development. For those who would claim to conduct Action Research, this is a real case of anthropology in action. I – and surely others – have blazed a trail (largely unwittingly and with little thought of altruism) that others can follow, should they choose to pick up the trail. My anthropological training has, rather than stymieing my deployment potential, provided me with an arguably unique springboard into areas of work that few – including me – could have anticipated.

In summary, then, I will be concluding that anthropologists choose to exclude themselves from government and associated work, possibly on spurious grounds. There is no 'hex' on the discipline, although many could claim fairly that other disciplines (e.g., International Relations, 'psychology') have become fetishised (at least in the anthropological sense of the word)!

## Aim and Objectives

The aim of this chapter is the relatively simple one of providing a view into the roles I have both currently and historically fulfilled in government through my application of anthropological approaches. I will seek to deliver this aim through the following objectives:

- to provide a flavour of the broad range of work to which I have contributed
- to encourage an informed view of what anthropology can contribute to government research and policy, and
- to provoke debate and reaction.

## The Daily Regime

I can provide some insight into what my work as an anthropologist has involved on a more-or-less daily basis. For the past six years I have been required to bring swift understanding of complex issues, many of them technological or, increasingly, related to policy. The aim of this understanding is to assist those in specialist areas who may, for example, have become stove-piped in their approach and hence lost sight of any wider strategic picture. In other cases, the absence of a concept-driven approach to a work or research programme has meant that managers have no means of progressing their work because they have lost sight of what it is that they seek to achieve. The freshness and innovation that anthropologists can bring – working in concert with others – means that such impasses can be passed. In these examples, the need is to assist customers with regenerating a sense of meaning pertinent to the work in question. They may know what they have to do (deliver) but not how (the means). By stripping problems back to the conceptual level, frameworks can be evolved that enable them to re-visit the assumptions of planned work and thereafter take things forward.

In terms of targeted research activities, anthropologists are skilled at assembling fragments of information – laid out on reconstructive tables – that enable the steady generation of wide and deep understandings of issues, problems, markets, companies, consumers, decision makers, adversaries, etc; the identification of commonalities, inconsistencies, contradictions, patterns, errors across large quantities of data. This has always been my task, whether as I currently work in, for example, designing and delivering scenario-driven events to test government and stakeholder preparedness for crisis, or in the profiling of a particular market sector for business clients in the past.

## 'The Different Discipline'

Anthropology is doubly exotic in my environments – of defence research and central government policy and operations. First, such environments remain relatively exotic ones for anthropologists to be working in. Our disciplinary colleagues may regard this as good or bad; they are unlikely to have a neutral opinion. Second, anthropology remains a discipline that is outwith the list of those subjects conventionally expected by those selecting applicants to interview, professional recruiters and career advice consultancies. This can also be either good or bad: good in the sense that novelty can attract attention, but bad in the sense that 'the shock of the new' can sometimes repel. This is especially the case when we might – rightly – express our professional dissatisfaction with any attempt to, for example, predict exactly human behaviour or attempt to speak with authority about groups such as 'the Muslims' or 'the British'. However, as this chapter aims to demonstrate, although anthropology is still relatively exotic, it has made its debut on the recruiting radar screen. In some ways this debut is all about helping enlighten others that those things which many take for granted (such as the inherent truth of the existence of a meaningful category of 'Muslims') is wrong and ultimately extremely unhelpful.

To my career path; I was recruited to DERA in 1998, fortuitously selected by an individual who became a close colleague, mentor and friend (J.P. MacIntosh). He was also a – relatively rare – social scientist (albeit a social psychologist) who realised the benefits that further social science input could offer. Five years later, we still work closely together and continue to represent a kind of 'effects-based proselytisation' demonstrating, through the benefits in outcomes, the advantage of drawing on social science and the advantage that social science presents in being able to access and problematise the findings of the other sciences.

The social science deployed in the domain of policy and decision-support has one particular standard: the need for it to be evidence-based. This is where anthropology is rather well placed to assist. Although we are all slightly cynical about the deficiencies of data collection, this cynicism is rather more healthy, and useful, than the assumption that the doxa – the orthodox view – is always right. In challenging assumptions, in testing claimed insights, we subject ourselves and our findings to rigorous review. If, as has been attributed to Huxley, amongst others, anthropology, like charity, should begin at home, then anthropological work has to pass our internal filtration systems first. The demands of non-teaching, non-research-led employers means that the standards we expect from ourselves in terms of quality and timeliness of product delivery must be raised.

## Anthropology's Asymmetric Benefit

Given that anthropology is a relatively exotic discipline to those in government circles, what is the advantage of involving those from such novel domains? Why does our blend of human sciences matter? The Performance and Innovation Unit (PIU[5]) of the U.K. Cabinet Office noted that the 'demand for social researchers has [already] increased across Whitehall' (PIU 2000: 46). But why is there a widening audience for the work of social scientists? For a start, we provide a good deal of 'spice' to what can sometimes be a very bland and over safe diet of sameness. In an effort to limit the damaging effects of Orwellian 'group think', approaches deployed by anthropologists and others can provide additional richness and breadth of insight to those required to make decisions, and those supporting those decision makers. Initially, this could be limited to what could be described as 'Devil's Advocate', 'blue skies thinker' niche roles – challenging assumptions; thinking widely. However, anthropologists and others can deliver so much more.

There is inherent value in what we find and in how we interpret and communicate those findings, adding rich, contextual insight where 'understanding is not of words or even of sentences and single statements, but is the communication of another way of understanding things about the world' (Overing, 1985: 20). Whether we are involved in the formulation of domestic policy, or inputing guidance to overseas policy (e.g., defence, international development), we can assist policy, and decision makers in understanding the worldview of others. Not least, this can avoid costly pitfalls that would otherwise occur in the real world. This has clear benefits to the conduct and planning of policy where planning is related increasingly to the expected needs and priorities of those whom we serve.

The business strategist Michael Porter is one of the most overt endorsers of the view that diversity within organisations is key to delivering product and service differentiation, i.e., competitive advantage. Not least, one could add, this is also about ensuring the agility and nimbleness of fit such that both business and service providers (including the public services) can adapt to changing requirements. As Porter puts it, this underpins competitive strategy, where '[c]ompetitive strategy is about being different. It means deliberately choosing a different set of activities to deliver a unique mix of value' (Porter 1998: 45). On a similar theme, although here explicitly related to the domain of defence and security, Tierfude is quoted as observing – I think correctly – that '[t]he great masters of warfare techniques during the 21st century will be those who employ innovative methods to recombine various capabilities so as to attain tactical, campaign and strategic goals' (Yier Tierfude cited in Liang and Xiangsui 1999: 124).

In an era defined by asymmetric risk and unconventional conflict, anthropology could bolster defence and security complexes through its practitioners' idiosyncratic 'take' on the world and events in it. With the requirement established that longer-term and more fundamental engagements are needed to begin to deliver truly collective security, anthropology should be at the fore of intellectual movements offering novel, convention-challenging appraisals. Let us not forget that: 'We will face adversaries who will not play by our rules and, indeed, who see our values as vulnerabilities. Make no mistake about it, technology cannot transform war into a genteel electronic exchange as some hope' (Dunlap cited in Lewer 1997: 12). The stakes are very high. Government is becoming aware of the need to involve the contributions of as many and as diverse a range of disciplines as possible. This involvement will not be a smooth process, skirmishes will have to be joined. There will be some pain. However, anthropology could exploit a particular juncture where every other scientific approach is flailing around wildly, largely incapable of mobilising any usefully integrated assessment of the world – or any part thereof.

## Network Enabled Capability (NEC)

Having claimed that we as anthropologists are well placed to benefit both our own discipline and those that we could serve through government, I will now sketch out a domain where this could usefully commence. In the U.K., the concept of Network Enabled Capability (NEC) – initially dubbed Network-Centric Warfare (NCW) by American defence strategists – encompasses:

An integrated Equipment Capability linking sensors, decision makers, and weapon systems so that information can be translated into synchronised and overwhelmingly rapid military effect at the optimum tempo. (developed from CM(IS) Scoping Note 29 May 02)

Manuel Castells is acknowledged to have propelled the term 'network society' (1996) into the wider public consciousness. Few have yet begun to absorb the full implications of an increasingly networked United Kingdom and world. Not least, anthropologists and our colleagues from the other social sciences need to become technologically aware – or be able to communicate with those that are – in order to better understand the socio-technical realities of the networked world. Such networks, which support, depend or comprise one another, represent a form of complexity that a new scientific discipline may need to be evolved to effectively engage with them. Indeed, Pagels neatly describes one perspective on the breadth of the challenge in observing that complexity theory begins from the view that – as all other areas (micro-/macro-cosmos) have been explored, and frontiers (space/molecular ...) have been opened – the 'great unexplored frontier is complexity' (Pagels cited in Lewin 1993: 10).

Systems of systems, such as a state or region's critical infrastructure, may appear to be stable and predictable, but there are likely to be all manner of buried assumptions, redundancies, vulnerabilities contained within them. We should not be trusting that a food distribution system – and its dependence on SCADA[6] technologies, employee availability, logistical resources (etc.) is resilient to challenges (security, availability, etc.). Those in the relevant sectors must challenge the resilience of those systems in as comprehensive and challenging a range of ways as possible. What appears to be stability is nothing more than an emergent property; it could ebb away, even as we may regard the disappearance of such systems as unthinkable!

Crucial to NEC is that decision makers, and elements of the systems that support them, are organic; they involve carbon-based life forms as well as silicon machines. In addition, given the inherent complexity of understanding such complicated socio-technical systems, and the relative paucity of concepts available for driving such thinking, anthropology could steal a quick march over its more established competitor disciplines in engaging effectively with information, where, as the U.K. Ministry of Defence puts it: NEC is the 'U.K.'s programme to enhance military capability by better exploitation of information.'[7]

## Anthropology and Me – Fearless in the Face of Incomprehension

I suppose one of the greatest – and most difficult to capture – strengths of the anthropologist is the ability to remain comfortable in environments of enormous uncertainty. I think we can be very good at surviving, even thriving, where we actually understand very little of what's going on around us. The key here is to be able to exist, learning incrementally, piecing fragments of information together to make a coherent narrative, without causing upset or massive change to those around us. We should not be fazed if we encounter languages, choices, actions that confound our expectations, which fail to fit into any pre-established frames of reference. Over time, things will surely become clearer. Just now, we'll absorb and observe. As we build social networks, so we are able to (re)examine these puzzling events from a range of perspectives, and thus gain a more measured view.

At a research level, and this is where our abilities can really shine in the workplace, this strength translates into our willingness to plunge into any new area of interest without fearing the consequences too much. Our passion – which no doubt somewhat self-selects some of us to become anthropologists – for finding and making meaning enables us to dive into new areas of research knowing that, given time and our ingenuity, we will prevail over current ignorance. In that sense, anthropologists may be able to tolerate a steeper learning curve than others. In the workplace, these skills are fundamental to any company or organisation, given that we now live in the knowledge-driven economy (cf. Department of Trade and Industry, Converging Technologies 1998). It is here, in particular, that holding a degree in anthropology could come to be synonymous with our abilities to be widely deployable, thus increasing our worth scores and overall value to any employer.

## Anthropology and Me – The Power of Empathy

Anthropology – as the sociable science – insists on its practitioners being empathetic. Although not all anthropologists are gregarious, bubbly, conversational polyglots, we all know that others' perceptions of us are very important. Thus, when we choose to be marginal, liminal, individuals, we know where the margins are, what we have to do to legitimately be 'on the edge' but still 'one of us'. In running through multiple scenarios of how our actions could be misinterpreted by others, we perform rather sophisticated work. Certainly, some of this work may be intuitive guesswork (and wrong), but some will be intuitive guesswork that is right, and still more will be correct because we have identified some pattern of behaviour, which reliably communicates to us how actions are being perceived. These skills are of enormous value to any manager, because management is becoming more about emotional intelligence (EQ) than playing hardball. Further, anyone who conducts any form of negotiation must have the best possible understanding of others, and the likelihood of them taking specific actions. Anyone concerned with the perception received by others (of a brand, product, organisation or political party) would do well to develop their empathetic understanding.

## How Anthropology Can Help in Supporting Decision-Making and Policy through the Delivery of Concepts

Even a casual reading of much of the literature or quotes in the media describing threats to national, business or cultural security – driven by those qualified in International Relations – indicates the substantial paucity of any concepts underpinning thinking. Those who comment on terrorism, asymmetry, risk, geopolitical change and so on, as well as being derivative and rather unexciting in their writing, are only good at one thing: lists. If insight was ever likely to be gained through the drawing up of endless lists of names, dates, organisational changes and groundless speculation about activities occurring at the neural level of our (real or imagined) adversaries – we would understand a good deal more than we currently do! Lists of the tens of pseudonyms that nasty enemies have had does not add anything to anticipating future problems or getting to grips with the *fundamentals* – as opposed to the *fundamentalisms* – which generate or sustain those who would seek to do us harm.

Chronologies of the development of organisations, disputes over the birthplaces of leaders, diagrams of who reports to whom, these are all things which may or may nor be accurate, may or may not reflect reality, and may or may not deliver anything approaching an option to any decision maker. Profiling 'cultures' or 'leaders' at a distance; relating activities to childhood experiences may or may not be significant. But whatever they are they are merely the recycling, or generation, of things that can pass as 'facts'. Even where such 'facts' are of relevance in constructing, for example, a chronology of use in supporting a criminal investigation (X bought Y dual-use materials on D date), they do not explain something crucial. That crucial thing is just why individuals have come to accept that a militant approach is the only option they have; or why people who may (or may not) have a good deal to lose fall in line behind certain leaders, perhaps turning 'normal' values or aspirations on their head! For example, the participation of ordinary people in genocide or ethnic cleansing or Shoah is still not well enough understood. It is not as though violence against minorities has gone away in the post Second World War era. What are the conditions that enable some to harness the minds of others to commit such crimes, how can this be anticipated and how can this be stopped? Let us do more than uncover 'the psychology of motivation'.

We have all, some of us perhaps more than others, received academic 'round robin' letters asking for support for some petition or other to prevent, say, Israeli armed oppression of Palestinian civilians, or vice versa. You may merrily sign statements supporting dissident voices everywhere. However, the real strength of academics (and anthropologists foremost amongst them?) should not merely be in making a mark on a page; it should be making a mark on a problem by evolving, and applying, what we do best, i.e., generating concepts to better understand which should then be followed through such that interventions can be made that improve a situation.

Given that all wars and conflicts are essentially wars about *meaning* – of identity, ownership of natural resources, of control, of purity, or profit, of greed, and grievance (Birdall and Malone 2000) – surely anthropologists concerned with the comprehension and generation of meanings should be claiming a role? Just as *Medécins sans Frontières* swing in to provide crisis medical care, so should not *Anthropologues sans Frontières* perform a similar role – preferably in advance – in providing crisis contestation of the meanings underpinning conflict and instability? These meanings can, and should, be contested, put in relief, have their inconsistencies shown through the application of concepts. These concepts could show, for example, that some unquestionable meaning thought to date to the earliest moments of a nation's history are, in fact, a recent, and cynical political invention.[8]

## Understanding Others – Communication Both Internal and External

Communication begins in the struggle to learn and to describe. To start this process in our minds and to pass on its results to others, we depend on certain communication models, certain rules or conventions through which we can make contact. We can change these models when they become inadequate, or we can modify and extend them (Raymond Williams cited in Carey 1989: 32–33).

C.P. Snow originally noted the existence of the two cultures of intellectual endeavour in a lecture given in 1959 (Snow 1993). They haven't gone away. Indeed, in some ways the boundary between them is more ossified than before. Anthropology, being about cultural translation, has much to offer in mediating across that boundary-membrane, to promote positive osmosis. In addition, because anthropology is about making sense of the ways in which people speak and write about their worlds, our familiarity and ingenuity in looking at and using metaphors and other devices can serve cross-cultural communication well.

For example, in providing input to a research programme on computer network security, I deployed material from sociobiological methodology. In essence, sociobiology examined the interaction between predator and prey animals concluding that ecosystems could sometimes adjust very quickly such that they combated invaders against which no prior defence existed. In particular, the case of the Cane Toads introduced to Australia, as a biological control of the cane beetle, highlighted that – despite their toxicity – predators learned how to deal with (dismember, select phase in toad lifecycle to eat) the toads in a matter of generations, rather than in very long evolutionary time. In the domain of computer security, then, the ambition would be to have an ecosystem-based approach that was able to react and learn much as the natural ecosystem of Australia appears to be learning. The inherently interactive nature of the contest between attacker and attacked also implied the necessity for systems to strive constantly to be as 'fit' as possible.

This sociobiological parallel was found to be a helpful and powerful aid to designing security protocols. Not least, it provides material to comprise a concept-driven architecture. Admittedly, there is little in this example which is anthropological *per se*. However, the identification of this as a parallel of value to the project in question does, I think, owe much to anthropology. There is – at least for those of us who have attempted to write in an experimental, reflexive and novel way – a certain ease with drawing on examples – to underpin arguments – from a range of disciplinary areas.

What is going on here is the explication of some rather tricky – but fun – science. As successive Governments, the Royal Academy and many others have noted, enhanced public understanding of science is a key area where improved communication needs to occur. For example, even medical practitioners observe that 'the microbial world is mysterious, threatening, and frightening to most people' (Holloway *et al.* 1997). We live in an era where science is all too often associated in the public mind with the perceived perils of a particular type of research and product (GM and GMOs); gruesome disease (BSE); medical side-effect (MMR); animal epidemic (FMD), let alone the 'particular dreads'[9] of chemical, biological, radiological or nuclear (CBRN) terrorism. Given this challenging ambient context, improved and novel ways of engaging in dialogue with the various segments of the general public in order to both educate and learn requires leadership from the qualitative sciences.[10] Anthropology, once again, could have all sorts of communication and marketing applications.

## Risk Communications: Another Opportunity

The area of what has come to be known as 'risk communication' is one where anthropologists have a lot to offer. Defined as follows, risk communication

> is essential in making decisions. It enables people to participate in deciding how risks should be managed. Communication is also a vital part of implementing decisions – whether explaining mandatory regulations, informing and advising people about risks they can control themselves, or dissuading people from risky, antisocial behaviour. (ILGRA 1998: 1)

What is it that anthropology can achieve here? Well, through its humanistic standpoint, anthropology can assist policy makers, communications planners, marketing managers and others to better understand the standpoint of others. We – or our customers – need not *agree* with those stand-points, but at least we can understand why, for example, the take-up of a new technology could be compromised; why a new technology could be applied to malign ends; why a new benefits framework is unsuccessful in improving targeted delivery, and so on. In terms of defence and security, as I noted when I wrote a paper for a NATO seminar, my assumption is that:

> a better appreciation of the drivers of peoples' fears and the motivations of those who attempt to direct them can assist Government in better engage-ment with its ultimate stakeholders: each and every citizen. These citizens are a frequently overlooked component of a state's critical infrastructure. It is hoped that lessons learned from considering the communication of Chem-ical and Biological (CB) risks may be equally applicable to risk communica-tions in other contexts. (Hills 2002: 3)

It is easy to assume that one's stakeholders or customers outside the institutions in which we serve think like us – or think nothing like us! Nei-ther is helpful and could lead to poor policy and ineffectual decisions. What the anthropologist can deliver to the institution is a view of the out-side world which, albeit probably based on relatively light and agile research rather than month or year(s) long activity, can guide formulation such that policy and decisions align with the socio-politico economic real-ities of the *lived* world rather than those of the *assumed* world.

## Evidence-Based Policy and Planning in Public Service

As noted earlier, the requirement for policy decisions of governments to be evidence-based, places a heavy burden on, and presents a glittering oppor-tunity to those who seek to improve the delivery of services. I am pas-sionate about the market opportunities where anthropology and anthropologists can contribute. I know that those from other disciplines who may have believed that they had something approaching 'all of the answers' concerning changes that needed to be made to the delivery of policy, and a complete understanding of their customer/consumer base are now, at the very least, aware of the limitations of psychology, opera-tional research, PPE, etc. Those who have been qualified in – or mutated into – generalists or specialists in any institution – save, perhaps, health-care – are unlikely to be able to support evidence-based policy. That is unless, and until, the realisation dawns that the world which could be administered, managed, made sense of, have profit extracted from is not that which those subjects and that training can any longer offer sufficient purchase over.

I can provide a flavour of what I mean. Much of my work for govern-ment, and business when my corner of the U.K. Government's research base was being prepared for flotation, has been about Forward Planning

(FP). FP supports decision makers by, for example, providing evidence-based scenarios of the ways in which a technology, even a policy could affect, and be affected by, the real world. This is not about double-guessing the future, or becoming trained seers. Those engaged in FP do not do anything as crude as 'prediction', psychic or otherwise. However, I believe that anthropologists are as well placed as any – and in many ways better placed than many others – to understand the variety of ways in which change can occur. Because anthropology is about the material as well as the semiotic world, we understand the role that technologies – concrete or ideational – can have on behaviour. Given our understanding of human behaviour, we may also be able to aid in the anticipation of ways in which the future could develop. For example, one might want to make extrapolations about how people could be changing their views of the need for personal protection, given the market-driven clamour for Ciprofloxacin during and after the anthrax mailing in the United States, and the seemingly ever larger self-dosing of Colloidal Silver and a range of other allegedly effective pills and potions in the United States and elsewhere.

In delivering richer, socially informed insight into events, technologies and meanings, I have adapted the approach pioneered by Gluckman and the Manchester School, namely that of situational analysis. The basic point here is that no matter where one starts – with whatever 'loose end' one has access to – one rapidly finds that links are made to all sorts of other things: predictable or otherwise. Rogers and Vertovec expressed this elegantly when they report that Gluckman, in giving an account of a bridge opening ceremony in Zululand, 'unpacks the nature of African social and cultural life within the context of white colonial domination, showing how elements in the wider social order are expressed by way of those in the situation' (Rogers and Vertovec 1995: 6). In my application of situational analysis, I have begun with an event, technology or meaning, and sought to identify the range of systems on which it is dependent. One way of describing these systems is in terms of the political, economic, social, technological, legal and environmental (PESTLE) realms. Whatever, one needs to encompass the meanings which drive, for example, the uptake of a piece of technology, the economic drivers – or barriers – and so on.

In addition, awareness of change needs to be incorporated into the core of any such analysis. Because all systems are dynamic, then the means of (better) understanding them has to both take account of change and, in fact, change in itself. The tools and techniques that we draw on must not be recuperated from a finite and stagnant pot. Rather, a constantly refreshed portfolio must be maintained from which 'best of breed' concepts can be deployed.

## Conclusion: Not Hard, Not Soft – Just Different

One of the brickbats, still, directed at the social sciences is that they are the 'soft sciences'. The descriptors 'fluffy, 'woolly', 'off the wall' are still in circulation as accepted (also tired, boring and derivatively) pejorative views of the social sciences. This despite the less than impressive track record of other sciences in delivering consistent and coherent views of anything. The words pot and kettle spring to mind. Nevertheless, we will achieve nothing if we do not attempt to engage and defeat these kinds of views. There is no point just complaining at the iniquity of it all. Rather, we have to show that through the conduits of opportunities such as the promotion of evidence-based research and policy, we can help deliver improved research findings that in turn support the delivery of enhanced services to the public. Anthropology can begin to work in the genuinely public interest, not least where working in government is a form of 'public interest anthropology', to adopt the term of Peggy Sanday (1998). Working in any area indirectly connected with defence and security aims at contributing the notion that *salus populi suprema lex est* (the welfare of the people is the highest law).[11] This work could be at a central, departmental, devolved, regional or local level. This is important work, aimed at increasing the sustainability of global and national security (not least because they cannot be sensibly disentangled).

Anthropologists need to acquire considerably more confidence in believing that they can help 'merging problem solving with theory and analysis in the interest of change motivated by a commitment to social justice, racial harmony, equality, and human rights' (Sanday 1998).

I strongly believe that through our empathetic understanding of others, our ability to enhance the robustness of thinking, tailoring/improving policy, anthropologists can achieve a lot for the benefit of policy and decision makers, the lot of those that government exists to serve and, finally, the recuperation of the reputation of anthropology. Unfortunately, if one has no stake in this domain, no participation in the evolution of policy and plans; no commitment to improving the knowledge base that sustains decision making, one can hardly complain about malformed outcomes. If we are not part of decision and planning processes, decisions and plans will still be made, and decision makers and planners will remain convinced of the belief that they understand the effects of their actions.

### Notes

1. Many thanks to my friends Jamie MacIntosh, Jas Mahrra, Jonathan Skinner, Tom Hardie-Forsyth and others for discussions that they may or may not realise aided my thinking.

2. The Defence Science and Technology Laboratory – DSTL.
3. In this chapter, please read every use of 'social anthropology' to relate also to any of the other anthropologies.
4. In the past couple of years, I would argue, there has been something approaching a sea change, and less of a burden of proof of value has been required.
5. Now re-branded as the (Prime Minister's) Strategy Unit.
6. SCADA – Supervisory Control and Data Acquisition.
7. www.mod.uk/issues/nec.
8. For hints of how this might be done, see Trevor-Roper (1984) and Gordy (1999).
9. A turn of phrase borrowed from Department of Health (1997).
10. Similar arguments could be advanced for a gamut of issues where public participation is sought: from neighbourhood renewal through to electoral turnout.
11. Thanks to Tom Hardie-Forsyth for bringing my attention to this phrase.

# References

Berdal, M. and D.M. Malone. (eds) 2000. *Greed and Grievance: Economic Agendas in Civil Wars*, London: Lynne Rienner.

Carey, J.W. 1989. *Communication as Culture: Essays on Media and Society*. London: Unwin Hyman.

Castells, M. 1996. *The Rise of Network Society*, Vol. 1. Oxford: Blackwell.

Department of Health. 1997. *Communicating about Risks to Public Health, Pointers to Good Practice*. London: Department of Health.

Department of Trade and Industry. 1998. *Converging Technologies: Consequences for the New Knowledge-Driven Economy* available at http://downloads.securityfocus.com /library/ecommerce/papers/converging.pdf, accessed 19 July 2004.

Gordy, E. 1999. *The Culture of Power in Serbia: Nationalism and the Destruction of Alternatives*. Pennsylvania: Pennsylvania State University Press.

Hills, M. 2002. 'Competing Against a Particular Dread: Novel Approaches to Risk Communication', unpublished Paper, NATO Brussels: NATO-Russia Advanced Scientific Workshop on Social and Psychological Consequences of Chemical and Biological Terrorism.

Holloway, H.C., A.E. Norwood, C.S. Fullerton, C.C. Engel and R.J. Ursano. 1997. 'The Threat of Biological Weapons: Prophylaxis and Mitigation of Psychological and Social Consequences'. *Journal of the American Medical Association* (JAMA), 278(5): 425–427.

Interdepartmental Liaison Group on Risk Assessment (ILGRA). 1998. *Risk Communication: A Guide to Regulatory Practice*. Suffolk: HSE Books.

Lewer, N. 1997. *Research Report No 1*, NLW Research Project Staff at the University of Bradford, November, available at http://www.brad.ac.uk/acad/nlw/research_reports/ researchreport1.php, accessed 19 July 2004.

Lewin, R. 1993. *Complexity: Life on the Edge of Chaos*. London: Phoenix.

Liang, Q. and W. Xiangsui. 1999. *Unrestricted Warfare*. Beijing: PLA Literature and Arts Publishing House.

Overing, J. (ed.) 1985. *Reason and Morality*, ASA Monographs 24. London: Tavistock Publications.

Performance and Innovation Unit. 2000. *Adding it Up: Improving Analysis and Modelling in Central Government*. London: PIU.

Porter, M. 1998. *The Competitive Advantage of Nations*. London: Macmillan Business.

Rogers, A. and S. Vertovec. (eds) 1995. *The Urban Context: Ethnicity, Social Networks and Situational Analysis*. Oxford: Berg.

Sanday, P. 1998. *Defining A Public Interest Anthropology*, address to the American Anthropological Association Symposium, Philadelphia, (available at www.sas.upenn.edu/anthro/CPIA/whatispia/pia1998.html, accessed 19 July 2004).

Snow, C.P. 1993. *The Two Cultures*. Cambridge: Cambridge University Press.

Trevor-Roper, H. 1984. 'Invention of Tradition: The Highland Tradition of Scotland', in E. Hobsbawm and T. Ranger (eds) *The Invention of Tradition*. Cambridge: Cambridge University Press.

Chapter 7

# SPEAKING OF SILENCE:
Reflections on the Application of Anthropology
to the U.K. Health Services

~~~

*Elizabeth Hart*


## Introduction

Reflecting on over twenty years' experience of fieldwork in the same
region of the U.K. (the Midlands), seventeen of which have been in the
National Health Service (NHS), this chapter draws out some observations
about the application of anthropology to such a politicised and volatile
organisation for others who might wish to take on the challenge and tread
a similar path. The chapter presents three of the seven studies in which I
have been involved directly since 1985, drawing on unpublished primary
data such as fieldnotes and end of award reports to illustrate what these
studies involved. The three studies reported below were conducted in four
different hospitals; three of them large teaching hospitals in two major
cities, and the fourth a small District General Hospital in a small town.[1] I
decided to write about what I know first-hand and as such this is a personal view and I do not claim to speak for anthropology. Nevertheless, I
hope by drawing out conclusions from a synthesis of three of my studies
to identify some points of general relevance for a future anthropology of
health service organisations that others might find helpful, building on
previous work (Wright 1994; Savage 2000; Gellner and Hirsch 2001a; Huby
2003), as well as contributing to hospital ethnography (van der Geest and
Finkler 2004).

Reflecting on these three research studies after a lapse of time I can see
connecting threads along the way, and also how my research developed in
response to opportunities that were offered to me or which I made for
myself. I cannot lay claim to anything as grand as a strategy but rather followed where the next research study seemed to lead. In common with

several of my anthropologist friends and colleagues, I have chosen to work as an anthropologist in a university but outside a department of anthropology. I am now a senior lecturer in social anthropology in a School of Nursing in a Medical School, where I have worked for over fifteen years, and where I established the Centre for Social and Cultural Research in Stroke and also run a programme on the anthropology of organisations for Master's and Doctoral students.

In reflecting on a series of studies in which I have been involved directly, I follow the examples of others such as Marris (1986) and Becker (1999) both of whom developed a conceptual theme from the synthesis of their various studies. A conceptual theme which runs throughout my various studies concerns people's experiences of speaking in organisational contexts where they feel themselves to be in some way suppressed, or marginalised, or even describe themselves as 'invisible' – as nurses often do when speaking of their caring skills (Colliere and Lawler 1998). Although the majority of my work in the NHS has been with women workers in a range of occupations, I have also worked with senior managers, the majority of whom were men, and who encountered similar dilemmas of speaking, displaying a confidence about the policies they were charged with implementing which often belied their serious misgivings (Laurance 1988; Pollitt et al. 1990). In this chapter such silences are explored by using the concept of 'cultural censorship', which is a 'socially shared silence' (Sheriff 2000) that may now be endemic in the health services (Hart and Hazelgrove 2001).

Cultural censorship is a concept developed by Robin Sheriff, a social anthropologist, to explain how it was that the racism observed in Brazil, and which was generally known to exist by shanty town dwellers and middle class Brazilians alike, was not spoken of publicly. Unlike other forms of communal silence where dominant views are naturalised and taken for granted, and people therefore lack the ideological means to voice dissent, cultural censorship does not mean that people cannot or do not speak: the silence produced by cultural censorship does not imply an acceptance of dominant ways of thinking, nor that people are coerced into silence. As in Brazil there may even be laws and procedures to protect people from racism and encourage them to speak out about abuse. But constrained by lack of consensus and motivated by a variety of political and psychological interests, people choose to forget what they know and withdraw into silence, and they do so collectively on the basis of tacit communal understandings. While in certain private contexts people may speak openly about their concerns, they stay silent in others, typically those contexts in which it might be possible to try to resolve the problems by speaking publicly: people fear that by seeking to resolve the problem by speaking out, they may only make the situation worse and create more suffering for themselves and others (Sheriff 2000; Hart and Hazelgrove 2001).

Although I do not work in the NHS, I have spent a long time researching in this one organisation but in diverse settings with a range of different groups and throughout a long period of enormous change, re-organisation and uncertainty under both Conservative and Labour governments. One of the advantages of having spent so long in one organisation but researching with different groups in diverse settings is that it becomes possible to see connections between apparently very different groups and their 'problems' that were not visible when viewing each in isolation, making it possible to distinguish the particular from the general. Reflecting on what underlies the organisational problems illustrated in each of the ethnographies below, these seem to be variations on the theme of 'speaking of silence' and, as such, may have archetypal dimensions which lend them to anthropological investigation and de-construction.

In writing a chapter in a book which is inevitably a 'shop window' for applied anthropology, I do so in light of current concerns in *Anthropology Today* (and elsewhere) about the discipline's apparent decline in popularity, and the need to regenerate its professional profile within and outside the academy (Sillitoe 2003). However, in an effort to promote anthropology, I do not want to overplay its advantages, overlook its limitations, or ignore the predicaments that the anthropologist may face when undertaking ethnography in an organisation as politicised as the NHS (Pollitt *et al.* 1990). My argument highlights the way that the anthropologist has constantly to work with and try to reconcile the contradictions and ambiguities inherent in the application of anthropology to modern organisational forms, being reflexively aware of the ambiguities of the anthropologist's own position at the interstices of a range of groups differently positioned in relation to power and authority (Batteau 2000; Gellner and Hirsch 2001b; Huby 2003). On the one hand, ethnographic research is attractive to managers and policy makers alike because the researcher 'steps into the shoes' of the research 'subjects' and understands 'problems' from their multiple perspectives, de-constructing them, and this in turn opens up possible solutions that organisations would otherwise struggle to comprehend. On the other hand, this may mean that managers perceive the anthropologist as voicing the views of marginalised and previously silenced groups within the organisation and of speaking of issues that were previously known about informally but unacknowledged formally. As Frankenberg points out, it also means that the anthropologist does not agree with funders and participants in advance what the outcome of the research will be, nor what viewpoint or outcome will be endorsed as the most important, but has the freedom to look at all the possible outcomes (Frankenberg 2003a). However, anthropologists have increasingly to obtain research-related work in organisational settings funded and driven by policy and practice-orientated institutions, and so there is likely to be even less room for manoeuvre than before (Mascarenhas-Keyes 2001).[2] During the 1980s and 1990s, when I conducted the studies discussed below, the climate was one in which criticism was silenced (as noted above). As Pollitt *et al* argued, such a situation arises when:

> a strong government has introduced a major new policy, backed it with substantial resources and invested it with high symbolic significance in terms of the currently dominant political ideology. This has always been the case, but since the mid-1970s … the rate of infection seems to have increased … in an era when public sector careers are more precarious than before, and resources more scarce, many senior officials can no longer afford the luxury of 'standing off', of taking a detached view of the policies they are supposed to be implementing … Their 'professional' views are increasingly demoted to the status of 'private' opinions, to be allowed out only to close friends or suitably harmless or remote strangers. (Pollitt, *et al*. 1990: 170)

If anything the above argument is even more true of the NHS today than it was when the Conservative government was in power, and so the dilemma of 'speaking of silence' could equally well apply to the twenty-first century. Indeed what Gledhill says in a different but related context also applies to anthropological research in the health services: 'Today we must focus less on silence than on the greater dilemmas of speaking' (Gledhill 2002: 439). I now present my three ethnographies in turn and then in the final sections discuss the issues raised.

## Three NHS Ethnographies

The three ethnographies are as follows: the first is a participant observation study with hospital domestic assistants funded by the U.K. Economic and Social Research Council (ESRC) which compares the social worlds of two groups of women who work part-time in two different organisations; the second is a participant observation study of nurses at two teaching hospitals focusing on the problem of turnover which was funded by a then Regional Health Authority; the third is an action research study of change at a District General Hospital funded by the same Regional Health Authority. The three ethnographies illustrate a process of transition, from lone anthropologist in the first to the principal investigator in a multidisciplinary team in the third. As I made the transition from one project to the next, the research itself became increasingly politicised so that by the time of the third study senior personnel from the Department of Health were involved in the project steering group.

# Ethnography 1: The West Midlands 1985 to 1986

*The Social Worlds of Domestic Assistants in the NHS*

I had not planned for the NHS to become my research field, but that was how my career developed as one project led to another. My doctoral research had been with pottery workers in Stoke-on-Trent and it had prepared me well to take on the ESRC research fellowship at a Midlands university on a comparative study of two groups of part-time domestic assistants, one group employed at a large teaching hospital, and the other at a university hall of residence. The research proposal was written by a senior anthropologist and I conducted the fieldwork and wrote the final report which was 'well received' by the reviewer (Tonkin and Hart 1986, Hart 1988). At that early stage in my research career this was an ideal post for me because I was able to research much as I had done as a doctoral student while having the support and guidance of a fellow anthropologist in making the transition to a university appointment. The research funding was for twenty months which provided the time and freedom to participate fully in work as a domestic assistant in both organisations, and also to spend time with the women at home, just as I was used to in the Potteries. Whereas in the pottery factory I only knew what the work was like second-hand, I came to have first-hand experience of domestic work in different contexts. I spent six months at the hall of residence before starting participant observation at the hospital and then, later in the research, I went back to the hall of residence to 'check out' my initial findings and do further comparative research.

This study aimed principally to use informal interviews and participant observation as evidence from which to grasp how part-time domestic assistants in two different organisations managed, co-ordinated and structured their lives. Initially I made contact with women in their workplaces, extending contact from there to their homes and neighbourhoods. At the student hall of residence, because there were only 17 domestic staff, it was relatively easy to get to know all of them, and of those I came to know four women very well (and am still in contact) and they invited me to their homes to meet their families. At the hospital there were approximately 220 domestic staff and so the situation was quite different from that at the student hall of residence, although I still established relationships with several of the women who helped me with the research. Indeed, some of the warmest relationships were with the African-Caribbean women with whom I worked, who also fed me at lunch time. For these friendships I was once criticised by one domestic supervisor for being a 'Blackie lover', a remark which I ignored.

Approximately six months into the research at the hall of residence, points of comparison emerged that affected the direction taken, and the approach of the subsequent hospital study. I became interested in differences in the commitment to cleaning work and identity between women who had recently started in the job, who worked shorter hours, and longer serving women who tended to work the longer shifts. At the hall of residence differences in hours worked and length of service had, in effect, divided the women into two main workgroups, each with its own identity. I was interested to see if this differentiation could also be found amongst women on different shifts at the hospital, and if so, to try and understand the conditions which gave rise to such distinctions as well as how these shaped a sense of identity and belonging.

I came to like the work and the women and became used to working early and late shifts so as to make the most of the limited time available for participant observation. As time went on I almost lost sight of the fact that cleaning was not my 'real job' and one day I was even asked by a supervisor at the hospital to work overtime. By working as a domestic, which in both the hospital and the hall of residence involved more than cleaning work, I felt the need to increase the satisfaction of the work by establishing some kind of personal contact with those for whom I cleaned. I felt this far more strongly in the hospital on the wards than in the hall of residence, although in both places such relationships were an important part of working life for the women alongside whom I worked. At the hospital I also had to deal occasionally with unpleasant and disturbing incidents and, like the other domestics, find ways to cope with my feelings of aversion or distress. Participant observation was enabling me to learn 'through the senses and in the body' and through those 'unconscious ways in which the fieldworker adapts and more fully participates' (Okely 1983 : 46).[3] The operating theatre domestics taught me how to walk in bulky theatre clogs, and although it took me a little time to move as confidently and smoothly as they did, I did learn to sweep along the corridors, commanding the space around me just like my workmates. These women considered themselves the 'elite' of domestics, had no time for patients, and were disdainful even of the porters; their reference group was not their fellow domestics but the operating theatre staff, of which they considered themselves a part (even though we rarely saw them). The operating theatre domestics' idea that they were different from those domestics who worked on the hospital wards seemed to draw on and reflect hierarchies within, and between, medical and nursing workforces.

Working alongside the women over several months, and also getting to know them outside work, helped me to understand how work, which they said 'stigmatised' and 'degraded' them, was also a source of respectability for them and their families (for a similar argument related to class see Skeggs (1997)). This in turn gave me insight into a cosmology of moral values and beliefs that underpinned many different aspects of women's lives and relationships (Hart 1988, 1991b), as well as into a 'theology' of cleaning work (Hart 2003a).

In relation to policy, the findings had shown that part-time work was not flexibly fitted around home and family, but that women did two or more part-time jobs in order to manage, often working long hours, including early and late shifts. Furthermore, the work involved far more than cleaning tasks and extended informally to patient care (Hart 1988). In relation to future developments in the NHS: the research anticipated that the privatisation of domestic services would erode loyalty to, and pride in, 'a ward of my own' which 'wasn't just clean but beautiful', and with it the job satisfaction that came from a sense of being more than a cleaner. The findings anticipated current concerns, widely publicised in the media and discussed in parliament, about the possible links between contract cleaning, 'dirty hospitals' and the so-called 'super-bug' MRSA (methicillin-resistant Staphylococcus aureus) (BBC.co.uk 2004).

## Ethnography 2: The East Midlands 1987 to 1989

### Why Do Nurses Leave the NHS?

The previous study with hospital domestic assistants led on to a two-year contract in a clinical management unit at another university as a lecturer in industrial anthropology. Although I got the post 'on the back' of the domestics research, I did not at first appreciate that this was largely because the research unit's manager (my boss) realised that in the current climate of major change not only to cleaning services but to the established nursing skill mix, there was a market for my findings amongst NHS policy makers, planners and managers who saw a use for my ethnography and were 'a locally-based…community of experts' (Kuper 1994: 551). There was also interest from nurse anthropologists (Hart 1991b).[4] By now, the contracting-out of cleaning services was a major issue for NHS managers and policy makers alike, and my research was featured in the *Health Service Journal* (Hart 1988). And so it was that shortly after starting my first lecturing post, I was presenting the findings at a national conference on 'Teamwork in the NHS' for NHS managers and health care professionals (Hart 1987) followed by two other local conferences; all three of which were well attended. As my post was 'self-funding', the profits from the three conferences helped to pay my salary as well as making a profit for the research unit. However, this also brought home to me what other anthropologists have found; namely, how difficult it was to anticipate how research findings might be used and interpreted by a range of 'users' in diverse contexts to support different arguments and how little control, if any, the anthropologist had over this process (Okely 1987; Goldschmidt 2001). As Okely argued, 'research may not be read in ways which the authors intended. It depends on the political circumstances and interests of those in power' (1987: 64). Brody observed that sometimes researchers only find out who they were working for many years later, and any research can be used by government as a form of control in ways the researcher cannot predict, and in ways which may even turn out to be harmful to participants (Brody 1981).

There was a market for my research skills and, including my doctoral research, I now had experience of research in both private and public sector organisations in three very different settings (a factory, a university, and a hospital). I was naturally keen to do some more research which built on my previous work, and so my boss put me in touch with a Regional Nursing Officer and I made an appointment with her to discuss possible research funding. Her major concern was how to stem the flow of nurses leaving the NHS, especially at the hospitals for which she was responsible. She talked about how frustrated she was by the findings of large-scale surveys, which highlighted general patterns and trends but threw little light, if any, on what was happening at ward level, and on what might be done by managers locally to improve the situation. Two of the hospitals about which she was especially concerned were in the East Midlands, seventy miles away from the university where I was employed, but close to my home and, as I was recently married, I had an interest in doing research that would enable me to live at home with my husband instead of in a campus flat on my own. In October 1987 I wrote my first research proposal for funding from which the following is an extract:

**From: A Comparative Study of Home and Workplace Factors Influencing Employment Continuity and Return Among Hospital Nurses. <u>Research Proposal</u>**

Synopsis of Research

A comparative study [is proposed] using social anthropological theories, observational techniques and semi-structured interviews of the influence of social and work factors upon employment patterns for selected groups of nurses, male and female. A major focus [will be] on their day-to-day experience on the wards in relation to their expectations of nursing and the satisfaction/dissatisfaction they derive from their work. The aim will be to produce a rounded ethnographic account of nurses that extends beyond the workplace by taking into consideration the implications of domestic and parental commitments upon their attitudes to work. The intention is to understand the ways in which nurses identify with their workplace, respond to different leadership styles and make decisions about when to leave and when to return to nursing.

I built twelve months of participant observation at two sister teaching hospitals into the costings, six months at each; a paediatric unit and a care of the elderly ward, respectively. I was directed by the Regional Nursing Officer to these particular sites because both specialities had serious problems retaining nurses: paediatrics because of a shortage of Registered Sick Children's Nurses nationally, and care of the elderly because newly qualified nurses did not want to work there: one staff nurse later reported that the then Matron sent those newly qualified nurses who, as students, had poor attendance records to care of the elderly as a 'punishment', which was why she was there.

The findings of the 'nurse turnover' study also turned out to be marketable. After leaving the field, I found myself running short courses on retention issues based directly on my research for NHS managers and senior nurses from across the country. An unanticipated advantage of these courses was that they enabled me to compare and contrast findings on aspects of nurses' employment situation in several different regions and build that comparative data into my final report for the Regional Nursing Officer. I began to realise that the picture varied markedly in different parts of the country, and that local context seemed to be a key factor in whether the problem was defined as 'high retention' or 'high turnover'.

Included below is an extract from the introduction to the final report to the then Regional Nursing Officer who sponsored the study. It is included here for two reasons: it shows how participant observation, with its focus on social processes at the micro-level, produced a new and different perspective on a long-standing problem, which also questioned the findings of large-scale surveys; and it demonstrates how easy it was, in an attempt to fulfil the sponsor's brief, to package what I did as 'qualitative' research rather than 'anthropology'. Another point that struck me when re-reading the report for this chapter is how it only alludes to what appeared to be nurses' deep-seated yet unspoken fear of becoming the subject of suspicion and fear akin to a witchcraft accusation. Unlike the Azande, witchcraft beliefs were not an explicit and ever present part of daily life for these nurses, but even so the coincidence of two happening – a particular nurse being on a particular ward when three patients died in a row – might be explained in relation to the presence of that particular nurse; very much as Azande might have done (Evans-Pritchard 1937). The three patients did not die because this nurse had deliberately killed them, but because her presence brought on their deaths; if she had not have been there then at least one, or maybe more, might not have died when they did. I was reminded of something a colleague had told me about her experience of fieldwork in Africa, when she had nearly become the focus of a witchcraft accusation because her position was marginal and ambiguous, and also she was in the wrong place at the wrong time. So I listened with a new ear to the stories of nurses who were leaving because they felt they 'didn't fit' in some way and/or were disliked by the sister or the unit manager, and I also became more conscious of the ambiguities of my own position.

*Extract from a Report to the Regional Nursing Officer about Why Nurses Leave the NHS*

Introduction

Recent large-scale surveys of nurses' attitudes have been concerned primarily with the reasons why nurses leave nursing and do not return. This present study is rather different. Using a qualitative approach, it focuses on the social processes which prompt a nurse to leave her present hospital, whether for promotion, a non-nursing job, to raise a family or for a range of other reasons, including leaving nursing altogether.

However, the focus is not on leaving reasons per se. Instead the concern is to understand the social and interpersonal factors which affect workforce stability or high turnover. For example, on the stability side, 'finding a niche' within your ward and 'clicking' with the other nurses; on the turnover side, catching 'itchy feet' from a colleague and 'getting bored' or feeling that your 'face doesn't fit' with the ward sister. These expressions and ways of thinking will be familiar to nurses and their managers. Yet it is noticeable that such widely used idioms are given no recognition in the official 'leaving' categories such as 'to widen experience', 'abroad', 'non-nursing job'. In translation these idioms lose their meaning and obscure the understanding of why it is nurses are leaving.

Statistically, for the purpose of manpower planning, the need to develop broad, workable leaving categories is understandable. It is of no help to the manpower planner to know that four nurses, all friends, left one ward within a few weeks of each other because they disliked their new sister. Neither is it necessary for the policy maker to know that all the members of a small student 'set' left within a year (after completing specialist training) because they believed themselves out of favour with their Unit manager. At the macro level such facts are statistically insignificant and irrelevant. But from the micro perspective of the ward or the Unit, the above events are significant; a new ward sister who loses four experienced nurses is in a difficult situation and their leaving may point to a possible problem in her management style. If the situation is not resolved her ward may become a turnover 'hot spot'. Or, a Unit manager may find it difficult to replace immediately all of the specialist nurses who left in turn as a 'set' and this may lead to a temporary imbalance in skill mix. This report is concerned with those factors from within the informal social organisation, which lead both to commitment and instability. The concern is with beliefs and perceptions and with social relations at the micro level of the ward.

As noted above the study found that one reason for leaving was to avoid the risk of being held to blame for something for which one was not responsible, i.e. the fear of a witch-hunt (Max Gluckman cited in Frankenberg (1982: 7)), and that there was a gap between what nurses said formally about why they were leaving and what was happening informally. In reporting these findings to hospital managers and the Regional Nursing Officer, as well as to the nurses themselves, I faced a dilemma: what not to say in order to say something which contributed to an understanding of why nurses were leaving, but without betraying the personal confidences of the nurses who had participated in the study. This was not just a personal but an ethical dilemma in that it would have gone against professional guidelines to present to nurses information about themselves that they might not want to know, or have known, in that way (Association of Social Anthropologists 2003). I was representing one group to the other, nurses to managers and managers to nurses, and so faced both ways. My situation was in certain respects analogous to that of the rate fixer in Lupton's classic shop floor study (Lupton 1963) and further discussed by Frankenberg (1990). As an outsider who had spent a relatively long time working with nurses, I was 'in but not of' the organisation, and my connection to the senior nurse (the Regional Nursing Officer) meant that I was almost in an intermediate position: 'the lowest in a hierarchy of leadership, who by representing their superiors to those below them, and their inferiors to those above them, pleased no one and were blamed by all' (Max Gluckman summarised in Frankenberg 1982: 14 )). Being blamed for the problems highlighted by the research both by nurses and their managers was a situation which I naturally wanted to avoid, and I resolved the dilemma as best I could by addressing my arguments to the evidence from quantitative data so far available, showing how the findings from the ethnographic study highlighted previously unrecognised dimensions of nurse turnover. In doing so, I included discussion of the power attributed to the number three, as well as to the widespread belief amongst nurses that things 'happened in threes', but did not refer directly to witchcraft beliefs.

As already mentioned, these ethnographic data challenged the findings of large-scale surveys such as those by Price Waterhouse (1988) in suggesting that these simply reproduced official leaving reasons and were thus misleading (Hart 1989). But they also challenged the received managerial wisdom that nurses left because of factors over which they had little, if any, control – such as a 'husband's job move' – when in practice it was likely to be the nurse who had initiated the move. In the event, the Regional Nursing Officer 'liked' the report and was 'fascinated' by some of the findings. My fieldnotes record that she said that it showed the importance of understanding the micro level of 'your ward' and 'your hospital' and that 'manpower data nationally is no good' (for those purposes). She reflected that when she was a hospital manager she used to collect that kind of data but 'doesn't think that managers do now' (although the manager of one unit certainly did because I used it in the final report).

As indicated above, a finding to emerge from this study was that nurses acted and spoke as if they felt themselves subject to powerful outside forces over which they had little direct control but to which there was some discernible pattern and logic. By intuiting these emerging patterns and anticipating the probable course of events, it became possible for a nurse, by leaving, to lessen the risk of damage to her professional reputation and career, as well as to her personal standing amongst her colleagues on the ward. I believe that these data suggest that such subconscious feelings were (and are) collectively held and that this might explain how it is that various attempts to 'retain' nursing staff, including pay increases, seem doomed to failure. It would be wrong to give the impression that fear of a witch hunt was the only, or even the main reason for leaving. Nevertheless, this and other 'findings' pointed to the 'hidden' dimensions of organisational life, and to the way that official leaving reasons were contradicted by what I observed to be happening in nurses' everyday working lives.

## Ethnography 3: The East Midlands 1990–1992

*Managing Change at a District General Hospital*

This study of the management of change at a district general hospital came about because the Regional Nursing Officer who funded the previous study on nurse turnover (ethnography 2) had liked it and found it helpful, and was now interested in a new proposal of mine that involved a developmental programme with ward sisters, focusing on their changing role. And so, in early 1990, I negotiated a new position on a short-term contract at a different university using this new research funding from the Regional Nursing Officer to 'buy myself in' as it were. I then became the principal investigator on a two-year action research project at a district general hospital, which senior people at the Regional Health Authority described as a 'backwater' in need of radical change (Hart and Bond 1995). An unfavourable report by external auditors on standards of care in one directorate had added to the Regional Health Authority's concerns. Unlike the two earlier studies where I had worked as a lone anthropologist and as 'chief cook and bottle washer', this project involved a team of researchers, one of whom was also my then Head of School, and a substantial budget far in excess of the two previous projects. In all, including myself, six people were involved in the research; a full-time research assistant, a research secretary, a research adviser; two outside consultants brought in at different stages of the project; one to work with me on the development and training component, and the other to undertake a financial analysis of staffing costs; and my then head of school.

This new proposal grew directly out of the time I had spent in the previous study working alongside ward sisters and I wanted to learn more about what their work involved and what 'nursing' meant to them in this changing context. The programme was intended to provide an opportunity for ward sisters to directly influence the direction of change, based on an understanding of their own development needs. In this the project was relevant to current policy but saw nurses as active players in the process rather than 'victims' of change. Transforming what were then perceived as 'traditional' ward sisters into 'progressive' ward managers was part of an attempt by the then Conservative government to challenge professional boundaries and undermine established professional strongholds. For nursing this involved an attempt to invert the established 60:40 nursing skill mix, trained to non-trained, including the establishment of a new breed of 'generalists' (Hart 1991a). The nursing workforce was, and is, the single biggest labour cost to the NHS and this top-down policy drive dovetailed with debates about the health care division of labour between doctors and nurses in relation to concerns about the rise of high-tech, high value interventions. In the early 1990s new visions for the relationship between medicine and nursing were being widely expressed in the media and professional journals. Dr Mark Baker, Chief Executive of Bradford

Hospitals Trust, in an interview with the *Nursing Standard*, talked of nurses taking on low level medical tasks, with a new group of 'sub-professionals' such as health care assistants taking over routine activities which had traditionally been 'owned' by the nursing profession. He argued that:

> The balance of nursing will shift from the care of the patient in bed to the application of technology to the patients … The old role can be done by non-nurses, and that obviously is threatening to those whose lives are tied up with that sort of work. (Naish 1991: 21)

However, the project did not turn out as I initially envisaged it, that is as an ethnographic study of ward sisters which would be used to inform an 'emancipatory' development programme. Following the involvement of a senior nurse from the Department of Health, the project expanded to become an action research study of organisational change. There are close links between action research and applied anthropology but the project became far more politicised than I had anticipated. Indeed the project began in a climate of considerable uncertainty within nursing about what the future might hold in the wake of the application of general management principles derived from the private sector to the NHS, and famously embodied in the so-called 'Griffiths Report' (Department of Health and Social Security 1983). Reinforcing this viewpoint, the publication of an influential ethnographic study of new management in the NHS observed that the new breed of general manager saw it almost as their mission to undermine the traditional 'tribal' culture, and the authors suggested that they were witnessing the emergence of a new culture, one which was strongly anti-professional (Strong and Robinson 1990).

During this research I had direct experience of what Pollitt *et al.* (1990) refer to as the 'discomforts' of ethnographic research in the health services, although at the time it felt more like suffering to me. As one senior manager put it, the hospital was in a difficult situation because 'we know we have just been a pawn in a bigger political game'. The project I describe here was one part of that political game, which senior managers at the Regional Health Authority saw as about using a 'backwater' hospital to show the big and powerful teaching hospitals that 'if they can do it, you can do it!'

The people at the Regional Health Authority believed they knew what the problems were, blaming 'old-fashioned' ward sisters, resistant to change, whom they referred to as 'dinosaurs', but they were cautious: hard won experience had taught them that 'top down' change does not work in the NHS and that the workforce has a knack of ensuring that whatever successive governments and managers try to do, nothing much changes. Action research, with its promise of 'bottom up' change, seemed an attractive option and an anthropologist like me, with a track record of research with nursing and domestic staff, seemed well placed to lead it.

My own first-hand experience of the culture of the District Health Authority concerned was that it could be almost brutal in its reaction to any kind of suggestion from 'below' that the 'problem' might not conform to the senior executive's view of it. Because I moved between the different worlds of the District Health Authority and the hospital, I was able to observe how structural inequalities reinforced the nurses' belief that they were 'second-class citizens' and to glimpse the scale of the problems faced by nursing staff. I observed that millions of pounds were available for new buildings to house new computers and people to feed them: but that this world of plenty co-existed with a world of relative poverty at the hospital. For example, one ward sister of a long-stay care of the elderly ward reported at the weekly ward sisters' meeting that the laundry budget was overspent and so there had been no clean knickers for her patients that morning. This situation had made her weep with shame and frustration. Thereafter, her fellow ward sisters, who empathised with her situation, referred to the ward ironically as 'Saint Knickerless Ward'.

The report about these problems that I had prepared with this group of ward sisters was negatively received, even though senior managers had specifically asked for a 'warts and all' approach. One finding was that ward sisters were unable to meet the requirement to provide continuity of care not because they were 'resistant to change' but because wards were short staffed and relied on agency and bank nurses, several of whom were nurses who had finished shifts at the hospital and then came back on the next shift 'on the bank'. This was supported by a separate analysis of the way staffing was financed and managed conducted by a finance specialist within the research team. The ward sisters themselves claimed that managers were trying to achieve cost savings by using the 'vacancy factor' (which meant that when a nurse left, the post would not be filled immediately). As a consequence, nurse staffing was so fragmented and depleted that 'continuity of care' was an unachievable ideal. Added to this, it was estimated by the 'IT' department that each day the ward sisters were seven hours short of nursing time, but they were then told by senior managers that 'nothing can be done'.

Ward sisters also highlighted the fact that senior managers, did not - or would not – listen to them when they raised these issues and that, charged with implementing a major change in their role, the ward sisters had no means of having their voices heard. One of the 'solutions' they proposed was to meet with senior managers to talk to them about their shared interests in improving patient care, to be listened to and listen in their turn. In the report, the ward sisters, the majority of whom were long serving, talked of the 'fear' they now experienced as an everyday part of their working lives. No longer was the hospital perceived as a safe and friendly place in which to work; rather these experienced ward sisters were fearful of senior managers (one of whom was described privately as a 'bully'), and were worried that they might lose their jobs (for which they were having to re-apply). In preparing the report the ward sisters and I had been careful to word it in such a way that for every problem identified there was a proposed solution, and to emphasise the point that the ward sisters would really welcome an opportunity to work with senior managers to improve standards of nursing care. At the time the negative response to this report seemed out of all proportion to its contents. Looking back, I can see now that in seeking to resolve the situation by speaking publicly to managers about such long-standing and widely recognised problems the ward sisters and I had unwittingly breached the constraints of cultural censorship and almost exposed the silence without which the wider organisational tensions alluded to in the report could not be contained: there was no means of resolution.

## Discussion: Dilemmas of Speaking of Silence

Drawing on the experience above, I now want to say a bit more about the extent to which the climate in which research is conducted impacts on the way findings are interpreted and received. I also want to say something about how my subsequent reflection on my work has enabled me to enhance my theoretical understanding of the problems I was studying at the time.

My experience is that the degree to which the anthropologist is seen as 'subversive' seems to depend on the extent to which the aims or conduct of the research challenge the current political or policy agenda, bearing in mind that that agenda can change even during the lifetime of a single project. In other words these challenges may be entirely unwitting: the anthropologist does not set out to be 'subversive'. In the NHS where managerial control is being increasingly centralised, employees are now 'empowered' self-regulating subjects (Brown and Crawford 2003), free to police themselves in ensuring the local delivery of corporate standards of service (Huby 2003). In the NHS, surveillance mechanisms such as 'quality audit' and 'clinical governance' are the mechanism of this control (Huby 2003) and are part of the global proliferation of 'audit cultures' (Strathern 2000). In these circumstances the hospital becomes a site of struggle (Navarro 1980; Scheper-Hughes 1990) with employees caught in the 'seductive doublethink of corporate culture' in which 'autonomy' does not mean 'freedom' but a tightly circumscribed 'obedience to the core values of corporate culture' (Willmott 1993 : 527). In such organisational contexts, Gellner and Hirsch argue, that despite a growing awareness that:

> careful ethnographic work is likely to bring far greater insight, there are reasons to believe that ethnography will always have an air of subversiveness about it. Alongside the postulated general cultural movement towards democratisation, there is a countervailing trend towards control, measurement and quantification of outputs. Any 'method' that insists it lacks a cut-

and-dried technique, any discipline that grants a central position to the voices of the 'client' and refuses to prejudge what they might say, will always be suspect to powerful organisations. (Gellner and Hirsch 2001b: 2)

The perception of 'subversiveness' also seems to depend on the extent to which the anthropologist is perceived as giving a voice to previously silenced groups, and in this respect 'bottom-up' approaches are perceived as tending to the subversive (Groocock and Maiteny 1997). Reflecting on my own research I have come to realise the importance of the concept of 'cultural censorship' in explaining how people are silenced (Sheriff 2000). As discussed above, this concept originally derived from Sheriff's fieldwork in Brazil and was developed to explain how it was that racism was simultaneously known about and concealed by a socially shared silence. At first sight a concept used to understand the experiences of Brazilian shantytown dwellers seems to have little direct relevance to the organisational problems of the NHS. However, when used to analyse the organisational context for 'adverse events' in the health services it proved a powerful analytic device which made it possible to find new ways of looking at old problems (Hart and Hazelgrove 2001). By using concepts developed in one context to address problems found in very different contexts the anthropologist is able to make connections between seemingly very dissimilar problems. The concept of 'cultural censorship' has enabled me to understand the silences I encountered during my three studies as 'socially shared silence' and to better explain how it is that the findings of ethnographic research in organisations such as the health services have the potential to be so disturbing for participants, sponsors and ethnographers alike.

The way in which cultural censorship operates is well illustrated by the third action research study (for a different perspective on the application of action research to the health services see Bate (2000b)). This action research study was different to the other two studies reported above in focusing specifically on organisational change, and because people at a senior level both at the Regional Health Authority and the Department of Health were involved. Both groups had a shared interest in a 'successful' outcome, as did the District Health Authority's senior executive, in that the hospital was applying for phase one Trust status. Politically it was in no-one's interests to bring longstanding problems to light, and especially not those which pointed to difficulties in the way the nursing workforce was being managed. Nevertheless, an external audit of one directorate had exposed less than satisfactory standards of nursing care, and the Regional Health Authority had a vested interest in showing that initiatives were in place to bring about change and improvement; hence the funding of an action research study. So in the third study the stakes were much higher and the context far more politicised than in the other two and the impact of the research process more direct and personal for all concerned, nurses, managers and researchers.

My own 'hunch' at the time, and nothing has happened to change that feeling, was that there were 'too many fingers' in the research pie – the research team included – which made the project very unwieldy. Between us the research team collected and analysed a huge amount of data, including ethnographic and financial, but in the end the credibility of the research rested not on the validity or extent of that evidence but on whether or not the senior executive was prepared to listen to, accept and act on, what the ward sisters were saying and take his senior managers along with him; which he was not. But his situation must have been a been very difficult one: the research was being funded by the organisation which was in a direct line management relationship to the District Health Authority and, what is more, the steering group involved personnel from the Department of Health.

So, how might things have been different? In the health services, as in any organisation, it is essential for the anthropologist to understand the working environment (Mascarenhas-Keyes 2001), and this includes recognising the need to establish strong vertical linkages with senior and middle managers to balance the strong horizontal linkages established with the participants most directly involved in the research (Hackenberg 1999). But in the health services this is easier said than done because senior staff move so often. In the directorate where the main study was conducted I had established strong (horizontal) linkages with the wards sisters and strong (vertical) linkages with both the lead medical consultant (Clinical Director) and the senior nurse manager, who together had arranged cover for the ward sisters to participate in a developmental programme (Hart and Bond 1995). In this directorate, where vertical and horizontal linkages were balanced and strong, as Hackenberg (1999) recommends, the findings were heralded as a 'new beginning' and were not perceived either as threat or criticism, and so were embraced. Yet, this was the directorate which had been the subject of a critical external audit, where it might be expected that people were less likely, rather than more, to welcome further recommendations for change. Managers and ward sisters at directorate level had participated directly in the research over the two years of the project, so that 'collaboration' had real meaning for them, whereas at District Health Authority level, over that time key people moved away, either to posts elsewhere or to different posts in the same organisation. This also meant that new people moved into key positions who knew nothing about the project, had no direct interest in its success, and had their own agendas. So, at a senior level there was no continuity of support and vertical linkages were fractured at a critical point in the feedback process. Indeed, so volatile was the situation in the NHS at that time, that at one meeting several months into the project, apart from one other person, I was the longest serving person there. Another difference between senior managers at the District Health Authority and those at the hospital was that the former were rendered temporarily powerless by being caught between the formal power of executive managers at the Regional Health Authority and the informal power of the university researchers. Drawing on case study analysis of organisational research, Klein and Eason explain the relationship between 'clients', in this case senior managers at the District Health Authority, and the 'social scientists', in this case the research team, as one in which power is fundamental:

> The word 'collaboration' trips easily from the tongue, but it is a complex process in which power plays an important part. The power of clients derives from the fact that they are the principal actors and 'own' the situation. The power of the social scientist derives from the fact that they are detached from the situation and not locked into it. Each has needs and may resent dependency on the other, or envy the other's power. This can lead to a cyclical process where those who experience powerlessness in one area avenge themselves by exercising power in the other. (Klein and Eason 1991: 225)

From a synthesis of a vast range of studies, Klein and Eason (1991) identified conditions tending to support or hinder success in relation to whether or not an organisation utilised social science research, and I have found their analysis helpful in generalising from my own studies. To illustrate this in relation to ethnography 3: there were several conditions tending to hinder success. First, the people funding the research were in line management authority to the 'subjects' of the research, reinforcing a situation in which 'they' (the Regional Health Authority) were perceived as doing something to 'them' (the District Health Authority), a situation which made senior people at the District Health Authority understandably defensive (if not to say fearful). Second, there was not a senior manager influential enough within the District Health Authority to act as an advocate for the research findings; a condition which hindered the take-up of findings through their lack of dissemination at management meetings and because there was no-one with the authority to ensure that findings were acted upon. A third condition hindering success was that there were a number of overlapping 'change management' projects taking place simultaneously, each with its own agenda, and each competing for the senior executive's approval. Since, for the managers in charge of these projects, success was tied through performance appraisal to individual ownership of outcomes, the researchers were perceived as threatening their interests.

Drawing on the three ethnographies above, I have tried to show that even in an organisation as large and complex as the NHS, anthropology's ethnographic method and theoretical insights can be applied to an understanding of organisational problems, and to research with a range of different groups. An anthropological understanding of people and events that springs from the field encounter may make it possible for even small-scale local studies to challenge the findings of large-scale national surveys (ethnography 2) as well as anticipating the unintended impact of policy changes on workers and organisations (ethnography 1). I believe this is because anthropological knowledge is constructed through what Terrell refers to as a 'human encounter metaphor', grounded in a quite different view of the nature of reality (irrespective of time in the field) than the 'crucial experiment metaphor' of positivist science (Terrell 2000) and it is from this that it derives its 'understanding power' (Frankenberg 2003b). Part of this power relates to the way anthropologists come to know by being there (Watson 1999), and this applies whatever is being observed. This point is illustrated by the study of nurse turnover (ethnography 2) where, by participating in daily life on the wards, I was able to observe how apparently unconnected events, beliefs and interactions, took on the meanings that became categorised as 'turnover'. In this respect the process of knowing is the same irrespective of whether the anthropologist is in a hospital observing the collective processes that imbue apparently unconnected events and beliefs with meanings which culminate in 'leaving' or in an Italian village observing the processes through which villagers come to a consensus about the appearance of the Madonna. As Apolito (1998) observed:

> Before what happened came to be called 'apparition', before it acquired this identity, there was an intense collective process that came to light. Above all it was the product of conversation, of gossip, of storytelling, of myth, all together produced ad hoc from the context. Between the first events, the first accounts, and the apparition as an established fact there was an infinite, detailed, intense activity of sustained linguistic interaction of the context. (Apolito 1998: 7)

Being there, Apolito was in the town for five days during the formative stage, before the appearance of the Madonna had become a 'real event' (Apolito 1998: 3). In a similar way, being there on the wards, I was able to document what happened in the formative weeks during which an apparently non-connected series of incidents, stories and resentments coalesced into the 'real event' of 'leaving'.

Even when funding only allows for short-term fieldwork of five or six months, it is still possible to retain a commitment to the 'field encounter' (Strathern 1991) as the origin of anthropological knowledge and understanding. Indeed this grounding of knowledge in day-to-day interactions with people in their workplaces, homes and neighbourhoods, though not unique to anthropology, is certainly distinctive for, as Frankenberg argues, what marks out the anthropologist is:

> the determination to engage over a period of time with people in action – people seeking both to create and to understand themselves and almost always to help others to understand them too. (Frankenberg 2003b: xiv)

Perhaps it needs to be more clearly recognised that for anthropologists who research in the same organisation over many years, as I have done, the process of engagement and understanding is necessarily cumulative (Goldschmidt 2001) so that the distinction between 'short-term' and 'long-term' fieldwork become meaningless: each period of fieldwork builds one on another, and reflection makes it possible to re-visit and re-think findings in light of later events. Indeed, this chapter is itself an illustration of this process, as in preparing it I have re-read and re-visited my fieldnotes, returned to 'check things out' with key participants and friends and engaged in the same kind of reflexive activity as Josephides does with the Kewa:

> With fieldwork, time and return are crucial factors. After such a long period of shared substances and emotions, I constantly carry my Kewa friends around with me, back to the field, to conferences, to classes, I reread my fieldnotes, their letters, I make constant connections when I read other writing, not only anthropological, which recalls a Kewa friend or event. In my own social relations and daily actions I constantly find parallels with Kewa situations. (Josephides 1997: 25)

When anthropologists study 'at home', as I have done, it is of course much easier to stay in touch with participants and return to 'the field' than for those who study 'abroad'. In my case, I now work in a School of Nursing, and so in that sense I have never really left 'the field', and am constantly in touch, including through my research students, with what is happening in the health services. This illustrates also how misleading it is to distinguish between 'pure' and 'applied' anthropology on the grounds that real anthropology is only practiced by those in university departments of anthropology, and to ignore the contribution of applied anthropologists not only to the theoretical development of other academic disciplines, but to the present and future development of anthropology itself (Mars 2004).

## Conclusion

The three studies reported here were conducted in four hospitals, and all involved periods of fieldwork of several months in order to explore issues in-depth and over time. They were selected to illustrate different ways in which I had worked in hospitals, independently and as part of a team, and to illustrate how 'traditional' fieldwork methods can open-up new ways of understanding issues and developing theory. In all three studies I was fortunate in that time and funding allowed for quite long periods of participant observation, including getting to know participants outside work, but I have since conducted research where fieldwork had to be costed in days and weeks rather than months and years. Nevertheless, I found that even a three-day period of fieldwork can be intensive and fruitful (as discussed elsewhere (Hart 2003b)). The fieldnotes of these three days, when combined with other relatively short but concentrated periods of observation and interviewing in six nursing homes, made it possible to trace the development of a service over two years and to produce a rich contextual background against which to interpret the interview data (Hart *et al.* 2005). In a different study of a community stroke services (Hart 2001), video diaries were used to enable two stroke survivors and their families to document their own experiences of what it was like to live with stroke on a daily basis over time to show to the project's steering group (Hart with Watling 1996). This illustrates that there are various ways in which anthropologists can and do contribute to organisational and health services research which do not necessarily involve long periods of fieldwork. Whether as principal investigator or as part of a team working with medical researchers and therapists, anthropologists continue to bring to bear a distinctive way of looking at issues in the health services, throwing light on the wider dimensions of organisational 'problems' and policy contexts (Savage 1995; Bate 2000; Parker 2001; Pulman-Jones 2001), and this includes contributing to debates about healthcare policy and health services research (see, respectively Savage (2000) and Lambert and McKevitt (2002)). By reflecting on my fieldwork in the NHS, without glossing over difficulties, I hope I have nevertheless demonstrated the value of an anthropological approach to problems that at first sight appear not to be within its domain, the relevance of anthropological theories developed in a different context to the current and future concerns of the health services, and the way in which these insights can be central to understanding and resolving problems old and new.

## Notes

1.  At the time I conducted these studies the current NHS procedures for applying for ethics approval did not exist, and I do not discuss them here. For ethical guidelines followed by anthropologists, see Association of Social Anthropologists (2003).
2.  For very useful discussions of organisational anthropology in relation to the development of organisational behaviour (OB) and management studies, see respectively Bate (1997) and Linstead (1997). For an account of a meeting between a group of organisational development practitioners and anthropologists which bears on these arguments see Groocock and Maiteny (1997).
3.  See also Jan Savage's account of how during participant observation with nursing staff she embodied what was involved in a new approach to nursing and was thus able to gain insight into how this differed from the way she had been trained to relate to patients (Savage 1995).
4.  In March 1986 the research was presented at the Nursing and Anthropology Conference, Centre for Cross-Cultural Research on Women, University of Oxford and later published in an edited collection, on Anthropology and Nursing (Holden and Littlewood (eds), 1991).

# References

Apolito, P. 1998. *Apparitions of the Madonna at Oliveto Citra: Local Visions and Cosmic Drama*. Pennsylvania: The Pennsylvania State University Press.

Association of Social Anthropologists. 2003. 'Association of Social Anthropologists of the Commonwealth: Ethical Guidelines for Good Research Practice'. http:// www.theasa.org/ethics.htm, accessed 4 April 2005.

Bate, P. 2000a. 'Changing the Culture of a Hospital: From Hierarchy to Networked Community'. *Public Administration*, 78(3): 485–512.

———. 2000b. 'Synthesizing Research and Practice: Using the Action Research Approach in Health Care Settings'. *Social Policy and Administration*, 34(4): 478–493.

———. 1997. 'Whatever Happened to Organizational Ethnography and Anthropological Studies'. *Human Relations*, 50(9): 1147–1175.

Batteau, A. W. 2000. 'Negations and Ambiguities in the Cultures of Organization'. *American Anthropologist*, 102(4): 726–740.

BBC.co.uk. 2004. Science and Nature: TV and radio follow-up. Should I worry about… MRSA http://www.bbc.co.uk/sn/tvradio/programmes/shouldiworryabout/mrsa.shtml, accessed 1 February 2005.

Becker, G. 1999. *Disrupted Lives: How People Create Meaning in a Chaotic World*. London: University of California Press.

Brody, H. 1981. *Maps and Dreams*. Harmondsworth: Penguin.

Brown, B. and Crawford, P. 2003. 'The Clinical Governance of the Soul: 'Deep Management' and the Self-Regulating Subject in Integrated Mental Health Teams'. *Social Science & Medicine*, 56: 67–81.

Colliere, M.F. and Lawler, J. 1998. 'Marie-Francoise Colliere – Nurse and Ethnohistorian: A Conversation About Nursing and the Invisibility of Care'. *Nursing Inquiry*, 5(3): 140–145.

Department of Health and Social Security. 1983. *NHS Management Inquiry* (The Griffiths Report), DA(83)38. London: DHSS.

Evans-Pritchard, E.E. 1937. *Witchcraft, Oracles and Magic Among the Azande*. Oxford: Clarendon Press.

Frankenberg, R. 1982. 'Introduction: A Social Anthropology for Britain?', in R. Frankenberg (ed.) *Custom and Conflict in British Society*. Manchester: Manchester University Press, pp. 1–35.

———. 1990. 'Taking the Blame and Passing the Buck, or, The Carpet of Agamemnon: An Essay on the Problems of Responsibility, Legitimation and Triviality', in *Village on the Border: A Social Study of Religion, Politics and Football in a North Wales Community*. Illinois: Waveland Press, pp. 200–223.

———. 2003a. Panel presentation: 'I can't get no satisfaction' or 'It ain't wotcher do it's the way tha'tcha do it' (or the way Thatcher did it?). Is it even possible for health services to seek to produce merely the absence of disease?' *Anthropology and Science: 5th Decennial Conference of the Association of Social Anthropologists of the UK and Commonwealth*, The University of Manchester, 14 to 18 July.

———. 2003b. 'Foreword', in A.C. Davies and S. Jones (eds). *Welsh Communities: New Ethnographic Perspectives*. Cardiff: University of Wales Press, pp. ix–xviii.

Gellner, D.N. and E. Hirsch (eds). 2001a. *Inside Organizations: Anthropologists at Work*. Oxford: Berg.

———. 2001b. 'Introduction: Ethnography of Organizations and Organizations of Ethnography', in D.N. Gellner and E. Hirsch (eds) *Inside Organizations: Anthropologists at Work*. Oxford: Berg.

Gledhill, J. 2002. 'Anthropology and Politics: Commitment, Responsibility and the Academy', in J. Vincent (ed.) *The Anthropology of Politics: A Reader in Ethnography, Theory, and Critique*. Oxford: Blackwell, pp. 438–451.

Goldschmidt, W. 2001. '2001 Malinowski Award Lecture – Notes Toward a Theory of Applied Anthropology'. *Human Organization*, 60(4): 423–429.

Groocock, P. and Maiteny, P. 1997. 'Anthropology and Organisational Studies Workshop'. *Anthropology in Action*, 4(3): 39–41.

Hackenberg, R.A. 1999. 'Advancing Applied Anthropology'. *Human Organization*, 58(1): 105–107.

Hart, E. 1987. 'Teamwork in The NHS: A Case Study Based Upon Two Research Projects About Domestic Staff. 22nd May 1987'. *National Conference on Teamwork in the NHS*. Central London.

———. 1988. 'Not Just a Cleaner'. *The Health Service Journal*, 98(5118), pp. 1066–1067.

———. 1989. *A Qualitative Study of Micro Level Factors Affecting Retention and Turnover Amongst Nursing Staff in Paediatrics and Care of the Elderly*, Clinical Management Unit, University of Keele.

———. 1991a. 'Ghost in the Machine'. *The Health Service Journal*, 101(5281): 20–22.

———. 1991b. 'A Ward of My Own: Social Organisation and Identity Among Hospital Domestics', in P. Holden and J. Littlewood (eds) *Anthropology and Nursing*. London: Routledge, pp. 84–109.

———. 2001. 'System Induced Setbacks in Stroke Recovery'. *Sociology of Health & Illness*, 23(1): 101–123.

———. 2003a. 'From Medieval Mystics to Domestics Assistants: Women, Stigmatisation and Cleaning Work'. *Paper presented to the Medical Anthropology Seminar*, University College London, 27 November.

———. 2003b. 'Panel Paper: A Culture of Contradictions in the NHS: a Perspective From Anthropology'. *5th Decennial Conference of the Association of Anthropologists of the U.K. and Commonwealth*, The University of Manchester, 14–18 July.

——— and M. Bond. 1995. *Action Research for Health and Social Care: A Guide to Practice*. Buckingham: Open University Press.

——— with R. Watling. 1996. 'Extracts from Video Diaries: Part of an Evaluation of a Pilot Community Stroke Service'. Nottingham: Department of Nursing and Midwifery Studies, University of Nottingham (video).

——— and J. Hazelgrove. 2001. 'Viewpoint: Understanding the Organisational Context for Adverse Events in the Health Services: The Role of Cultural Censorship'. *Quality in Health Care*, 10(4): 257–262.

———, M. Lymbery and J. Gladman. 2005. 'Away From Home: an Ethnographic Study of a Transitional Rehabilitation Scheme for Older People in the UK.' *Social Science & Medicine*, 60(6): 1241–1250.

Holden, P. and J. Littlewood (eds). 1991. *Anthropology and Nursing*. London: Routledge.

Huby, G. (2003). 'An Overview of Current NHS Organisation and the Role of Research Within It: Towards the Matrix as a New Organisational Metaphor?' *Anthropology and Science: 5th Decennial Conference of the Association of Social Anthropologists of the U.K. and Commonwealth*, The University of Manchester, 14 –18 July.

Josephides, L. 1997. 'Representing the Anthropologist's Predicament', in A. James, J. Hockey and A. Dawson (eds) *After Writing Culture: Epistemology and Praxis in Contemporary Anthropology*. London: Routledge, pp. 16–33.

Klein, L. and K. Eason. 1991. *Putting Social Science to Work: The Ground Between Theory and Use Explored Through Case Studies in Organisations*. Cambridge: Cambridge University Press.

Kuper, A. 1994. 'Culture, Identity and the Project of a Cosmopolitan Anthropology.' *Man, New Series*, 29(3): 537–554.

Lambert, H. and C. McKevitt. 2002. 'Anthropology in Health Research: From Qualitative Methods to Multidisciplinarity'. *British Medical Journal*, 325(7357): 210–213.

Laurance, J. 1988. 'Silencing the NHS'. *New Statesmen and Society*, 10 (June): 14–15.

Linstead, S. 1997. 'The Social Anthropology of Management.' *British Journal of Management*, 8: 85–98.

Lupton, T. 1963. *On The Shop Floor*. London: Pergamon Press.

Marris, P. 1986. *Loss and Change: Revised Edition*. London: Routledge and Kegan Paul.

168 | ELIZABETH HART

Mars, G. 2004. 'Guest Editorial: Refocusing with Applied Anthropology'. *Anthropology Today*, 20(1): 1–2.

Mascarenhas-Keyes, S. 2001. 'Understanding the Working Environment: Notes Towards a Rapid Organizational Analysis', in D.N. Gellner and E. Hirsch (eds) *Inside Organizations: Anthropologists at Work*. Oxford: Berg, pp. 205–232.

Naish, J. 1991. 'Would You Trust the Doctor's Regime?'. *Nursing Standard*, 6(2): 20–21.

Navarro, V. 1980. 'Work, Ideology and Science: The Case of Medicine'. *Social Science and Medicine*, 14c: 191–205.

Okely, J. 1983. *The Traveller-Gypsies*. Cambridge: Cambridge University Press.

———. 1987. 'Fieldwork up the M1: Policy and Political Aspects', in A. Jackson (ed.) *Anthropology at Home. ASA Monographs 25*. London: Tavistock, pp. 55–73.

Parker, M. 2001. 'Stuck in GUM: An Ethnography of a Clap Clinic', in D.N. Gellner and E. Hirsch (eds) *Inside Organizations: Anthropologists at Work*. Oxford: Berg, pp. 137–156.

Pollitt, C., S. Harrison, D.J. Hunter and G. Marnoch. 1990. 'No Hiding Place: On the Discomforts of Researching the Contemporary Policy Process'. *Journal of Social Policy* 19(2): 169–190.

Price Waterhouse 1988. *'Nurse Retention and Recruitment: A Matter of Priority'*. Report for trent Regional Workshop, 12 July.

Pulman-Jones, S. 2001. 'Observing Other Observers: Anthropological Fieldwork in a Unit for Children with Chronic Emotional and Behavioural Problems', in D.N. Gellner and E. Hirsch (eds) *Inside Organizations: Anthropologists at Work*. Oxford: Berg, pp. 117–135.

Savage, J. 1995. *Nursing Intimacy: An Ethnographic Approach to Nurse-Patient Interaction*. London: Scutari.

———. 2000. 'The Culture of 'Culture' in National Health Service Policy Implementation'. *Nursing Inquiry*, 7: 230–238.

Scheper-Hughes, N. 1990. 'Three Propositions for a Critically Applied Medical Anthropology'. *Social Science and Medicine*, 30(2): 189–197.

Sheriff, R.E. 2000. 'Exposing Silence as Cultural Censorship: A Brazilian Case'. *American Anthropologist*, 102(1): 114–132.

Sillitoe, P. 2003. 'Time to be Professional?' *Anthropology Today*, 19(1): 1–2.

Skeggs, B. 1997. *Formations of Class and Gender: Becoming Respectable*. London: Sage.

Strathern, M. 1991. *Partial Connections*. New York: Rowman and Littlefield.

——— (ed). 2000. *Audit Cultures: Anthropological Studies in Accountability, Ethics And the Academy*. London: Routledge.

Strong, P. and J. Robinson. 1990. *The NHS: Under New Management*. Milton Keynes: Open University Press.

Terrell, J.E. 2000. 'Essay: Anthropological Knowledge and Scientific Fact'. *American Anthropologist*, 102(4): 808–817.

Tonkin, J.E.A. and L. Hart. 1986. *Working Women's Social Worlds: an Anthropological Study in the West Midlands*. London, Economic and Social Research Council. End of Award Report Ref: G00232171: 29.

van der Geest, S. and K. Finkler. 2004. 'Hospital Ethnography: Introduction'. *Social Science and Medicine*, 59(10): 1995–2001.

Watson, C.W. 1999. 'Introduction: The Quality of Being There', in C.W. Watson (ed.) *Being There: Fieldwork in Anthropology*. London: Pluto Press, pp. 1–24.

Willmott, H. 1993. 'Strength is Ignorance; Slavery is Freedom: Managing Culture in Modern Organizations'. *Journal of Management Studies*, 30(4): 515–552.

Wright, S. (ed.) 1994. *Anthropology of Organizations*. London: Routledge.

# PART IV

# ANTHROPOLOGISTS IN THE PUBLIC DOMAIN: ANTHROPOLOGY MEDIA AND LAW

*Chapter 8*

# ANTHROPOLOGISTS IN TELEVISION:
A Disappearing World?

———— ∞∞∞ ————

*Paul Henley*

## From the Ethnographic Case Study to the Personal Story

The application of anthropology to the production of television programmes in Britain has taken two principal forms: first, the provision of
specialist ethnographic knowledge by career academics to documentary
film-makers; and second, the application of an anthropological training by
graduates seeking to develop a career in television as documentary film-
makers themselves.[1] These two applications have occasionally overlapped
in the sense that anthropology graduates working in television have sometimes used the specialist knowledge they acquired whilst studying for
their anthropology degrees. But this is the exception that proves the rule
and typically applies only in the early stages of a career, when an anthropology graduate might be taken on as a researcher specifically on account
of this specialist knowledge. However, if an anthropology graduate then
wants to go on and develop a more long-term career in television, he or
she will need more than just ethnographic expertise. Television is an
industry in which fashion and circumstances are constantly changing, and
no graduate can hope to build a career in it simply on the basis of a particular body of specialist knowledge acquired in the course of a degree.

This is where a series of more generic skills and attitudes come into play.
Whilst not exclusive to anthropology and by no means sufficient to guarantee a successful career in television, they are nevertheless qualities that in
the ideal case should be fostered by an anthropological education. Most
obviously, these include an interest in exploring cultural worlds other than
one's own, which surely every student who perseveres through to the end
of an anthropology degree must possess. Somewhat more significantly,

———————————
Notes for this chapter begin on page 188.

there is the ability to think critically about culture and its relationship to social and political realities, coupled with an attitude of cultural relativism that encourages one to investigate these connections rather than take them for granted in one's own society whilst dismissing the cultural practices of Others as mistaken, morally outrageous or somehow simply 'natural'. But perhaps most important of all is the idea that in order to understand these connections fully, it is not enough just to interview official spokespersons or to read official documents and other texts produced by elites. Nor is it enough to go from door to door conducting surveys, no matter how sophisticated the sampling procedure. A defining principle of anthropology as a form of knowledge about the world is that these connections between culture and society must be examined from the inside, on the basis of an extended first-person immersion in the day-to-day life of the ordinary people whose world it is. If they have engaged seriously with the subject, this awareness of the crucial importance of 'fieldwork' should distinguish anthropology graduates from those emerging from other humanities fields such as history, literature, political science and even some forms of sociology. Moreover, I would argue that there is a clear overlap here with the concern of many television documentarists to make their general points through following the particular experience of individual protagonists. The distance from the academic 'ethnographic case study' to the journalistic 'personal story' is not as far as one might think.

## Decline and Fall: the 'Golden Era' of Anthropology on Television

In a recent guest editorial for *Anthropology Today*, Professor Paul Sillitoe laments the fact that 'anthropology has scarcely any media presence, compared, for example, with its sister discipline of archaeology'. In a somewhat black humorous aside, he suggests that the only time that the discipline is likely to come up on television is as a quiz show jackpot question; 'what is anthropology?' (Sillitoe 2003: 2). I suspect that he is purposefully overstating the case for polemical effect. Certainly it was not always like this. For in a 'golden era' lasting about 25 years, from the late 1960s until the early 1990s, anthropology had a distinctly high profile on British television. During this period, perhaps as many as 100 hour-long television documentaries were made for British television based directly on the fieldwork of one or more consultant anthropologists who advised the film director on location and also, to varying degrees, in the edit suite later. This approach to anthropological programming was pioneered by Brian Moser, the first series producer of the Granada Television series, *Disappearing World*, which broadcast its first film in 1970. Series based on similar principles and often executively produced or directed by film-makers trained on *Disappearing World* were later developed by the BBC, Channel 4 and even by some satellite broadcasters.[2]

If the average budget for these productions is estimated conservatively at around £100,000, in effect this means that during this period, British television invested at least £10 million in programming based on anthropological research. Allowing for the effects of inflation, in real terms this is equivalent to at least half as much again today. Moreover, this figure could be considerably higher if one also included all the programmes that were based indirectly on the work of anthropological consultants, i.e. series featuring an on-screen presenter in the David Attenborough mould in which anthropologists, amongst others, might have been consulted prior to the making of the programme. These films represent a remarkable bequest by the television industry to academic anthropology and they continue to be used actively in teaching, even if some colleagues have reservations about their true worth.[3] However, for most television executives, they represent the day-before-yesterday's format and are therefore of little or no interest today.

The reasons for this decline in programming which is readily identifiable as 'anthropological' have been multiple and it is not my intention to discuss them here at any length. However, one particularly important point to make is that these reasons were not exclusive to anthropology. The reluctance to schedule programmes about the developing world unless they involve celebrity travellers, game-show contestants, furry animals or some combination of two or more of these has been widely commented upon. It is not only anthropology, conventionally defined, that has disappeared from the schedules, but a whole raft of serious documentary programming on such matters as development, global environmental issues

**Figure 8.1:** Lamahalot fishermen set out in open boats to hunt sperm whales around the islands of eastern Indonesia. Production still for the *Disappearing World* film 'Lamalera' (1988) directed by John Blake, on which Robert H. Barnes of the University of Oxford acted as anthropological consultant. © David Wason.

and Third World politics. Nor has the general 'dumbing down' of television documentary applied only to culturally exotic subject-matter. Even on the domestic front, life-style programming on such subjects as the DIY metamorphosis of houses and gardens or on what not to wear to a dinner party has shouldered documentaries on heavy-duty political and economic subjects out of many of the prime-time slots.

It is also important to remember that the 'golden era' of anthropological programming unfolded in a television environment of no more than three or four channels, in which all franchise holders had to offer a certain proportion of 'informative' programming in order to meet their legal obligations. Anthropological documentaries represented merely one way of meeting these obligations and programmes about ballet or natural history could also serve the same purpose.[4] But as British television became more influenced by free market principles, the educative-informative component declined, and in the battle for ratings in a much more competitive multi-channel environment, a documentary about celebrity make-overs or police forensic methods was always going to be more favourably looked upon by commissioning editors than, say, a study of symbiotic relationships amongst East African cattle herders.[5] Eventually, in 1993, even the flagship of the anthropological series format, *Disappearing World*, itself disappeared, having become progressively marginalised in the schedules. In its heyday, it was scheduled for the prime-time slot immediately before *News at Ten* on ITV (playing against *Nine O'Clock News* on BBC1) thereby ensuring an audience of up to eight million. But as the series was moved increasingly later in the schedules, audience figures predictably began to fall and in the Catch-22 logic of television programming, its extinction was thereby justified.

Meanwhile the BBC's self-defining 'anthropological' strand *Under the Sun*, launched in 1987 and, originally modelled on *Disappearing World*, continued to broadcast until as late as 2000. But by then it had long since abandoned the principle of basing each film on the fieldwork of an anthropological consultant. Under pressure to maximise ratings, successive series editors had filled many of their slots with films based on strong journalistic stories rather than on academic research. The subjects they dealt with were those most likely to attract large audiences, such as unusual sexual practices or eccentric Americana, or best of all, eccentric Americans engaged in unusual sexual practices. A film based on an individual anthropologist's field research had become the exception that proved the rule.[6]

To some extent, programmes on anthropology, development and Third World ecology have been replaced by programming on history and archaeology, as Paul Sillitoe's remark quoted above suggests. But it is surely significant that apart from certain ancient sites, so well established in the British imaginary that they are almost domestic (such as the Pyramids or the Inca Trail) these programmes seem to be predominantly about the European past when they are not actually about the world of ancient

Britain itself. A concern with the culturally distant Other, be it in the past or the present, has apparently simply slipped way down the mass media agenda. And although anthropologists themselves will vociferously claim that they now have as much to say about Us as about Them, they have yet to convince many television commissioning editors that they can provide

**Figure 8.2:** Consultant anthropologist Terry Turner, right foreground, interviews a Kayapó leader for the *Disappearing World* film, 'Kayapó' (1987), directed by Mike Beckham. Cameraman Mike Blakely is in the left foreground whilst the windcover-clad microphone of sound-recordist David Woods is visible top right. © Peter Connors.

insights into domestic affairs that are not already available from other more familiar social and cultural commentators. The only self-consciously anthropological series focusing exclusively on British society that I can recall was the Channel 4 six-part series *Native Land*, co-written and presented by Nigel Barley as long ago as 1989.[7]

## Preparing for New Opportunities

However, the disappearance of anthropologists on television has not necessarily coincided with the disappearance of anthropologists in television. That is, although self-definingly anthropological programming may have been effectively all but eliminated, at least from terrestrial screens, there were and are a significant number of people with some sort of background in anthropology currently working in television. Indeed, the prospect of a career in television or a related media field continues to be attractive to many anthropology graduates. For despite all the supposed 'dumbing down', many clearly feel that there are still certain areas within television that can provide a creative and challenging career. Although there may no longer be any self-defining anthropological strands, it can still offer the opportunity to become actively involved in a broad variety of social worlds, both at home and abroad. This is often what attracts students to anthropology in the first place and television can provide a means of taking this interest further and building a career on the back of it.

An ambition to get into television certainly continues to motivate many of those who apply to do the M.A. in Visual Anthropology which we offer at the Granada Centre for Visual Anthropology at the University of Manchester. Since the course was launched in 1988, our general aim has been to provide a documentary film training of a kind that we consider to be particularly appropriate to the general intellectual project of anthropology as well as to the practical conditions under which anthropologists normally work. However, as the director of the programme from its inception until 2004, it was my concern that although we normally require applicants to have a first degree in social anthropology or a closely-related subject, we should not restrict ourselves to meeting the needs of those who intend to use film in further academic research. We have also striven to cater for those who wish to put practical film-making skills together with an anthropological first degree in order to pursue a film-making career outside academic life. In the majority of instances, in practice this usually means working in some capacity for television. Nor is this simply an idle ambition: over the last ten years about two-thirds of our graduates have gone on to work in some branch of the media.

In early the years of the course, whilst I was happy that a significant proportion of our graduates were finding their way into television, I used to worry at the disparity between this figure and the mere 30 per cent of graduates who remained in academic life. But then some time in the early 1990s, the distinguished television documentarist, Melissa Lewellyn-Davies, herself with a first degree in anthropology from University College, London rebuked me – in the politest possible way – for being apparently concerned only with the reproduction of visual anthropology as an academic sub-discipline. Instead, she suggested, I should take pride in the fact that we were training anthropologists to enter a highly influential and economically extremely significant industry. She was, of course, entirely right, particularly when her view is considered in the light of the recent calculation that in the period from 1970 to 1994, the chances of a successful doctoral student getting an academic job in anthropology was no better than roughly one in four.[8]

In designing the film training course which forms part of the M.A in Visual Anthropology at the Granada Centre, we have sought to encourage an attitude of flexibility so as to enable students to take advantage of a range of different post-graduation possibilities. Rather than insist, in a doctrinaire fashion, on one particular approach to documentary film-making, we encourage students to develop, on a substratum of transferable technical and editorial skills, a repertoire of film-making styles which they can accommodate to the requirements of the subject-matter, the nature of the relationship with the protagonists, the audience, and the budget .

**Figure 8.3** *Disappearing World* cameraman Mike Blakely demonstrates a 16mm camera at a workshop in the Granada Centre for Visual Anthropology. However, in practice, most student projects have been shot on video, particularly following the arrival of cheap digital technology in the mid-1990s. Dominic French, centre, is now a free-lance director-cameraman working in British television whilst Penny Harvey, right, later became head of the Department of Social Anthropology at the University of Manchester. © Ricardo Leizaola, 1994.

In the first phase of the course, we require students to work according to the procedures of observational cinema. The reason for starting with this approach is that we believe it has many affinities with characteristically anthropological ways of working. It is based on the careful observation of everyday life over a prolonged period of time and it involves following action rather than directing it according to some predetermined script or intervening to make things happen for the camera. It also involves long, considered takes out of respect for the rhythms and spatial configurations of the world being represented and typically entails what one might call an aesthetically puritanical editing style, eschewing artificially dramatic narratives and special effects. The technical instruction is supported by the regular screening of films made in this style.[9]

On the other hand, as a practical film-making strategy, observational cinema is in many ways entirely antithetical to the standard procedures of British television in that it does not allow interviews, narration or music, all of which provide the scaffolding of most current television documentaries. However, we continue to insist on these self-denying ordinances because we believe that rather like life-classes in an artist's education, this way of making films requires the students to observe intensively what is there before them, and build their filmic narratives out of that, rather than re-inforcing a series of preconceived notions about what should be there with an all-too-readily applied series of cinematic devices. Making an engaging film in the observational manner can be very difficult, but we reckon that if our students can learn to make a film without the conventional supports, they will use the latter in a more discriminating and effective way later. As such, we consider observational cinema to be a good initiation to documentary film-making, not just for those who want to use film for anthropological purposes, but as an effective underpinning for a variety of different styles.

Only when we have thoroughly inculcated students with the observational way of working, do we then introduce them to a range of other styles and the techniques necessary to achieve them. These include the interview-based and commentary-led styles that are standard fare on British television. But we also introduce them to the work of European auteurs, North American independents, film-makers working in community contexts, and so on. To the degree that budgetary considerations allow, we also invite film-makers working outside the academy to come and talk about their work. Many of these speakers are graduates of the Granada Centre now working in various different branches of television or other media industries. In devising projects at this stage of the course, we encourage students to be discriminating in their selection from amongst all these alternatives now being presented to them, hybridising or following the conventions of one particular style as appropriate to the nature of the particular projects they intend to pursue. In this way, we aim to prepare them to adopt a similarly flexible attitude in their post-graduation careers.

## Anthropologists Wanted: Digital Technology, Docu-soaps and the Free Market

This flexibility is particularly necessary for those who plan to go into television because programming fashions come and go with seemingly increasing rapidity in the industry. However, it is a curious fact – if our experience at the Granada Centre is at all generalisable – that it was at precisely the time that anthropology was disappearing from the programme schedules that there seemed to be greater opportunities for anthropology graduates to enter television. Two factors in particular would seem to explain this apparent paradox, one to do with changes in the organisation of television as a whole, the other to do with a more specific technological change that had particular significance for the training in anthropological film-making that we offer at the Granada Centre.

In relation to the first of these factors, it was the promotion of increasingly free market principles in the regulation of the television industry by successive Thatcher governments that was primarily responsible for the changes that began to take place during the 1980s. Whilst leading to the progressive casualisation of labour in the industry as a whole, they did at least have the positive effect of producing both a greater number and a greater variety of opportunities for young film-makers to get into television. In the 'golden era', the prominence of anthropological programmes in the schedules had led to the recruitment of a number of anthropology graduates to work on these programmes as researchers. But in statistical terms, the number of anthropologists who could enter television through this highly specialised route was actually very small. Otherwise the principal route into a television career for anthropology graduates, as for graduates in any field, was via one of the production traineeships offered by the BBC or by large independent companies such as Granada TV. But even these schemes only recruited a handful of people from a large field of applicants.[10]

But the obligation imposed on the BBC to buy in 25 per cent of its programming, and a similar outsourcing of production by the large independent companies, coupled with the proliferation of channels with the coming of satellite and cable, meant that there was suddenly an increased number of openings in the small production companies that had sprung up in and around London. It still required a mixture of steely persistence and straightforward good luck to graduate from lowly paid jobs as runners and researchers to positions that were more rewarding both creatively and in terms of income. But compared to the 'golden era', there were certainly more opportunities to get your foot in the door, not just for anthropology graduates, but for everyone.

The technological change that specifically facilitated the entry of Granada Centre graduates into the television industry was the emergence of cheap, broadcastable lightweight digital video. When we first ran our film-training programme in the academic year 1988–1989, the technical gulf between our equipment and that of the television industry was vast. Whilst the industry standard for production equipment was the 16mm film camera plus Nagra taperecorder or, alternatively, a BETACAM video camera (each kit costing at least £25–30,000 depending on the quality of lenses, etc.), we could not afford anything better than the most sophisticated models of what was essentially domestic VHS equipment (approx. cost £2000). Similarly, at post-production, industry editors were using 16mm Steenbecks or hugely expensive three-machine BETA edit suites whilst we were training our students on very primitive two-machine VHS systems.

But with the appearance of the new technology in the mid-1990s, the gulf suddenly narrowed as it became possible to shoot a broadcastable documentary on a digital camera that cost only slightly more than our upmarket VHS models had done in the early days of the course. At the same time, edit suites of a quasi-professional standard, once prohibitively expensive, had undergone a similarly precipitous fall in price. By the late 1990s, with less than £4000, you could set up a non-linear system that would have cost you £40,000 only three years previously. In order to keep production costs low, many of the new small television companies began to acquire this technology which also now fell within the budgetary range of academic institutions such as ours. As a result, by the academic year 1998–1999, our students were shooting and editing on more or less the same quality of equipment as was being used in the very sectors of the television industry in which they were most likely to get their first jobs.

But perhaps even more significant than this technological change was the accompanying change in production practices. This too had the effect of narrowing the gap between the Granada Centre and the norms of the television industry. In 1988, professional documentary production for television was still typically carried out by large crews. It was only by special agreement with the technicians' trade union, the ACTT, that *Disappearing World* productions could be crewed with a 'light' crew of only four production staff: camera, sound, director-producer and 'researcher' (not an academic researcher, but rather a sort of director-producer's assistant, responsible for reconnoitring and general logistics). In conventional documentary production, a crew of at least seven production staff was more normal, with a director's PA, camera assistant and electrician being the most common additions to the basic roster of a light crew.

In contrast, at the Granada Centre, we trained our students on the assumption that they would be working alone or at most in teams of two. But by the mid-1990s, as a result of the pressure on production costs and with the *de facto* emasculation of the ACTT, a significant number of television documentary series were also being produced in this way. Many of these were 'docu-soaps', i.e. series constructed narratively around the day-to-day experiences of a limited number of protagonists, often within some given institutional context such as hospitals, hotels, cruise ships, airports, Mediterranean holiday resorts, even certain urban environments such as

Soho or Manchester. In the manner of a soap opera, each programme cut back and forth between a number of different story-lines. Other series made by film-makers working solo or at most in pairs had somewhat more elevated editorial ambitions. These included the series *United Kingdom* produced by Mosaic Pictures for BBC 2 in which I was involved myself. This aspired to provide a snapshot of modern Britain through a series of films about particular individuals or small groups from all over the country. The same company had previously produced a similar series about Russia and would later give the same treatment to the European Union. In contrast to the docu-soap format, in series of this kind each film was normally dedicated to a single central story-line.

**Figure 8.4** Nigel Farage, chairman of the secessionist United Kingdom Independence Party and newly elected to the European Parliament, stands in the central courtyard of the parliament building in Strasbourg. Production still from 'The Enemy Within', a film made by the author for the series *Europa Eutopia* (2000). This series about the European Union was produced for the BBC by Mosaic Pictures and was typical of the documentaries shot on lightweight digital cameras by single person crews which became commonplace on British television in the latter part of the 1990s. © Mosaic Pictures.

Granada Centre graduates were well adapted to this new television environment. Not only were they familiar with the new technology, but they were also used to working on their own and had a range of skills to match. By contrast, there was a tendency for students emerging from conventional documentary film courses to have been trained as specialists in one of the various functions distributed around a traditional crew – camera, sound, production, direction and so on – and therefore to be more accustomed to working in teams. But the producers at Mosaic Pictures also noted that anthropology graduates had other skills which although less tangible than their technical abilities were, nevertheless, highly advantageous in this solo production environment. These included the ability to immerse themselves in the world of their protagonists and to establish the necessary relationships of trust and understanding. Although it seems very likely that the disposition to engage with the world in this way might have been something that the students concerned brought with them to the study of anthropology, it is certainly an approach that an anthropological training would have further encouraged.

## Adapt and Survive: Anthropological Career Trajectories in Television

For a short period then, in the mid to late 1990s, anthropology graduates were able to use a particular mix of skills to gain entry into the world of television. Although they typically did not have final editorial control over their work, those working on docu-soaps and other solo production formats were actively involved in the process of shooting and directing films on location right from the beginning.[11] However, not all of those who were able to get their foot in the door of the television industry in this period were then able to convert this initial entrée into a satisfactory career.

Whilst the casualisation of the television industry may have greatly increased the opportunities for getting into television, a major downside is that the hours associated with these first jobs are generally long and the wages generally low or even non-existent. Perhaps even more problematic, individual contracts are usually very short term (they may be for no more than three months and are rarely for more than a year) and it is often very difficult to build up a systematic and coherent career. These insecure conditions may be acceptable to twenty somethings with no responsibilities; they can simply enjoy the buzz of working in television, at all hours of day and night, and, if they are lucky, all over the world. But these conditions become much less acceptable to those same people as they reach their thirties and feel the need for career continuity. As a result, a number of Granada Centre graduates, having made a start in television under the favourable conditions of the mid- and late 1990s have subsequently left it because of the endless uncertainties associated with this kind of work.

There has also been another factor adding to the disillusionment. After an initial period of enthusiasm arising from working in a professional environment, some of those who entered television in the late 1990s began to look not just for greater material rewards, but also for greater opportunity to make documentaries that called on more than their ability to handle the new technology, and to get on with people from all walks of life. Typical of this point of view are the following comments of Tom Sheahan who first started working in television after completing an M.A in Social Anthropology at the School of Oriental and African Studies in the mid 1990s. Initially offered in reaction to an earlier draft of this chapter, they capture so well a mood shared by many Granada Centre graduates who entered television at about the same time that I quote them here at length:

> It seems to me that while the needs of the once ubiquitous docu-soap happily coincided with several of the anthropological film-maker's key technical skills, it provided a much less satisfactory role for those film-makers than once appeared. Of course, it was in many ways a great time for the one-man-band young film-maker when every production company in Soho needed them to go out and befriend a transvestite illegal immigrant or an air steward with ambitions as a presenter, but what they never asked of the anthropology graduates was for them to demonstrate their hard-won analytical ability. They never asked them to put the behaviour they were observing in a socially meaningful context – which is surely the aim of the anthropological endeavour. In fact, although the docu-soap needed 'people people' who could shoot, the last thing it required was an actual anthropologist. In retrospect, I think it was something of a chimera. It looked like an explosion of documentary film-making, even to some, an explosion of ethnographic film-making. In fact, it was the opposite. And once the explosion was over, it was inevitable that the opportunities that had briefly proliferated for your graduates (and others like them) would vanish.

> In the current climate ... the opportunity for people to explore an anthropological sensibility in documentary is now limited in the U.K. to one single slot – *Storyville*. Any of the other spaces supposedly opened up by the proliferation of cable channels on closer examination turn out to present mere simulacra of ethnographic films. Like the docu-soaps of the past, the 'ethnographic' films shown on National Geographic or Discovery rely on many of the techniques of the anthropological film-maker – in this case an ability to gain the confidence of non-industrial peoples, to negotiate permissions in foreign countries and to keep a camera working in a humid climate – but like docu-soaps, they refuse to allow a genuinely anthropological engagement with the subject.

In the last couple of years, getting employment in television has become more difficult for everyone. At the same time, documentary programming fashions have been moved on and in ways that are no longer particularly advantageous for anthropology graduates. By and large, documentary programming fashion is very fickle and subject to high levels of copycatting, so that once one broadcaster launches a successful format (as measured by audience ratings), every other one seems to feel that they have to have their version of the same thing. Thus docu-soaps and other formats based on solo production, once ubiquitous, have now been largely displaced by 'reality show' formats in the Big Brother mould, not necessarily set in a closed house, but in pop-star 'academies', hair-dressing salons, on tropical islands or in deserts. Even this format is now showing signs of decline and commissioning editors of factual programming are currently casting around for the Next Big Thing. Under these rapidly changing conditions, any anthropology graduates aiming to get into television will have to seek other vehicles in which their skills are likely to give them an advantage over all the other wannabes who hope to develop a television career.

Nor will it only be to gain entry that they will have to show such flexibility. Even in the heyday of the 'golden era', it was rare for television filmmakers to be able to work exclusively on anthropological series. Although anthropology graduates might have been recruited in the first instance to work as researchers on a particular anthropological series, they would then typically be sent off to current affairs and other factual programming departments for further training. Pending the commissioning of another anthropological series, they would be expected to work on a broad variety of other factual programmes. Those who had had these broader experiences were later well equipped to deal with a television environment in which specifically anthropological programming had disappeared entirely. Similarly, the Granada Centre graduates who have been most successful as freelancers in building a career amidst the vagaries of present-day British television, have done so by diversifying their work, looking to pursue any interests or approaches that they might carry from their anthropological background under a variety of guises and formats; for example, in travel and exploration programmes, in science programmes, or youth-oriented lifestyle programming.

An independent production company that has been particularly active in exploring the boundaries of what constitutes television anthropology is KEO films. One of its directors is Andrew Palmer, a member of the first cohort of Granada Centre graduates in 1989 who came to us after a first degree in Human Sciences at Oxford. He takes a decidedly positive view of the possibilities for anthropologically informed film-making on British television. His comments were also offered in reaction to an earlier draft of this chapter and also deserve to be quoted at length:

> I don't entirely agree that anthropology has disappeared from terrestrial television: in the past three years KEO has filmed with the Evenk in Siberia, the Afar in Ethiopia, the Tubu in Niger, the Baka pygmies in Congo, the Kombai (lowland Papua), the Matses in Peru to mention only the most obvious cultural destinations. It is true that none of these films would count as anthropology *per se* – but they have been made to satisfy the public's curiosity for the way other cultures live/survive. These films have cost the broadcasters

**Figure 8.5** Anthropology on British television today: in 'Jungle Fever', produced by KEO films for Channel 4, a young Englishman, right, is followed on his quest to the Peruvian Amazon to try out the mind-altering drug *ayahuasca*, here being prepared by the shaman Don Guillermo. Both the director, Andrew Palmer, and the principal cameraman, Gavin Searle, were graduates of the Granada Centre, and the film was advised and partially presented by the Cambridge anthropologist Françoise Barbira. In a manner reminiscent of the format of make-over shows such as *Faking It* and *WLTM*, before the protagonist gets to try Don Guillermo's potion at the climax of the film, he is advised along the way by a series of 'experts' on drugs and drug-taking. © KEO Films.

well over £2m. and they sell very well – and that is just our output. So I would argue that there is an appetite for anthropology but how we nourish that need is subject also to a requirement that the films are entertaining and accessible (hence presenter as cultural barometer and voice-over in place of indigenous voice).

The other thing I instinctively feel but can't back up is that television hasn't dropped anthropology – rather a lot of the changes that have gone on in television reflect changes that have also gone on in anthropology – whether behind, running in parallel, or dare I say it, ahead of, is open for debate. Just as anthropology became more introspective – or became more interested in the personality of the anthropologist than the culture that the anthropologist studied – the same has happened in television: individuals are our mediators/investigators.

The other thing is that anthropology and television have both moved towards subject-matter which I would call 'niche' – I was speaking to a Cambridge Ph.D. student the other day and she gave me a list of theses in production ... very few of them were set in obvious anthropological terrain.

Instead it was the likes of gay sub-culture in Berlin ... I remember thinking anthropology has even lost its subject-matter. I guess anthropology would retaliate [by] saying you are going to learn more about the bigger picture by looking at containable sub-cultures. And that is certainly what television does. 'Karachi Cops', 'Lagos Airport' – I could go on and on – are small windows onto other cultures but anthropologically valid. They just happen to tick more than one box on the commissioning editor's wish list.

Whether one agrees with Sheahan or with Palmer, it is clear that if anthropology graduates want to pursue their interests in television in the future, they will have to remain constantly on the lookout for new opportunities for doing so. A particularly interesting example here, involving the presentation of an anthropological subject in an innovative format, was the screening, in 2001, of a series of films on Channel 4 about the Kumbh Mela, a pilgrimage involving up to 50 million Hindus which takes place every twelve years at Allahabad at the confluence of the Ganges and Jamuna rivers in northern India. The deviser and series director was Michael Yorke, now a freelance director, who completed an anthropology doctorate at the School of Oriental and African Studies in 1976. Yorke carried out his anthropological fieldwork in India and has a wide interest in the subcontinent. He had previously made a number of films on Indian subjects for British television. These included 'Dust and Ashes' about the previous Kumbh pilgrimage in 1989, which was an early film in the *Under the Sun* series. This had been made in the conventional television one-hour format with voice-over narration.

Suspecting that another standard one-hour documentary would be turned down as 'an old-fashioned ethnographic film', instead he proposed a television 'event' to BBC 2. This would involve a series of 10-minute 'as-if-live' pilgrim video diaries, along the lines of *Canterbury Tales*, to be shown in the *Video Diaries* slot. These were to be shot and edited *in situ* on a daily basis and sent back by satellite up-link, involving a very large crew on the ground. The BBC Video Diaries Unit liked the idea but wanted to expand it and run the films for twenty minutes, fronted by the entire cast of the comedy programme, *Goodness Gracious Me*. As Yorke explained in a response to an earlier draft of this chapter:

Their argument was not just that celebrities would bring in more viewers, but that understanding other peoples' way of life and cultural reference points is made easier with an interlocutor or translator, and if that person's outlook and viewpoint is known, understood and familiar to the audience – a celebrity whose onscreen personality everybody knows – then the audience can identify with the presenter and gain access to the 'other' culture more easily ... Perhaps the problem with anthropologists making films for the mass media is that they have spent a great deal of time, energy and dedication getting under the skin of another culture and fail to realise how difficult it was for them to do it and that it is even more difficult for a mass audience.

However, even whilst recognising the force of this argument, Yorke did not pursue the proposal any further with the BBC because he sensed that rather than providing a means of communicating an indigenous Indian experience of Hinduism, as he had hoped to do, the series would, in effect, become a vehicle for a British Asian exposition of Hinduism.

He then took the idea to Channel 4 to discover that they also had their own ideas about the appropriate format. Rather than each daily broadcast being the video diary of one pilgrim, they wanted a magazine-style programme after the *Channel 4 News*, that would not only hold on to the preceding *Channel 4 News* audience, but also capture the 13–17-year-old audience of the next broadcast, the teenage soap-opera *Brookside*. Also, it had to conform to Channel 4's concept of 'Friday Night Is Music Night'. In this sense, it was very different from Yorke's original idea of indigenous video diaries. But he was open to the idea of using this format, and appealing to a youth audience as a novel way to get ethnography onto prime-time British television. For its part, Channel 4 accepted that the indigenous voice should be present in the form of subtitled dialogues and that voice-over narration should be minimal. This in itself was a considerable achievement.

In the event, the series opened with a one-hour introductory and explanatory programme, based in part on the old 'Dust and Ashes' material, followed by eighteen daily 'as-if-live' broadcasts from the Kumbh Mela, each of eight minutes duration, over a period of three weeks. At the end of each week, there was a presented thirty-minute omnibus programme summing up the week's events. Finally, a one-hour special was shown the following Christmas. Far from losing the audience from the *News*, the daily broadcasts actually more than doubled it, bringing it up to 1.6 million. In total, over six hours of 'as-if-live' ethnographic 'event television' on the Kumbh Mela was screened. This was an extraordinary amount of time for what might be conventionally regarded as an ethnographic subject, even if some academic purists might have winced at the series title, *The Greatest Show on Earth*.

## Conclusion

The general conclusion that one must draw from these recent developments in the television industry is that there is no point in preparing anthropology graduates for any very specific niche in the world of television. It is possible that in the general ebb and flow of television fashion and circumstance, there may be moments in the future when either expert anthropological knowledge or some specifically anthropological approach to understanding the affairs of the world may be much sought after. At the time of writing, the expansion and development of BBC 4 to carry serious documentary programming of the kind that used to be screened on BBC 2 might offer some openings for documentaries based in some sense on anthropological ideas or methods.

But whatever the immediate possibilities, one can be certain that there will also be prolonged periods when anthropology is certainly not in vogue. An anthropology graduate going into television for the long term therefore needs to develop ideas and skills to offer when anthropology is out of fashion just as much as for when it is in. In particular, this means keeping an open mind about the formats through which anthropological subject-matters and approaches might be pursued.[12]

We conceive of the anthropological film-training that we offer at Manchester as providing certain foundational skills, representing a platform on which to build rather than some definitive set of competences. Similarly, I would argue that one should think of the intellectual formation given to students of anthropology more generally, not as a specific body of knowledge that can be applied to a television career, as medical students might apply a knowledge of physiology to curing patients, or as engineering students might apply a knowledge of materials science to building bridges, but rather as a set of generic attitudes and strategies of the kind outlined at the beginning of this chapter. Provided they are prepared to adapt to the constantly changing circumstances, I believe that an anthropological training continues to provide anthropology graduates with a firm foundation from which to develop as documentarists working within the complex, multi-channel television environment of today.

## Notes

1. There have been other applications of anthropology to television, including ethnographic studies both of the process of programme production (see, for example, Silverstone 1985 and more recently, Born 2002 and 2004) as well as of the reception of television programmes in domestic contexts (see Roberts, this volume). However, in this article I will be concerned exclusively with the application of anthropology to the actual making of television programmes.

2. See Loizos (1980), Henley (1985), Singer and Woodhead (1988), Turton (1992), Ginsburg (1995) for various accounts and analyses of the *Disappearing World* series.

3. See, for example, Banks (1994) and Taylor (1996).

4. André Singer, one-time series producer of *Disappearing World* and subsequently an influential independent producer of anthropologically-informed documentaries reports that there was an informal division of labour between broadcasters. Thus whilst Anglia Television specialised in natural history programming, Granada Television 'took the tribes' (Singer 1992: 270).

5. In an interview with Rachel Greenwood, Leslie Woodhead, director of sixteen *Disappearing World* films, offered this description of his 1982 film, 'The Kwegu', based on the work of consultant anthropologist David Turton in the Omo river valley, Ethiopia, as an example of the arcane subject matter about which it was once possible to make films for prime-time television (Greenwood 2002: 3) According to David Wason (personal communication), later to be the series producer, the irony was that the film idea originally pitched to Granada Television executives had been along the lines of 'Hippo Hunters of

188 | Paul Henley

the Omo'. But, as Wason points out, what is significant is that such was the attitude at the time that Woodhead was not criticised for coming back with a story-line that would be more likely to appeal to an academic audience.

6. Audience figures from the *Under the Sun* series broadcast between December 1997 and February 1998 make the point very eloquently. Publicity material for the series indicates that a film about fox-hunting, *The Hunt*, made to very high production standards and based on the advice of anthropologist Garry Marvin (though he was credited as 'associate producer' rather than 'anthropological consultant', see Marvin, this volume), was watched by 1.4 million people. This may be large by academic standards but it was dwarfed by the 3.5 million who watched 'Painted Babies', Jane Treays' film about American child beauty pageants and even more so by the audience for her other film in the series, 'What Sort of Gentleman Are You After?'. This followed the activities of a heterosexual male prostitute in Melbourne 'with over 1200 female clients across the city' and registered a remarkable 4.8 million viewers. I am indebted to David Pearson, then the executive producer of the series, for arranging for me to be supplied with the publicity material from which these viewing figure statistics are taken.

7. There had been a number of earlier series in which certain aspects of British society were directly compared with those of other societies within the general framework of an anthropological analysis. Perhaps the first of these was the BBC series *Family of Man*, directed and presented by John Percival, and screened in the late 1960s. This was followed by *Face Values*, screened in the late 1970s, presented by a former student of anthropology, one Charles Windsor, Prince of Wales, and involving the comparison of British society with that of Gypsies, the people of Chole Island off the coast of Tanzania, a parish in Malta, the Kayapó of Central Brazil and a village in Bali (see Sutherland 1978). In 1984, Granada Television produced *The Human Jigsaw*, a more popular series presented by Ray Gosling which intercut sequences shot in Britain with footage from the *Disappearing World* series. However, I think I am right in saying that whilst all the sections on the Other communities in these series were based on the research of anthropological consultants, the sections on Britain were researched by the programme makers themselves.

8. See the correspondence in *Anthropology Today*, 19(1): 25. In a subsequent edition of the same journal, David Mills (2003) produces more detailed figures which suggest that the chances of a newly graduated Ph.D. students getting an academic appointment in the U.K. are still no more than 'slim'.

9. I myself was trained in the methods of observational cinema whilst I was a Film Training Fellow at the National Film and Television School (NFTS). This fellowship scheme was set up by the Film Committee of the Royal Anthropological Institute with the aid of funding from the Leverhulme Trust. It ran from 1984 to 1987, during which time four fellows were trained in basic documentary production techniques. As well as myself, the others were the ethnomusicologist John Baily (now at the Department of Music at Goldsmiths College, University of London), Marcus Banks (Institute of Social and Cultural Anthropology, University of Oxford) and Felicia Hughes Freeland, University of Swansea. Elsewhere, I have discussed both the affinities and disjunctures between the canons of observational cinema and the anthropological project at much greater length (see Henley 2004 and forthcoming).

10. These general traineeships were still being offered in the 1990s but they remained very difficult to get. In 1998, when I was asked by the BBC to give a reference for one of our graduates, I was informed that he was one of nine successful candidates out of a field of 1,800 applicants.

11. This compares favourably with the lengthy apprenticeship typically served by those entering television through traineeships or researcher roles within the BBC or the large independent companies. Howard Reid, who became a researcher on the BBC Bristol anthropological series, *Worlds Apart*, shortly after completing an anthropology doctorate at Cambridge in 1979, informs me that the seven years he had to wait before directing his first programme was not unusual for those entering television at that time (personal communication 2003).

12. In another example of innovative thinking in this regard, Michael Yorke is currently working with a professional animator funded by Scottish Screen on a series of animations of Indian mythological subjects.

# References

Banks, M. 1994. 'Television and Anthropology: An Unhappy Marriage?'. *Visual Anthropology,* 7: 21–43.

Barley, N. 1989. *Native Land*. London: Viking.

Born, G. 2002. 'Reflexivity and Ambivalence: Culture, Creativity and Government in the BBC'. *Cultural Values: Journal of Cultural Research,* special issue on Culture and Governance, 6 (1–2): 65–90.

———. 2004. *Uncertain Vision: Birt, Dyke and the Reinvention of the BBC*. London: Secker and Warburg.

Ginsburg, F. 1995. 'Ethnographies on the Airwaves: The Presentation of Anthropology on American, British, Belgian and Japanese Television', in P. Hockings (ed.) *Principles of Visual Anthropology,* 2nd edition. Berlin & New York: Mouton de Gruyter, pp. 363–398.

Greenwood, R. 2002. Anthropology on British Television in the Present Day: Is There Any? Unpublished assessment essay, M.A. in Visual Anthropology, Granada Centre, University of Manchester.

Henley, P. 1985. 'British Ethnographic Film: Recent Developments'. *Anthropology Today,* 1(1): 5–17.

———. 2004. 'Putting Film to Work: Observational Cinema as Practical Ethnography', in S. Pink, L. Kürti and A.I. Afonso (eds) *Working Images*. London: Routledge, pp. 109–130.

———. forthcoming. 'The Origins of Observational Cinema: Conversations with Colin Young', in B. Engelbrecht (ed.) *Memories of the Origins of Visual Anthropology*. Frankfurt, New York, Bern, Brussels: Peter Lang.

Loizos, P. 1980. 'Granada Television's Disappearing World Series: An Appraisal'. *American Anthropologist,* 82: 573–594.

Mills, D. 2003. 'Quantifying the Discipline: Some Anthropology Statistics from the U.K.'. *Anthropology Today,* 19(3): 19–26.

Sillitoe, P. 2003. 'Time to be Professional?' *Anthropology Today,* 19(1): 1–2.

Singer, A. 1992. 'Anthropology in Broadcasting', in P. Crawford & D. Turton (eds) *Film as Ethnography*. Manchester: Manchester University Press, pp. 264–273.

Singer, A. and Woodhead, L. 1988. *'Disappearing World': Television and Anthropology*. London: Boxtree in association with Granada Television.

Silverstone, R. 1985. *Framing Science: The Making of a BBC Documentary*. London: British Film Institute.

Sutherland, A. ed. 1978. *Face Values*. London: BBC.

Taylor, L. 1996. 'Iconophobia: How Anthropology Lost It at the Movies'. *Transition,* 6(1): 64–88.

Turton, D. 1992. 'Anthropology on Television: What Next?', in P. Crawford and D. Turton (eds) *Film as Ethnography*. Manchester: Manchester University Press, pp. 283–299.

*Chapter 9*

# RESEARCH, REPRESENTATIONS AND RESPONSIBILITIES:
## An Anthropologist in the Contested World of Foxhunting

*Garry Marvin*

The main theme of this chapter is that of responsibility and the differing forms of responsibilities that have emerged as a result of a research project on English foxhunting in which I have been engaged for the last few years. Although my ethnographic example here is rather specific, my concern is not with foxhunting as a social or cultural practice, nor with issues pertaining to foxhunting *per se*. Rather, I will use this case as an illustration to consider some wider questions associated with applying anthropology. In particular, I am interested in issues of responsibilities and representations, that arise when the anthropologist facilitates the access of others to her/his area of research, and where s/he is needed or called on for advice because of particular contacts and levels of knowledge and expertise. In keeping with the themes of this book, my central focus will not be that of my responsibilities as an anthropologist engaged in an academic study of fox-hunting with the aim of writing academic texts about this event and the social/cultural world in which it is embedded (although aspects of that will be important), but rather on the responsibilities that emerged from the access that my anthropological involvement in foxhunting offered to other interested parties. In none of the examples that I will discuss was it simply a question of others making use of written material that I had produced as an anthropologist, but rather that my anthropological perspectives were those out of which I was asked to create, or help to create, new material for purposes that were not specifically anthropological. What I have attempted to write here is a case study and, given the individual and particular nature of the research, and my involvement in the processes that grew out of it, this is, necessarily, a personal, reflexive, account.

Notes for this chapter begin on page 207.

## Access to Foxhunting

Prior to my present academic appointment I spent ten years as a free-lance researcher and producer of documentary films in the commercial television world. During the research for an unrelated series of programmes I met someone who was a member of a Hunt[1] and who, when I expressed an interest in attending a foxhunt, offered to take me along. As a result of this experience I became keen to embark on a study of the event, both because I was intrigued by it, and because I was looking for a research project in order to, as it were, keep my anthropological mind active. I was introduced to key members of his local Hunt who were friendly and welcoming, but they would not agree to any formal interviews with me until I had obtained permission for such research from a representative of the official body of foxhunting – The Masters of Foxhounds Association. I spoke with the most senior official by telephone and explained the sort of anthropological research I would like to carry out. He explained to me that the MFHA needed to consider this carefully because of the way that foxhunting was generally represented at a time when there was considerable pressure by some people and groups to have the event prohibited by law. Anticipating that this most powerful gate-keeper needed to check on my credentials and possible trustworthiness,[2] I offered to send him a copy of a book I had published on the basis of my Ph.D. about bullfighting and Spanish culture. I suggested that it offered a 'fair' account of an event that was also perceived in a negative light in Britain. He read the book and agreed with my claim about it. At a subsequent meeting he asked me how I wanted to carry out the research, and about the sorts of questions/issues in which I was interested. He was interested in my anthropological perspective and his concern was to try to establish whether I had an animals rights agenda rather than whether I was actively pro hunting. As a result of that interview, and another with someone responsible for public relations for the MFHA, I was given permission to begin the research. I was allowed to return to the first Hunt to begin participant observation. Whenever I wished to visit another Hunt or interview people, all I had to do was to telephone the secretary of the MFHA, who would prepare the ground for me by explaining to the people concerned that my research was known about, and, I suspect from hearsay, that I was probably a 'safe' person to speak with. That was at the official level.

On the ground, I still had to work on how I presented myself, because there was often a suspicion that as someone who was attempting to gain access to their world in order to write about them, rather than attempting to gain access in order to participate directly in hunting, I might be an animal rights activist in disguise. I was ever-conscious that they would perceive me to be an urban academic, assume that I had political views associated with such a position and think that I might regard them as what

Lee (1995: 25) refers to as an 'unloved group' from that perspective. At the beginning of my research I was working with two Hunts, and with one of them it took months before people began to lose their suspicions. This became an interesting problem – how could I prove to them that I was not someone whom some people feared I might be; an animal rightist or a member of one of the anti-foxhunting associations in disguise? It was no good simply *stating* that I was not such a person. All I could do was to act in a manner that made it difficult to hold such a view of me, and my intentions. But, in a sense, that was never going to be enough for people who were suspicious. Individuals from organisations opposed to hunting, but disguising their true affiliation had, in the recent past, been accepted into Hunts, and then later revealed, as part of their political campaign, what they considered to be unacceptable practices associated with hunting. Some members of the Hunts with which I was seeking to be involved, adopted a strategy of keeping themselves or keeping me at a distance, and simply waited to see whether their suspicions were true. What was interesting was that with members of one Hunt I had a much easier time because of my initial friendship with the person who first introduced me to this world. He became one of the Masters of the Hunt, and I would stay in his home on the weekends when I was able to attend hunts. There I would meet members of the Hunt who came for dinner, and I was invited to dinners, parties and social events with others. I came to be known as a person rather than simply as a researcher, and I believe that for most of the time they forgot or paid little attention to the fact that I was also there and present as an anthropologist. As Hammersley and Atkinson have put it:

> … whether or not people have knowledge of social research, and whatever attitude they take towards it, they will often be more concerned with what kind of person the researcher is than with the research itself. (1996: 83)

It is important to indicate the position I have adopted with regard to foxhunting. I have only ever researched this event from *within* hunting. This is a perspective and position on which I have often been challenged – perhaps rightly so. I have never explored foxhunting from the perspective of those who are opposed to it (although I have read many books and articles against hunting), I have never interviewed opponents of hunting, and I think that I have never asked anyone in the hunting world to justify why they participate in hunting. This might seem odd, because for many people, the fact that foxhunting is a highly polemical and contested event is the most significant and important issue. What I wanted to do was something different – I wanted to understand what foxhunting is *per se*. I sought to understand the social and cultural processes that constituted foxhunting. As an anthropologist I have a particular interest in human/animal relations, and it seemed to me that at the heart of hunting were some complex configurations of such relations – humans, horses, hounds, and foxes

– enacted within the spaces of the English countryside. I regularly heard those who participated in foxhunting defend hunting against attacks from the outside but that defence never seemed to tally exactly with how they spoke about hunting, the experiences they had of it and the meanings it had for them when they were talking amongst themselves. My interest was in understanding that talk and those practices, experiences and meanings.

This research was conducted at a leisurely pace whenever I had free time from my other work. Once I was able to attend foxhunts as a participant observer the personal relationships I developed further created trust in me as an individual and in the work I was seeking to do as an anthropologist. Once my presence was known in the hunting world I was never refused any request to participate in an event, to interview someone or to access information I needed. Indeed I was often contacted and invited to events I had no knowledge of, but which people in the hunting world thought would be of interest to me. Later in the research I was introduced to another Hunt, and I began to think about the possibilities that such close contacts might offer for a film about foxhunting. If such a film could be commissioned then I would have created an ideal link between my anthropological interests and my daily work. There were several unsuccessful attempts to raise money for the project. Sometimes the money was potentially available but I was usually unhappy with the political and social agenda (normally expressed as disapproval for the event and a desire to 'expose' its practices) of the film company concerned, and each time I withdrew the proposal. Finally there was a general agreement with a company. The money was raised, permission was given by the Hunt authorities and members of the Hunt concerned, a director with an interest in the social world and cultural practices of foxhunting was contracted, and the process began. However, just at the moment of securing the funds and the permission I accepted a university lectureship, and my work as co-producer of the film had to run in tandem with my teaching commitments.[3]

## The Hunt Filmed – the Anthropologist as Gatekeeper

I had worked for years to build up good relations with a large number of people connected with hunting. I was welcomed to participate in the event, I was always given privileged and unprecedented access to activities, a large number of people had become close personal friends, and I socialised regularly with them. I was regarded, I think, as a slightly odd member of their community. As a responsible anthropologist I always tried to be completely open about my intentions, aims, objectives and interests, and I believe that those in the Hunt world who took any notice of my research trusted me to represent the world of hunting fairly. I was always clear, when speaking with them, that I was not interested in polit-

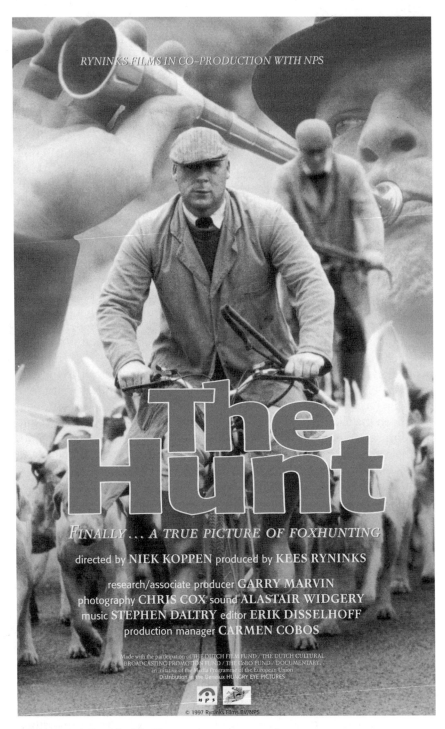

**Figure 9.1** A flyer for *The Hunt*

ical or ethical issues relating to hunting; that this was not investigative journalism and that I was not primarily interested in questions about whether hunting should or should not be banned. This, of course, was a political and ethical stance in itself. I was clear in my own mind that when I began to write about foxhunting I would be able to do so in terms of what is generally perceived as good practice among anthropologists. I had obtained, at least at some level and in some senses, informed consent from those I was seeking to study although I never asked anyone to sign a consent form. I would be the sole author (this leaves aside the question of how much the people with whom we work are also authors of our texts) of any articles and books, and I would be able to capture, at least within the limits of my abilities as an anthropologist and writer, the complexities of the world I was studying. Within written texts I felt that I would be able to disguise specific Hunts and particular individuals in the Hunt world if I thought this was necessary to preserve anonymity, and to preserve them from any harm that might result from my representation of their actions or opinions. Such issues are, of course, not unique to my research. All anthropologists will be involved with similar concerns and issues relating to the people amongst whom their research is conducted.

A different set of problems quickly emerge if the anthropologist acts as a conduit by which others are introduced into a social and cultural arena to which entry would otherwise be difficult. Of particular concern in this case is that a film obviously makes visible, it reveals, and it can, in the negative sense, expose. What then are the responsibilities of the anthropologist, who has moved into a 'gate-keeper' position, towards the people who have been the focus of the research, and what responsibilities are owed to the company which contracts the anthropologist and pays, at least in part, for their skills, their knowledge and understanding, their contacts, and access to the people and the activity to be filmed? Here I need to stress that the film with which I was involved was not an academic, ethnographic, film with the central focus on anthropological issues, nor was the project to make an investigative television programme or a balanced documentary, but rather is was to be an aesthetically pleasing, character-driven film, which explored the social and cultural world of a particular Hunt.[4] Although it was expected that the film would eventually be shown on television, it was expressly filmed (and post-produced) for showing in 'art cinemas' in Europe and the United States. It was both an artistic and a commercial venture, and as such the producer, the director, and the company had certain expectations and demands.

After a long period of negotiation we obtained permissions to film over the course of about a year. These permissions were of different orders – permission from the Hunt authorities at different levels, permissions from the officials of the Hunt that was to be the focus of the film, and permissions from the individuals who would actually feature in the film. Permission, however, is only the beginning of the access necessary for making a film of this length. What then had to occur was a process similar to an anthropologist becoming accepted in their fieldwork area, but without the same anthropological concerns. The crew had to slowly, and sympathetically journey into the world of this Hunt, in such a way that they would be trusted. This was a process fraught with difficulties, and as the anthropologist responsible for important areas of the film I was often sorely tested. My knowledge, expertise, and understanding of foxhunting and the people of this particular Hunt was initially the bedrock for the film. I had mapped out significances and interpretations for the producer and director, and together we had produced a set of themes and potential storylines to be explored and filmed. In an important sense I had promised them things, and these had to be delivered. My access to the foxhunt world (at all levels) had allowed access for others, and I was paid to supply this. I had responsibilities to my employer. That which I knew about, and had spoken about to the director, had to be filmed. However, seeing and representing as an anthropologist is different from seeing and representing with a camera present. For example, it was of crucial importance that we were able to film all the aspects of animal deaths that occur in hunting or which are connected with hunting. I had been present many times at all such events, and my presence as a lone anthropologist never seemed to cause any problems, but it was to be a very different matter when such deaths had to be filmed. Officials of the Hunt were rightly sensitive about requests to film such events, which, although everyday occurrences, were likely to carry a huge emotional weight when captured on film and, in their view, could lead to a negative portrayal of them and their practices. Often then there was a tension between officials who wanted to protect and restrict access[5] and the director/producer who pushed to be allowed to film what they felt they needed to make a successful film. My role was, in part, to try to negotiate between these two positions.

Although I was aware of my responsibilities to both parties, my central concern was with how the people with whom I studied would be represented. While it was not my place to make decisions for them, these were not people who were unaware of the power of the media,[6] I did often find myself reminding individuals that they were being observed in all their actions and to consider that before they acted. Perhaps oddly for an anthropologist who was always seeking trust for his own work, I sometimes felt that people were perhaps 'too trusting' (see Lee 1995: 25 for a discussion of this dilemma in another context). In my anthropological research I had taped interviews with people and taken photographs of hunting events, just as the film crew was about to do, but I would be solely responsible for how such thoughts, opinions and images would be used in my written ethnographic text. I would be able to disguise, make anonymous and hide individuals – something that is not possible when a film needs to have its characters seen expressing their views: a difference that the people of the Hunt did not always seem to make. Therefore, whereas in my strictly anthropological work with members of the Hunt I did not feel the need to continually draw attention to the fact that I was studying them, during the course of filming I often felt the need to remind people of the project in which they were involved. For me there was a continual tension between my anthropological understanding of foxhunting and the world in which it was embedded, and how I wanted to represent that, and how the film might capture and represent the event and the people who participated in it. I was certainly conscious of my self-censorship and what Lee (1995: 38) has called 'disutilization strategies' that might be resorted to by some researchers in certain circumstances.

This was not to be an ethnographic film exploring and explaining the nuances of a highly complex cultural and social event, but a more 'popular' one that worked at a very different level, and in which the director was seeking to create a strong, dramatic narrative, full of interesting relationships among the main characters to engage the interest and attention of the audience. In an ethnographic text, the anthropologist, through a discursive practice, is able to carefully work through the social and cultural processes and practices in which they are interested to reveal subtle shades of meaning, and overlapping, multifaceted, perspectives, in his or her representations, and interpretations of the complexities of the life worlds of others. A documentary film, of the sort I am describing here, is, I think, in a sense a more simple production. The primacy of the visual gives it an immediacy, but also a fixity of view or perspective. It creates or offers an emotional engagement for, and with, the viewer, and is the more powerful for this, but in this power lies its potential for misrepresentation. This film was never planned as an exposé of the hunting world, nor did it set out to portray its peoples and practices in any negative way, and the finished product was a sensitive and sympathetic rendering of the lives of those who participated in it. However, during the whole process of producing the film I felt that there were issues, elements and interpretations better left with the anthropologist, to be considered in a more strictly anthropological setting.

Before leaving this example I would like to touch on an issue relating to ethics and responsibility – that of the consent that anthropologists seek from those with whom we work, and the consent involved in the sort of film I have been discussing. I am sure that most anthropologists seek the consent of those whom they wish to study, and attempt to explain, at least in part, the nature of the research in which they are engaged, and what they are going to do with the material they obtain. Perhaps they do not always follow exactly all the ethical guidelines of bodies such as the American Anthropological Association (AAA) or the Association of Social Anthropologists (ASA), but they do always try to ensure a fair representation of the people they study, and ensure, to the best of their abilities, that nothing that they write about them will cause them any harm. I think, however, there are all sorts of problems with the notion of 'informed consent' and how informed that consent is. Do the people anthropologists study always, and fully, understand exactly what it means or might mean to have articles and books written about them or to have their lives, beliefs, opinions, and actions discussed in books, articles, conferences or lecture rooms? They might offer their consent for us to ask things of them, and for us to collect information from them, but within that relationship of consent is there any implied notion or expectation about *how* that information will be used? Do we, for example, tell them what we are going to write about them, and why we plan to write in such a way? This seems hardly possible because at the moment of gathering information we are unlikely to have a clear idea, or any idea at all, about how such information will be used. As Howard Becker has commented on the difficulties of informed consent for film-makers and social researchers:

> ... they cannot know when they begin their work what they will end up with, since that will depend on what material they finally have and how their ideas have evolved (in Gross *et al.* 1988: xiii).

We seek consent to question them, but most of us, I suspect, do not seek any consent for what we write and publish about those who have given us this first level of consent.[7]

In the case of this particular study, I felt that I had obtained information, views and explanations only because I was perceived as someone who was not opposed to hunting and who attempted to understand and interpret hunting in a particular way. The trust given made me feel bound by a moral obligation (one that I was happy to accept) not to represent the people with whom I worked in any negative (not that there was ever any reason to do so) way. I think that if I had in some way announced that I was intending to portray them 'warts and all' then they would have been concerned about what I might decide were the 'warts', and consequently been less open, and responded to me in a more circumspect manner.

Generally there is a notion of personal trust at the heart of our research practices. We do not ask each and every person we speak with during the course of our research to sign a legalistic document, which clearly sets out what the respondent is agreeing to when agreeing to answer our questions, when freely offering opinions, views or information, or when the anthropologist listens in on people's conversations. Trust, however, is more problematic in the world of ordinary commercial documentary-making.[8] Here, what is generally required is that those who participate in a documentary must sign a 'release form' that allows the producers of the film to use the person's voice and image in any way, within the limits of the law, they choose. Although such release forms differ in style and content with each production company or broadcaster, they all cover similar issues. The person who signs the form gives his or her permission for the producers to film them; agrees that their contribution may be edited and incorporated into the film at the discretion of the company, that any interview might be edited, and added to or taken from, and agrees that the finished product can be distributed in any known medium or medium yet to be discovered. Usually the person assigns all copyrights or other rights from their contribution to the company, and sometimes even waives the right to be credited or acknowledged in the finished film.

Asking participants in this project to sign such a form made them aware that they were the focus of attention, because in an important sense they are being asked to give themselves up to others, and to release those others from any liability as to how their image, opinions and actions were used or represented. Whether or not those who signed the form, and without it no one could be used in the film,[9] fully understood the implications of what they were signing was ultimately irrelevant, because the company held a legal proof of an agreement, and could claim that the signature represented a full agreement based on understanding.[10] As I have commented above, the officials of the Hunt were not naïve participants, and they insisted on some control about how the filmed material was used in the finished product. The film company also wanted to operate in a friendly, cooperative and conscientious manner, and welcomed the input of people from the Hunt as the filming and the editing progressed. There was a written agreement between the Hunt and the production company to allow nominated people from the Hunt to see the film as it was edited, and to make suggestions and requests for changes before a final version was produced. What the company retained, however, was ultimate editorial control; they were, in the end, legally entitled to make the film that they wanted to make.

In this whole process I had a series of concerns. I wanted the film to represent, as closely as possible, my individual anthropological perspectives of, and insights into, the hunting world, but I could not be fully and solely responsible for these. Others in the production team also had their views, which would inform what was filmed, how it was filmed, and, finally, how that world was represented. I also wanted, as a professional working in television, to be one of the creators of a successful film. I was contracted by, and so had responsibilities to, the production company. I only had this job because of my position (*vis-à-vis* the hunting world) and the people who had agreed to allow me to work with them, and I felt I had enormous responsibilities towards them – even if I did not make this explicit to them on all occasions. In this case I felt that if there were any conflicts of interest or problems of representation that my primary and overriding responsibilities were to the people of the specific Hunt involved and to the hunting world in general. I had promised them that, as an anthropologist, my agenda was not that of exposure, but that of understanding, or rather that the anthropological exposure I would bring would be one of understanding. That was my unwritten contract with them – a contract that, for me, implied a set of personal, moral obligations. There was also self-interest. I wanted to continue with my ethnographic research with them, something that required their continued trust and acceptance of me as an anthropologist. My concern was always that if they felt threatened or misrepresented in the film then my claims for my anthropological work would be questioned or disbelieved, and my access to them would be curtailed. How could I be associated with a portrayal or representation in one medium, and make claims for a different agenda, and a different set of representations and interpretations in another?

In the end I think the project was successful. The film was not an anthropological account of foxhunting, and was not something that could easily find a place within the genre of visual anthropology or ethnographic film, but it was never premised on a set of anthropological or ethnographic concerns. There were many difficulties that had to be resolved along the way, but such difficulties occur in the making of any documentary film. Simply titled *The Hunt*,[11] the finished film depicted many of the intersecting lives of members of a Hunt, and was a richly visual account of their relationships with the animals and landscapes that are brought together, and bound together, in the complex event that is foxhunting. Others certainly felt that the film was successful. It was shown, to critical acclaim, in film festivals, broadcast on many television channels, and in 1999 it was awarded the Prix Italia for the best European television cultural documentary.

## Hunting Scrutinised – Anthropologist as Consultant

My next example of the use of my anthropological research outside the area of academic anthropology very much depended on my position within the academy. In 1999 Lord Burns was commissioned by the Home Secretary to set up a major inquiry into hunting with dogs[12] – the Lord Burns Commission of Inquiry into Hunting with Dogs. Soon after his appointment he invited me to meet him to discuss my research, and to ask what sort of research had been undertaken in this area. He wanted to know what was known in terms of academic research, about foxhunting, and he asked what, in my opinion, were areas that needed new or further research. Once the inquiry team began its work I was asked to produce a paper for the committee. This was to be an interpretative description of what occurred during a 'typical' hunting day. It was to be interpretative in that after each section in which I described the events of a hunting day I offered a commentary on meanings and significances.

As I understood it, the reason that my report was requested was that other interested bodies, those pro and anti hunting, would be allowed to submit their own accounts of hunting, and that the committee needed an independent, outsider, account of the event. It is important here that I was asked to produce this report specifically for the committee, and I was paid for it – it was treated as a research report commissioned by them. Other interested bodies were invited to submit papers arguing their particular positions and perspectives to the committee, but I was expected to produce a neutral account. It was not expected that I would produce a highly theoretical anthropological piece, but rather one more akin to a close ethnographic description. Such a request did not seem particularly problematic because I was hired directly, and specifically, because of my experiences and perspectives as an academic anthropologist, and I was expected to offer these sorts of perspectives. As it was to be a general description of the practices that constituted hunting rather than the specific activities of a particular Hunt I was able to use the classic ethnographic techniques of depersonalising and anonymising.

In terms of my responsibilities here, I felt that I had been hired for my professional anthropological knowledge, and that my responsibility was therefore primarily to anthropology, to the requirements and demands of the discipline, and to good academic practice. My report was different from, for example, an article I might submit to a peer reviewed journal – the committee did not need that level of complexity – but it had to have some academic credibility in order to have the required status for their purposes. Linked with this was my responsibility to the government committee, which expected to read my account and interpretation as a nonpartisan document. I could not be seen to be advocating a position in the debate, although once again, my perspective *was* a position in the debate. In accepting this request I had to think carefully about the nature of the report that would, inevitably, become part of a public political debate rather than an internal, academic, debate.

Finally, there was my responsibility to the hunting world. I knew that my report would become a document to which they would have access, and I needed them to see that I had fairly set out an anthropological account of the sort that I had promised them. I knew that I would not write the sort of report that they might, ideally, have liked me to have produced, and that I would probably not choose to highlight all the aspects of hunting that supported their arguments and positions. For example, in my work I have always focused on issues to do with the performative, ritual, and ceremonial aspects of hunting; hunting as a cultural practice, rather than stressing the elements such as effective vermin control, the usefulness of hunting, that are emphasised by those supporting and defending hunting. I suspected that any omission of such arguments in my report might be seen by the hunting world as a failure to give a full account of why they hunted.

I did produce my account, it was accepted as a useful document by Lord Burns' committee, and my anthropological perspectives were commented on, and incorporated into the final report. In the end I felt that what I wrote was not a partisan piece, and much of the description of hunting practices produced for my report will be incorporated, with more complex anthropological commentary, into the book I am writing on foxhunting. My responsibility here was to produce a description and an interpretative account of a practice. I was contracted as a form of consultant because of a claim I made for the value of anthropology, and a claim about myself as an anthropological practitioner, as offering a particular perspective and a particular understanding, which I felt would enhance the committee's understanding of an event on which they were sitting in judgement.

## Hunting Defended – Anthropologist as Ally?

My final two examples come from within the hunting world itself. In the spring of 2002 the Scottish Parliament banned the hunting of foxes by packs of hounds followed by people mounted on horseback. The Countryside Alliance planned a legal challenge to this law, and contracted a legal team to contest it. This team requested material on the potential social and cultural impacts of such a ban in the sparsely populated Border Region of Scotland where there are five Hunts. I was asked by the Countryside Alliance[13] to conduct research, and write a report on this – a report for which I was paid. I strongly suspect that I was approached by the Countryside Alliance because they were aware of my previously published work that stressed the cultural practice aspect of foxhunting rather than engaging with the political and ethical debates about the acceptability or otherwise of the practice.

This project really demanded anthropology on the run for I had only a week to do any first-hand research. What I was offered, however, was an enormous range of material from the Countryside Alliance from other studies, and invaluable, non-public documents, about the social composition of Hunts, and a breakdown of all their social activities throughout the year. I had, independently, through my other ethnographic work, come to some views about the importance of local Hunts for rural communities, and I would not have accepted this research if I had not already been convinced that the banning of hunting in most rural areas would constitute a form of social and cultural impoverishment. This research allowed me to investigate the specific forms that the social and cultural impact might take in this particular part of the country rather than attempting to discover whether a ban on hunting would have any social and cultural impact at all. In my final report, I examined the totality of the hunting world in the region (i.e. not simply the hunting of foxes *per se* but the social world in which it is embedded), and came to the conclusion that hunting was a major focus of social life for a large number of people, and that a ban would have a major impact on sociality and the structures and practices of community. This report formed part of the case that the legal team submitted to the court in their defence of hunting and their challenge to the legality of the ban.

Once again there was clearly a set of issues to do with responsibility and the sorts of representations I was engaged to produce. Although the Countryside Alliance never discussed with me what they were hoping for from my report, never pointed out that they were paying me for it, and never asked what was going to be in it when I reached the writing up stage, I once again felt a set of responsibilities to the world they represented. In terms of the specific research in Scotland, although I had the responsibility of the anthropologist to represent fairly those with whom I had spoken in the region about how hunting figured in their lives, in this research I did not have a close and enduring relationship with these individuals, and it was therefore easier to make more general statements about them. It could be argued that what I was doing was merely applying anthropological knowledge acquired elsewhere to this specific case, and using the information and perspectives I obtained in interviews there as examples to support or illustrate my previously formed arguments. There was a process of investigation here, but it could scarcely warrant the term 'fieldwork' and all that that implies for an anthropologist. The other responsibility was, once again, to the hunting world in general, and I was clear in my own mind that I needed to represent as clearly, and as forcefully as possible, the importance of the relationships between hunting and the local community for the participants in, and active supporters of, hunting.

I feel that in this case the responsibilities involved were of a different order from those previously considered. I was not being asked to adopt an overtly political, advocational, position. Indeed, I understand from discussions with members of the Countryside Alliance that this is exactly what they do not expect or want from me. When they do express any interest in my work it seems to be because it represents part of an academic endeavour written by someone who is not perceived as opposed to them. I was, however, trusted by them to be the author of a significant document that would be used in a court of law in their defence. It was important, however, that this could not be a political document masquerading as a neutral anthropological one, because there was the possibility that I might have to appear in court as an expert witness to be cross-examined about my findings, interpretations and opinions. I did not want to be put in a position of defending an anthropological position in court that I would not be equally willing to defend in an academic seminar. Here, though, I could not avoid recognising that I was researching and writing for an interested party rather than for an academic institution or publication. This research was clearly going to be used to support a particular case, and to argue for a particular position. However, I had not been asked to comment, or to take sides in a moral debate, but rather to offer an anthropological view on how the event related to local communities and the social and cultural lives of those communities, and I felt that this could be done whether or not one approved of hunting itself.

# Hunting Debated – the Anthropologist Talks Back

My short concluding example focuses on being an anthropologist directly responding to, and talking back to, senior representatives of the hunting world. In the summer of 2002 I was invited to attend a series of private seminars convened by the Countryside Alliance. The purpose of these seminars was to discuss a range of issues associated with all forms of hunting with hounds. On this occasion I was asked to give my opinion on the social and cultural aspects of foxhunting, and to comment on what I thought the hunting world needed to concentrate on, and the types of arguments they ought to advance, in order to explain to their practices to outsiders. This was a rather odd position to be in. I was, as it were, being asked to speak to those from whom I had drawn my information, about who I thought they were, and what I thought they were doing. Here my responsibility was purely to anthropology, but in a rather peculiar setting and context. Having seen their practices, and sought their opinions I was now in the position of suggesting to them what I thought were the 'real' significances of their world. I was invited to interpret them back to their practitioners.

In these seminars I often disagreed and debated with them about what they thought were the most important issues of foxhunting, and the reasons for their practices, and they often disagreed with me about my view of the primacy of the performative and ritual nature of hunting, and generally that of foxhunting as a cultural practice. My view was that they needed to find a way to communicate this aspect of hunting to a largely anti-hunting population. I suggested that stressing this aspect of hunting, and building on some popular notions of tradition and heritage, might help to create an image of the event that reduced the focus on the death of an animal as the central feature of a leisure and pleasure pursuit. This was an approach that fitted very well with my anthropological view that foxhunting had little to do with fox killing – a view that is probably diametrically opposed to that of most people who disapprove of the event. It was a view that was perfectly well received within the seminars, but it was felt to be little use to them either as an explanation or defence.

My anthropological view was accepted, or at least listened to, as just that, my view, but it did not seem particularly significant for them as relevant to or as an answer to their concerns. In terms of the issues of responsibility I have touched on here, what was interesting was that I could offer this contested representation of hunting, and those who hunted, to representatives of the people I had studied and I could do so in a safe, private, environment among those charged with representing and defending hunting in a political arena. However, I think I could only do this, and I was probably only invited to participate, because of the trust I had built up during the course of my anthropological fieldwork, and because I had not abused that trust in the form of writing negatively about them in my anthropological work.

## Anthropology Applied: a Concluding Comment

In this chapter I have dealt with different ways in which I, as an anthropologist, led others into an individual area of fieldwork or engaged with that terrain in ways and for purposes which were not immediately related to the intellectual and academic concerns of anthropology. I am convinced that there are particular responsibilities that derive from the quality, intensity, and duration of fieldwork-based studies that begin life as academic projects. We attempt to make ourselves experts of particular things, and represent ourselves as having specialist knowledge of particular peoples, their societies, and their cultural practices. Sometimes others, with non-anthropological interests, will seek our help in gaining access to them and their worlds and I believe we have some compelling responsibilities in such processes.[14] Those amongst whom, and with whom we study, allow us to develop relationships with them which in turn allow us to develop our academic careers, and it seems only right that, in most cases,[15] they and their interests should take priority over any others. However, not all those who define themselves as working anthropologists will have exactly the same responsibilities; they will have responsibilities of a different order. Many will be hired by companies, organisations and agencies because of what those employing them might rightly recognise as the skills of social/cultural understanding and social/cultural sensitivities characteristic of well-trained anthropologists. Here, though, the name or title 'anthropologist' might not be that which defines them. For example, in my case I always thought of myself as an anthropologist working in television, but those for whom I worked usually judged me as a more or less skilled, and a more or less successful general researcher. In working environments outside academia anthropologists might not be judged or held to account for their opinions, interpretations, decisions or actions in terms of a purely academic anthropological discourse, but because of other interests, demands and concerns connected with the nature of the work in which they are involved. The issues involved in fulfilling and negotiating such interests, demands and concerns are rightly topics for the experiences and expertise of other anthropologists in this volume.

# Notes

1.  Throughout this chapter the use of the word Hunt, with a capital letter, refers to the fox-hunt as the social entity, or association, rather than to the activities that constitute hunting itself.
2.  See Lee (1995) especially pages 16–20 for access to research settings in which there is potential social conflict.
3.  Although I was initially a co-producer of the film, my new full-time job meant that I could no longer fulfil the obligations that this entailed. I was finally credited as the researcher and associate producer.
4.  I think it was significant that the producer and the director were Dutch. I believe that many people involved with the filming thought that this would mean that these key figures would not automatically hold what they regarded as stereotypical 'outsider' views about the social world of foxhunting.
5.  This is not to suggest that the Hunt authorities were uncooperative. Far from it and, as far as I am aware, the director was never refused permission to film anything. At the beginning of the process, however, the Hunt authorities sometimes needed time to consider the implications of when and how certain things might be filmed. Throughout the filming process there was a continual negotiation between the Hunt and the film crew.
6.  See Winston (1995) especially chapter 34, for a discussion on who is, or might be, aware of what in the documentary filming process.
7.  I cannot claim to have sought permission from those whom I have written about each time I produce an article, but I have usually tried to offer such articles to members of the hunting world who have expressed an interest in my work in order to benefit from their comments, suggestions, criticisms and corrections.
8.  An exception here would be investigative, journalistic, documentaries in which it would be impossible to obtain permission from some people featured in the programmes.
9.  In fact it is a little more complex than this. Although the ideal might be to have permission from everybody, this is, in practical terms, impossible. For example, it would be almost impossible to obtain the permission of every one of a score or so of riders who are filmed galloping across a field. It might even be impossible to identify each one of them.
10. I must emphasise that this is only a theoretical point here for no such conflicts ever arose. I remember one occasion when a person was filmed as she fell from her horse and was asked to sign a release form. At the time she agreed only reluctantly but months later when the film was edited she was happy, although a little rueful, to be the representative image of the danger of riding horses.
11. *The Hunt*, 1997 Ryninks Films, Amsterdam. Directed by Niek Koppen and produced by Kees Ryninks.
12. I think the term 'dogs' was used as a politically neutral one. Within the hunting would such animals are called 'hounds' see (Marvin 2001).
13. The Countryside Alliance is an organisation that campaigns on rural issues and promotes country pursuits. Part of the Alliance has a particular interest in hunting and other field sports.
14. I am leaving aside here, because I have no specialist knowledge of the area, the issues which arise when the anthropologist and the people with whom s/he work negotiate a position in which the anthropologist acts as an advocate for them.
15. The issue becomes much more complex if the anthropologist is working, perhaps covertly, with, for example, criminal or racist groups or those involved in the violation of human rights.

# References

Gross, L., J.S. Katz and J. Ruby (eds). 1988. *Image Ethics: The Moral Rights of Subjects in Photographs, Film, and Television*. New York and Oxford: Oxford University Press.

Hammersley, M. and P. Atkinson. 1996. *Ethnography: Principles in Practice*. London: Routledge.

Lee, R. 1995. *Dangerous Fieldwork*. London: Sage Publications.

Marvin, G. 2001. 'Cultured Killers: Creating and Representing Foxhounds'. *Society and Animals*, 9(2): 273–292.

Winston, B. 1995. *Claiming the Real: The Documentary Film Revisited*. London: British Film Institute Publishing.

*Chapter 10*

# 'CULTURE' IN COURT:
## Albanian Migrants and the Anthropologist as Expert Witness[1]

*Stephanie Schwandner-Sievers*

With some disappointment I enclose the adjudicator's determination. Perhaps you would like to comment on the ways your report has been handled? (solicitor's letter regarding the court's rejection of an asylum case concerning a victim of war rape fearing social ostracism upon return to Kosovo)

There is no way that I can ignore the expert's report. (adjudicator admitting a claim for asylum of an Albanian victim of human trafficking in opposition to the Home Office's representative)

The expert explained my culture correctly. (Kosovo-Albanian murderer in a criminal case)

We would like to speak to you immediately about the possible cultural background of murder as it will shape our investigations. (police Detective Inspector investigating murder among migrant Albanians)

He got out of detention thanks to your report. You saved his life. (Human Rights activist, asylum case regarding a refugee from blood feud in Albania)

These examples are just some of the reactions noted in the aftermath of, or in connection with, asylum and criminal court cases involving Albanians from Albania and Kosovo[2] in conflict with the law in the U.K., for which I have produced anthropological expert reports. In recent years I have received approximately 150 requests to give expert evidence regarding asylum cases and occasional requests regarding criminal cases. Usually, in both types of cases, I was asked to explain various issues involving 'Albanian culture', either in a written report or, on some occasions, as an expert witness in court during trial. Such requests assumed a particular expertise based on my ethnographic research among Albanians in Albania and Kosovo from the early 1990s until the present day. Usually it is the solicitor who seeks an independent expert to support their client's case, but in rare cases I have also been approached directly by asylum seekers themselves. I was usually asked to comment on the risks involved if an asylum seeker were to be returned to his or her home country, and how socio-cultural issues at home would affect that risk. Regarding criminal cases I was often approached by police detectives during the criminal investigation process. In such cases I was usually asked to explain the 'Albanian culture of violence' or particular aspects of Albanian culture and how these would give cultural sense to a violent deed and help explain its motives.

Although randomly selected, the above-cited examples of legal professionals' responses are fairly typical. They highlight the ethical and other questions at stake in producing expert statements. These include the extent to which the anthropologist involved as an expert in the legal process interferes with other people's lives, people who in other circumstances would be our fieldwork interlocutors. Most generally, it therefore could be asked whether it is acceptable at all to challenge our anthropological ethos of non-interference – assuming that the anthropological expert can, sometimes, make a difference in the legal process. More specific questions of an ethical nature have long occupied social and cultural anthropologists dealing as 'expert witnesses' with courts, particularly in the U.S. from the late 1970s, and these have included the following: How can we adequately convey theoretical insights on contextuality, cultural change, ambiguity and fluidity? How, for example, to reconcile the seductive possibility (particularly in the U.S.) of using 'cultural defence' in representing an 'ethnic community interest' that may, at times, be at odds with its often most vulnerable social actor's, individual experiences and aspirations? (Alvarez and Loucky 1992; Kokot 2000: 1; Koptiuch 1996; Rosen 1977). How should we cope with the court's demands for 'facts', 'evidence' and 'proof', categories themselves based on particular concepts of rationality, textuality (as, for example, the only permissible proof of history, Clifford 1988: 277–346) and causality? Or is it possible to take the 'opportunity to phrase testimony in terms that are no more definite than the data permit' (Rosen 1977: 572), for example that are of a non-textual nature? How should we cope with categorical terms such as 'tribe', 'culture', 'identity', 'acculturation', etc., 'that courts might regard as conclusory' (ibid.: 566) yet that appear much more ambiguous to us? More recently, such questions have been turned around in asking whether, and in what ways, the legal process validates anthropological knowledge in our societies (Donovan and Anderson 2003). Yet, lastly, if observing the anthropologist as just one of the actors in the legal arena, the following question remains valid: How can both 'self-serving relativism [and] the moral self-righteousness to which both anthropologists and lawyers may fall prey' be avoided in legal procedure? (Rosen 1977: 557).

Regarding contemporary asylum cases in the U.K. and the anthropologists' involvement as 'expert witnesses' in these, Anthony Good has suggested that although British anthropologists 'have been regularly approached by immigration solicitors seeking expert reports on their clients ... little has been written on asylum from an anthropological perspective' (Good 2003a: 93). His ethnographic research on anthropological expert witnessing in such cases has addressed this deficit, and – with extensive reference to Good's work (2003a, 2003b) and to my own experiences – in the following section I will explore the role of the anthropological expert witness in the legal process involving migrant Albanians to the U.K. In more detail I will then question the concept of 'culture' in the ways in which I have encountered it in the legal realm in both asylum and criminal cases involving Albanians in the U.K. Not only are there general issues of power, representation and ethical academic responsibility at stake when the anthropologist is challenged to describe and communicate 'the culture' of someone else to the various legal actors who will decide on this person's future and who commonly operate on the basis of certain assumptions about the 'other's', the client's, 'culture'. There are also highly specific issues such as the particular 'risk' which may affect an individual asylum seeker, who for example, has escaped death threats, often locally justified in the name of 'tradition', in the informal realms of Albania or Kosovo, if returned home. How can 'culture' be explained in such cases while avoiding that 'culture shifts from something to be described, interpreted, even perhaps explained, ... [to being] treated as a source of explanation in itself' (Kuper 2001: xi)? How can the dangers of 'Albanian traditions of violence' be represented to a court without reproducing generalised, stereotypical outside assumptions of Albanians as well as a culturalist discourse of the most radical local (and transnational) perpetrators of violence to whom this served justifying crime? Indeed, implicit complicity in representing Albanian culture as being particularly prone to violence, can be traced between Albanian enactors of 'traditions of violence' and the legal professionals (cf. Schwandner-Sievers 2001; cf. Giordano 2000: 12n). I have suggested elsewhere that such representations can act as self-fulfilling prophecies as they empower those who profit from a strong reputation of violence and who, at the same time, produce those victims who then can be encountered as asylum seekers abroad (Schwandner-Sievers 2004). At the same time the victims of the real consequences of enacted 'Albanian traditions of violence', face mass rejection of their asylum claims abroad because the host country's asylum policy also justifies itself through the populist feeling of threat evoked by a generalised image of Albanian violence abroad.

I would like to claim that the fluidity of transnational and transitional societies such as those of Albania and Kosovo offer a field for investigating the ways in which individual agency negotiates structure, driven by varied interests such as to revitalise, consolidate, manipulate, subvert or escape 'culture', its options and its constraints. Blood feuding and social ostracism, explained in terms of Albanian or Balkan 'traditions of violence' or 'patriarchal culture', thus 'pinpoint ... the difference between people's perceptions of what is proper and appropriate in different contexts of conflict. This explains why it is praised by some and condemned by others' (Stewart and Strathern 2002: 3) both at home and in the transnational context. As one homosexual male Kosovo-Albanian research respondent – interviewed in the U.K. regarding gender issues and social vulnerability at home – put it: 'in Kosovo, murder still goes as legitimate in certain contexts, and being homosexual goes as criminal'. This respondent, drawing from alternative knowledge and possibilities available in the exile situation – equally as many other 'refugees from tradition' interviewed in the U.K. – strongly disagreed with such local manifestations of 'culture'.

The scope of agency within structural constraints can be exemplified through the following examples[3] of Kosovo-Albanian asylum cases of young married women who had become victims of war rape during the Kosovo war (1998–1999). The technique of rape in the wars of former Yugoslavia seems – as the sheer number of such cases suggests – to have been systematically orchestrated. In Kosovo it effectively undermined local and family patterns of social cohesion. Perpetrators were mostly Serb paramilitaries before and during the 1999 war and, perhaps to a lesser extent and certainly much less known, radical Albanian gangs who 'punished' the families of political deviants in post-war Kosovo.[4]

In two, here paradigmatically juxtaposed, cases a nusja (the Kosovo-Albanian 'bride' or 'young wife' living with her husband and her extended family-in-law under one roof in a village as a result of the comprehensive structural rule of post-marital virilocal residence), was raped by Serb paramilitaries in front of her mother-in-law. The presence of family witnesses is crucial to make this technique of war socio-culturally effective. In one case, the mother-in-law (vjehrra) left the nusja in the looted house to die; in another case, vjehrra consented, in solidarity with nusja, to keep the event a secret from the men and the wider community in order to avoid social consequences such as expulsion, ostracism, and perhaps, as in the most extreme cases, honour killing. In both cases the same cultural references informed the vjehrra's choice yet it differed according to the personal decision made. According to tradition, the nusja – although involuntarily a victim of symbolically nationalised rape – had forfeited her value as a 'faithful' and 'pure' woman to the family and become a reminder of the men's failure to protect their sacred and secret 'world of intimacy' (cf. Bourdieu 2002: 10–22, 90, 93) – their honour, ndera. She transformed into kurve (a woman outside the man's control, i.e. unfaithful, a 'whore') who, if this transformation were to be known to the wider family and local community and according to traditionalist discourse, would need to be ritually expelled (or killed) as a means of social purification if the others were not to share her 'disgrace' (marre or turp). Threats of 'honour killings' (or actual murder in the most extreme cases), severe social ostracism, the blaming of the women themselves and suicidal tendencies of war-raped women in Kosovo have been associated widely with such cultural expectations (Igric 1999; Milner and Schmidt 1999; Refugee Women's Resource Project 2002; Smith 2000).

Denying cultural references as the basis of the consequences and risks faced in such cases would be a liability at the expense of the victims (cf. similiarly for 'honour killings' in a Kurdish exile community in Sweden; Kurkiala, 2003). However, 'clearly, every Albanian family makes choices which may contradict the voices of the past, and conflict, dissent and dysfunction are very much a part of the social fabric' (Reineck 1993). In the first case, the witnessing vjehrra chose to execute 'propriety' in the traditional sense, in the second case the vjehrra chose to resort to a strategy of consensual silence in order to avoid the social consequences if the deed were to be known in the wider family and community, and to protect her daughter-in-law, nusja (who, however, remained forever at the vjehrra's mercy). The anthropological expert report in both cases would need to explore the local social patterns in order to address the risk to either nusja, who each managed to flee to the U.K.

I also encountered a number of similar cases in which, for example, the Kosovo-Albanian husband, asylum seeker in the U.K., knew about his wife's ordeal and decided to support her and to stay with her. However, in such a case he would always fear the enormous social pressures for divorce and separation if returned to the home community. In contrast, I also encountered a number of cases in which the husband, upon learning of the rape history of his wife (for example, through kinship contacts while in Britain), immediately turned violent, separated from her or in some cases threatened to kill her – particularly if he were to see her back home in Kosovo. These examples further show the scope and variety of individual choices that some Kosovo-Albanians make in relation to their 'culture'. They also show that migration not only offers protection but also emerges as an avoidance strategy from cultural constraints at home, and the social consequences they invoke. Similiarly, many cases of Albanians from Albania suggest such strategies of escaping the constraints of 'culture' enacted at home (cf. Schwandner-Sievers 2001). For example, Albanian refugees from blood feuds, fearing to be the next victim in the circle of violence, were of approximately equal number as those who fled in order to avoid pressures having to kill or being 'pre-emptively killed by the more powerful adversaries although, according to traditional ideal-type logic, it would have been ritually their turn to kill in a given feud. In such cases, local reference to 'culture' helped in covering up underlying conflicts over informal power and economic resource distribution (Schwandner-Sievers 2001).

Individual agency encountered in the face of cultural constraints, wider identity politics and the instrumentalisation of reference to 'culture' in order to cover up local and transnational informal interests stand in contrast to outside essentialist assumptions of Albanians as being shackled by 'traditions of violence' as part of their cultural 'essence'. However, such images can be traced both within the legal process and the wider socio-political climate within which it operates. Indeed Albanian asylum seekers from both Albania and Kosovo appear as refugees from struggles over power and social norms at home in which reference to 'tradition' enforces social and political pressures to comply or serves, such as in the Kosovar case, wider processes of traditionalist inspired national homogenisation. At the same time, the generalised outside images of Albanians as shackled by 'traditions of violence' in the asylum seekers' host countries helps to justify a policy of exclusion with little space for recognising individual coping strategies. How can the anthropologist, called upon as an expert, counteract such generalised outside representation in court without denying the dramatic social effects of cultural references enacted within the asylum seeker's home context?

Whether the anthropologist can make a difference in asylum or criminal cases at all and how to communicate culture in the legal process will be the core questions underpinning the following sections. I will begin by exploring the role of the anthropologist consultant or 'expert witness' in the legal arena and then discuss the linkage between power, policy and representations in legal cases involving migrant Albanians in the U.K. Here I am particularly concerned with exploring the interface of contradicting representations of 'the other' both as violent perpetrator or victim of violence within the legal arena; and, lastly, I will revisit the question of how culture can be communicated within the legal process while avoiding harming the victims or supporting the perpetrators of violence.

## Making a Difference?

There is no guarantee that an expert report will make any difference at all in the legal process. 'Expert status in the strict sense is inapplicable to asylum cases' (Good 2003b: 5) because,

> applicants are in no position to call witnesses or extract documents from the state [or other agent] which persecuted them. There is consequently no essential difference between experts and other witnesses: it is simply a matter of how much weight the court attaches to their evidence. (Good 2003b: 5)

However, citing a solicitor with whom I cooperated on numerous occasions regarding Albanian asylum cases, 'expert evidence wins cases more than the legal argument'. The admission of expert witnesses actually enables courts and lawyers to include and 'offer opinions otherwise inadmissible under strict rules of evidence' (Good 2003a: 114) and to show how human rights abuses impact on this particular person or persons of their particular social group in drawing 'attention to general evidence that supports (or not) the applicant's account' (ibid.). Expert reports relate the individual circumstances of a particular case to the wider country information available and thus help the court in assessing individual risk. 'Experts can assess how the appellant might be treated if returned,' (Good 2003b: 7) and 'confirm that they [the claimants] would face unacceptable risks if returned' (ibid.: 6). A report will particularly comment on, or challenge, statements in the Home Office's Reason of Refusal Letters (Good 2003a: 114). However, as Anthony Good has repeatedly and strongly emphasised, it is not the expert's, but the adjudicator's task to judge the 'credibility' of a particular asylum claim. 'Whereas in academia "consistency", "plausibility", and "credibility" may seem virtually interchangeable terms, in legal circles "credibility" is a term of art, denoting a judgement that only the court is entitled to make' (Good 2003b: 7). Legal interpretations, such as defining someone's identity as a genuine refugee, are solely up to the court to decide. The transgressions of the country's expert's legal competences in, for example, judging 'credibility' of a claim, may, in fact, harm a claim and devalue a report as the court may feel its authority appropriated (ibid.). Furthermore, the court alone will judge whether asylum or, possibly, a particular period of Leave to Remain on the basis of humanitarian protection or discretion can be granted by taking conventional or other 'compelling' reasons, possible individual and country risk of persecution and Human Rights into account.

Usually the expert witness in asylum procedures receives only 'the bundle' (see below) and hardly gets to see the asylum seeker (in criminal cases a court appearance is more likely). However, I have also appeared at asylum appeal and tribunal hearings or spoken to clients personally. Such personal encounters normally happened at the request of the solicitors in order to strengthen the chances of their client in court, particularly if these had advanced to a hearing at the High Court, and I generally welcomed such opportunities from an ethnographic point of view. 'The bundle' usually includes documents such as the initial Immigration and Nationality Directorate (IND)'s SEF (Statement of Evidence) interview forms laying out the basis and circumstances of the asylum claim, and any follow-up interview transcripts and witness statements of the asylum seeker him/herself as well as the Home Office Letter of Refusal, which usually contains a pretty standard set of reasons for refusal (Anthony Good calls the quality of most of these letters 'abysmal'; 2003a: 105), as well as any other material related to a case, such as psychological or medical reports. The expert witness is required to address the information in both general and in case-specific terms in the report.

Legal processes are open processes and may, as observed in asylum appeal procedures, depend more on the personality and compassion of the particular adjudicator on duty than on 'objective evidence'. Yet the anthropological commentary increases the chances that the legal agencies' judgements, decisions, and strategies of engagement will be in favour of a person's asylum claim, as it provides new arguments and information. It may therefore indeed have an effect on someone's real life. The expert writes and signs a statement owing duty to the court, confirms his or her independence from the financial source of remuneration, in asylum cases, usually Legal Aid raised through the claimant's solicitor (Good 2003b: 5) and waives any responsibilities of his or her home institution (in accordance with the particular university's rules on consultancy).

I found that the cases themselves offer deep anthropological insights into social processes in Kosovo and Albania, which have informed my ongoing ethnographic fieldwork projects in the region. As has already been mentioned, I have dealt with cases which included those of both female and male victims of sexual assault, during and after the 1999 Kosovo war (war rape, attempts at castration, and persecution of homosexuals) who feared stigmatisation, social ostracism or assaults if returned.[6] Other cases included those of victims of domestic violence who feared reassertion of control over them by their spouses and in-laws if returned to Albania or Kosovo; furthermore, with victims of abduction, trafficking, and forced prostitution mainly from Albania, who feared for their security if returned; 'deserters' from the guerrilla 'Kosovo Liberation Army' (KLA) who feared reprisals as a result of the prevailing post-war radical cultures of ethno-national homogenisation; members of inter-ethnic marriages or families in Kosovo and members of ethnic or religious minority groups such as Roma, Gorani, Serbs, Catholic or Orthodox Albanians, in fear of radical nationalist Albanians, and various cases in which the asylum seekers were in fear of blood feud and its ritual demands, and/or in fear of criminal interest groups across the region. In all cases I was usually asked to comment on possible risks and the security situation for a prospective returnee, and the chances of relocation and protection by the home authorities.

In contrast to asylum cases, in criminal cases the anthropological expert opinion can only serve the court's wider understanding of the deed. In fact, offering an interpretation in terms of 'cultural sense' – for example in cases of revenge killings or blood feuds – usually suggests the premeditation of murder in British courts rather than serving as a 'cultural defence'. Incidentally, the contemporary Albanian penal code itself – a fact commonly neglected by culturalist explanations – defines murder in revenge or blood feud as premeditated murder, to be punished by no less than twenty years in prison (Stoppel, 2003: 83, article 78). The anthropological comments were mainly sought to assess possible motives for murder among migrant Albanians, which would then shape the direction of police investigations and the court's understanding of the case.

In the context of criminal cases I was asked for comments in cases of Albanian young men/gang conflict over prostitution, the murder of a previous girlfriend and of an illegitimate child, for all of which police suspected 'cultural reasons', such as 'codes of honour' and blood feuding.

However, in many cases, social peer-group pressures, prestige systems, generational changes in reference to 'tradition', and (informal) business interests in migrant niche situations, suggested brutalised codes of conduct similar to any violent Western inner-city gang cultures (cf. Bourgois 1995) rather than roots in 'historical traditions of Albanian blood feud' – although criminal perpetrators in court were found to be fond of this reference in culturally justifying their deed (similarly as with contemporary Albanian crime in Albania, cf. Kikia 1999). Sometimes such justification existed simply in retrospective discourse, in others it was symbolically marked as part of a reinvented discourse of honour within the deed itself, for example through deliberately leaving signs (cigarettes, cartridges, business cards) behind at the place of the deed that identified the murderer. However, in most cases, following alternative suggestions based on assumptions of transformed, modernised codes of conduct, the police uncovered various informal, entrepreneurial, and transnational interests groups, inter-group and intergenerational conflict over propriety of conduct rather than uncontested ancient customs as the background to homicide. Nevertheless, the reinterpreted 'traditions' sometimes provide a source of information, of symbolic references, and ideological justification to the perpetrators (cf. Schwandner-Sievers 2001).

There are personal and moral choices the anthropologist must make when engaging in legal procedures. Indeed, not only is our professional ethos of non-interference challenged if we agree to participate, but equally, the decision not to produce a report may have implications for someone's life. This may limit the chances of an asylum application, and may put an individual at real risk if returned home. However, in owing duty only to the court, the expert is required to take 'account of points calling the appellant's story into question as well as those tending to corroborate it' (Good 2003b: 6). Since I personally rebut the idea of becoming an accomplice in someone's asylum rejection, I dealt with this moral dilemma by taking on only those cases that I felt I could possibly support through reference to my ethnographic understanding of the home situation. In addition to such ethical considerations, there are also emotional experiences. There is personal pride when a case succeeds and, by the same token, disappointment and hopes betrayed when a person believed at high risk is returned despite the report. The responsibility weighs particularly heavily in such cases, and one becomes aware of being part of a wider 'industry', which negotiates the inclusion and exclusion of other people in the legal realm. The representation of 'culture' is part of wider relations of power.

## Power and the Interface of Representations in Court

In legal procedures and in court, particularly in asylum cases, individuals from different cultures and legal background come into contact. Here the anthropologist both participates in, and observes, relations of power for/in the courts, policy is challenged or consolidated by perceptions, rituals and practices within the legal arena. It is through policy that,

> the individual is categorized and given such statuses and roles as 'subject', 'citizen', [asylum seeker] ... 'criminal' and 'deviant'... people are classified, shaped and ordered according to policies, but they may have little consciousness of or control over the processes at work. The study of policy, therefore, leads straight into issues at the heart of anthropology: norms and institutions; ideology and consciousness; knowledge and power; rhetoric and discourse; meaning and interpretation; the global and the local – to mention but a few. (Shore and Wright 1997: 4).

Power rests generally with the host country's legal institutions and its representatives in court which make decisions about the criminal delinquent's or the asylum seeker's future in what has been described as a process of 'objectification' (ibid.). Furthermore, relations of power rest also in the interaction between various individual subjectivities in court; and lastly, power rests in the relation of victims and perpetrators of violence, preceding, and located outside, the legal procedures.

The power of interacting subjectivities in the legal realm is more subtle and less visible than the power of institutional structures. For example, it rests with the interpreters (translators). I observed negligent translations which provoked doubt about the asylum seeker's credibility, thus endangering the case, as well as individual translators whose empathy encouraged the asylum seeker in court to a more genuine, sympathetic narrative in front of the adjudicator. Similarly, the solicitor's engagement or lack of engagement, the experience and expertise of the 'case worker' or individual solicitor, and the construction of the legal 'argument', can make a difference. Not least, sympathies and chances depend on the client's own capacity of self-representation as well as on the adjudicator's personality, political convictions, and his or her compassion towards the individual asylum seeker. Every single 'House' of the Immigration Appellate Authority where asylum appeals are dealt with, and the various adjudicators, have a 'reputation'. For example, in an appeal case involving a sexually-abused young Albanian girl, her solicitors deliberately did not request an 'all-female court', as one might expect, because of the tough reputation of the female adjudicators of the particular House in which this case was heard. Equally, the Home Office representatives, seeking to meet government targets of reducing asylum numbers, have varied reputations. Individual engagement, professional skills, time and funding, chances, risk, and reputation of any of the legal professionals involved are thus an integral part of the legal procedures and account for the unpredictability of the outcome of a case.

There are also predictable principles, rituals and roles in legal procedures of asylum cases that are part of wider power structures. For example, the Home Office does not legally recognise risks that are not described in the 1951 United Nations Geneva Convention on Refugees and its 1967 protocol. These categories describe a genuine refugee as someone:

> owing to well-founded fear of being persecuted for reasons of race, religion, nationality, membership of a particular social group or political opinion, is outside the country of his nationality and is unable or, owing to such fear, is unwilling to avail himself of the protection of that country.[7]

Those Albanian asylum seekers who fear blood feuds, criminal revenge or gendered abuse thus do not qualify for 'conventional grounds' of asylum, and are thus categorically rejected by the Home Office. However, from 1998 appeal procedures could make reference to the European Convention on Human Rights (ECHR) which was integrated into UK law in 1998 and 2000.

> Protection under ECHR article 3 (freedom from torture, inhumane or degrading treatment) is potentially wider than under the refugee convention, because the ill treatment does not have to be related to a person's race, religion, nationality, political opinion or membership of a social group. Nor can anyone be excluded from protection under ECHR whereas certain people, such as war criminals, can be denied refugee status. (Refugee Council 2002: A.2./ii)

Fear of degrading or inhumane treatment upon return for 'unconventional reasons' such as organised crime, patriarchal gender roles or blood feuds have thus received a fresh chance for success on Human Rights grounds. However, the Home Office may not just be guided by 'objective categories' but by government policy and the public opinion of the electorate. Indeed, 'Home Office procedures seem designed to undermine credibility rather than verify it. For example, despite the traumatic past experiences … [or] the clandestine circumstances under which many have travelled, staff are told to query their credibility if they have not applied for asylum "forthwith"' (Good 2003a: 94; cf. IND 1998: 1, 2, 11.1).

Questioning the credibility of an applicant has become the decisive issue for rejecting an asylum applicant. The Home Office can use any indication of inconsistency of a claim to reject it. Unfortunately, so-called 'bogus claims' have been commonly made by asylum seekers from Albania pretending to be Kosovar war refugees (UNDP 2000: 36), a fact which has made such asylum seekers liable to immediate deportation. However, I have produced a number of last-minute reports, which suggested that such 'inconsistency' in the asylum cases can actually indicate the claimant's genuine need of asylum, and some claimants were, subsequently, released from detention (normally preceding deportation).

From 1990, 'Albanians have emigrated by all means, legally and illegally' on a mass scale (ibid.). In subverting existing structures of exclusion migrants shared the best strategies of gaining access to otherwise legally inaccessible countries. 'Bogus claims' increased with the 1998/1999 peak of the Kosovar crisis. Albanian migrant strategies of identity mimicry have been documented as a common strategy for subverting both wider structures of exclusion and negative stereotypes for a variety of reasons mostly, but not only, economic (Hart 1999; Mai and Schwandner-Sievers 2003; Kretsi 2002; Schwandner-Sievers 2004). For example, in seriously dangerous cases such as flights from a blood feud or from organised crime, adopting a different identity has always served as the most efficient form of self-protection where the home state did not provide alternative means of protection.[8] Even more commonly, victims of sexual abuse, including the inter-ethnic violence of the 1999 Kosovo war or the abduction and forced prostitution of women from Albania, chose silence for psychological, social and cultural reasons of 'shame', and as an avoidance strategy of the social consequences indicated above.

An abused woman's vested interest in not disclosing her ordeal to her family could be seriously damaged in legal procedures, particularly in situations of claims as a dependant on the husband. There are no guarantees that such exposure will lead to the success of an asylum claim particularly if issues of credibility are at stake. However, exposing ordeal and identity can also constitute the last chance for asylum of a victim otherwise potentially returned to a hostile environment. Sometimes such hidden and painful stories have suddenly emerged when inconsistencies in the testimony provided in the 'bundle' led me to ask further questions via the solicitor. Inconsistencies encountered can thus lead to additional arguments in support of a case. Such arguments have helped abused women to receive permits to stay but have also exposed them to a debate of their ordeal within the legal process.

Previous critiques on the Home Office included 'its lack of transparency and its "culture of disbelief"' (Good 2003a: 7) which, de facto, have helped exclude asylum seekers on a large scale. In fact, although 'expert witnesses and IND use broadly the same sources of factual information', there is a fundamental difference in the ways in which these texts are interpreted (Good 2003a: 94). While the expert witness is not guided by targets of exclusion, the Home Office appears to respond to prejudiced guidelines of government policy.

In early 2003 'under pressure from the growing public and right-wing media antipathy towards asylum seekers' it was announced that 'the [British] government is hoping to cut the expected final total of 100,000 asylum applications for 2002 in half by the end of next year' (Bolton 2003). Although, by comparison with other EU member-states, U.K. asylum figures are rather low (Good 2003b: 3) as with many other nationalities also Albanians from both Albania and Kosovo were included on the so-called 'White List'[9] introduced under the Nationality, Immigration and Asylum Act of 2002.

The white list system, allows the government to presume that any asylum applications from those countries are clearly unfounded, and so reject them – unless the applicants can provide evidence to rebut that assumption... However, the parliamentary joint committee on human rights has warned that the white list amounts to an 'unacceptable' threat to human rights, adding that the UN does not accept that any country can be declared safe. (Bolton 2003)

The 'white-listing' of Albanians from Albania and Kosovo in January 2003 immediately led to a considerable increase in requests for anthropological expert reports by rejected asylum applicants seeking new evidence for their appeal procedures.[10] Some of them were likely to be in genuine fear of dangerous consequences if returned home, others perhaps just seeking better chances for their and their children's future, and yet others simply hopeless 'economic refugees' with few alternative legal routes available to them but to formally seeking asylum (Robinson and Segrott 2002; cf. Mai and Schwandner-Sievers 2003).[11]

On the one hand, Albania and Kosovo were 'white-listed' as safe for returnees, although the UNHCR and other organisations have repeatedly warned against the premature return of members of ethnic minority groups or victims of sexual abuse to Kosovo (OSCE and UNHCR 2003; Refugee Women's Resource Project 2002, 2003; UNHCR 2002). On the other hand, 'ethnic Albanian organised crime' was acknowledged in the U.K. National Criminal Intelligence Services as a 'potential threat' to the British nation although it is known by police and the Home Office that the majority of victims of such crime have always been Albanians themselves (NCIS 2003; cf. for the Italian case Bonifazi and Sabatino 2003). Albania and Kosovo are also not yet considered safe for tourist travel (Foreign and Commonwealth Office 2003).

In other words, Albania and Kosovo are considered safe for the most vulnerable victims of recent war, fragile transitions and criminality, but unsafe for British travellers. At the same time Albanians are generally perceived as a potential threat if encountered abroad. Negative press coverage of Albanian 'cultures of violence' has supported populist calls for the deportation of all Albanian asylum seekers. '*The Sun* printed what was meant to be an amusing reinterpretation of the children's Mister Men characters and included a Mr Asylum Seeker and his friend Mr Albanian Gangster' and 'the *Daily Mail* ... claimed Britain was a "haven" for "Albanian gangsters, Kosovan people smugglers and Algerian terrorists"' (Morris 2003). Such images of Albanians proved so all-pervasive in early 2003 that an Englishman accused of murdering his two young sons first tried to blame a gang of three Albanian gangsters in order to divert attention from his crime,[12] and tabloid journalists were found to instigate a story of an Albanian/Romanian criminal gang plot to kidnap celebrity Victoria Beckham, alias 'Posh Spice' (Byrne 2003). [13] At the same time, various documentary films focused on Albanian blood feuds, gun trafficking and prostitution rackets, consolidating the image of Albanian gang violence and crime in the absence of any alternative media representation of Albania, Kosovo and Albanians in general.[14]

Noticeably in such representations, the term *kanun*, or more specifically, the *Kanun of Lekë Dukagjini* (Gjeçov 1989), serves as an exotic short-cut explanation and symbolic signifier of violent Albanian culture of feuding, violence and revenge killing. *Kanun* historically was a generic Ottoman term of indirect rule for any local set of rules governing village and tribal life in parallel to the religious law, *Sharia*, according to principles of self-regulation, in the Ottoman Empire. One of various flexible variants – orally transmitted and interpreted differently in various mountain valleys[14] – were first 'standardised' in text and paragraphs in a failed patriot attempt by a Franciscan priest, Shtjefen Gjeçov, to produce the basis of future Albanian national constitutional law (Fishta 2001). Gjeçov's early twentieth-century version of the *'kanun* of Lekë Dukagjin' was translated into English in 1989 and has since become the major source of reference for explaining Albanian crime and customs of blood revenge by any foreigner engaging with 'Albanian cultures of violence' (cf. Blumi 1998; Pandolfi 2002). However, local conflict regulation has never been governed by a fixed text in print but rather by oral transmissions and local negotiations of principles and rules with interpretations always subject to the local prestige economy (cf. Hasluck 1954). Undoubtedly a fascinating source, the use of Gjeçov's print *kanun* commonly ignores the historical context and political agenda of its original production (romantic patriotism at turn of the nineteenth/twentieth century producing ideal-type norms), social and political changes since (note the brutal Communist struggle against local patriarchal structures, Schwandner-Sievers 2001) and the methodological limitations of the author's research.[16] Legal professionals, including the Home Office, commonly mistake the English, printed, Gjeçovian version of this historical source as having 'laid out a code of "laws"'[17] when requesting explanation in terms of *kanun*. Some requests or material received by legal professionals for an expert report have included the following statements:

1. ...The Secretary of State is aware that there is a centuries-old tradition of blood feuds in Albania, the practice under which members of one family were permitted to take revenge against another family who were responsible for the death of one of their number, and the rules under which such matters were settled were laid down in the Canon of Lek Dukajini [sic]. Blood feuds were suppressed under communist rule, but have re-emerged since the return of democracy. ... The Secretary of State has noted that your stated problems, which caused you to leave Albania, are with members of another Albanian family, and your fears of being killed as a result of a blood feud. However, he would point out that in general such people cannot be regarded as 'agents of persecution' within the terms of the 1951 United Nations Convention relating to the Status of

Refugees … (Home Office: Letter of Refusal rejecting an Albanian asylum seeker to which the claimant's solicitor requested an expert response in support of the asylum seeker).

2. … our client has become subject to death threats because his father worked for the Serbian council in Pristina in the 1990s. We believe that these were informed by the Albanian traditional code of Lek Dukagjin. We particularly request evidence of how this informs the concept of the traitor. (Solicitor's letter requesting support in an appeal procedure of a Kosovo-Albanian).

3. … we would need information about the Albanian traditional customary law, known as *kanun*. It would be particularly helpful, if you could explain to us under what circumstances women can be killed according to this law… (Criminal court's instruction via telephone regarding a case in which an Albanian asylum seeker had killed his ex-girlfriend, a national of the European host country).

4. … our police are currently investigating the murder of an Albanian national. Many witnesses as well as the prime suspect are also Albanians. Since the investigation began it has become evident that the *kanun* has governed the actions of the Albanians within the inquiry. It will therefore be necessary for us to evidence the impact of the *kanun* and it is this area we seek your expertise. … (Police, crime investigation department, investigating the killing of a young Albanian migrant by another).

*Kanun* of historical Ottoman times has thus become a common identifier of an assumed 'Albanian culture of violence' within the arena of asylum policy and law. It has served to explain criminal violence as well as victimhood in the migrant situation, exotic fascination as well as populist calls for exclusion of Albanian asylum seekers in public media, independent of the fact that these may actually be the victims of local political processes and informal economic interests justifying violence under the label of 'tradition' at home.[18]

In summary, asylum and immigration policy emerge as being guided by targets of exclusion if not, as Teresa Hayter (2000) suggests, by explicit racism. The Albanians both from Albania and Kosovo provide a paradigmatic example of how selectively employed, stereotypical images of a country and a people can have an impact on Home Office asylum policy and court decisions regarding asylum seekers. If the construction of an hetero-image of Albanians as being shackled by crime and violent traditions has contributed to a stricter re-shaping of government admission policy then the Albanian victims (and not the perpetrators) of violence are multiply punished. They are identified with those who reproduce 'cultures of violence' for their own interests and have thereby contributed to the consolidation of a negative image.

## Communicating 'Culture'

How can 'culture' be communicated in expert commentary for legal decision makers without reproducing stereotypical images and giving sense to murder on the one hand and denying the victims a chance of verifying their ordeal suffered, often executed in terms of 'cultural propriety' by their perpetrators, on the other? There is no space for delving into further ethnographic detail here, but there are some general points that can be made.

The expert's chance of communicating 'culture' (and its social consequences) without reproducing essentialist representations, appears to me as situated in the anthropological, differentiated understanding, both in terms of time and space, of the home context of the asylum seekers or criminals encountered in the legal process. An ethnographic understanding of historical and contemporary social and political processes of social exclusion and inclusion in localities, and possible scopes of individual agency, of scopes of difference in generational, gender, social and other background variables, of experiences of statehood and the relations between the local and other power holders in shifting contexts, seems to me an essential tool to juxtapose any generalised images. Yet, historicity, fluidity and contextuality of 'culture' need to be reconciled with the demands of the legal professionals who usually appreciate an expert report, which is clear in argument, source-referenced, but understandable to someone not trained in anthropology. In fact such demands have forced me to sharpen my own understanding of particular problems regarding Albanian societies in flux.

For example, through fieldwork I found 'tradition', particularly any self-essentialising *kanun* references similar to the outside representations described above, served as a resource and local pool of information on the one hand as well as informing local power politics and helping various interest groups to justify the use of violence on the other. 'Tradition' can thus appear transformed as 'criminalised' in certain realms of Albania, and 'nationalised' (which may also include criminalisation) among radical actors of Kosovo. At the same time, in a situation of a vacuum of state power in both Albania and Kosovo during the 1990s, processes of re-patriarchalisation helped create substitute social orders. In an expert report, the individual experience of an asylum seeker needs to be studied carefully, and set into the context of such general insights. It is the ethnographic engagement with the individual case itself, which not only prevents essentialist generalisations but also participating in the violence of 'objectification' of the individual asylum seekers. There is ethnographic gratification in this. Not least through such engagement I have learnt that short-cut representations of 'culture' create an implicit complicity between the legal professionals in the U.K. and the most radical actors in the migrants' home country; that victims (asylum seekers) and perpetrators of violence (criminals) tell the same stories from different perspectives, and also that the real consequences of reference to 'tradition' and its enactment, have influenced Albanian migration patterns, thus functioning as a self-fulfilling prophecy.

## Notes

1. This chapter has profited from many collegial comments when presented in parts or in various earlier versions to anthropological audiences at Krakow: EASA conference (2000), Sussex University (2001), Brunel University, SOAS and University of Loughborough (2003). I owe many thanks to all those patient enough to listen and comment.

2. The choice of how to spell the name of this region is highly disputed within the region. Albanians generally prefer to use the Albanian 'Kosova' in order to distance themselves from the Slavic, particularly the Serb, usage 'Kosovo' or 'Kosovo-Metohija'. As this is an article written in English, I am using 'Kosovo' here in line with the general international usage of designation without political or nationalist prejudice.

3. Under duty of confidentiality contractually acknowledged with every involvement in a legal case, I have to protect the identities of any individual legal professional, company, asylum seeker, criminal or case and can only show wider patterns.

4. I dealt with approximately fifty cases involving inter-ethnic war rape and about five cases involving intra-ethnic, politically motivated rape. Typically, all cases involved gang rape.

5. Cf. for a strict example of traditional expectation according to historical *kanun* local customary law, see Gjeçov (1989: 38, 40); for critical contextualisation regarding *kanun* applicability today, see further below.

6. For some cases I was supported by former research students of the Albanian Studies Programme, London School of Slavonic and East European Studies, which I directed from 1997 to 2003; namely by Julia Pettifer and Ellie Pritchard who both have vast fieldwork experience in the region.

7. According to Article 1A(2) of the 1951 UN Convention on Refugees and the 1967 protocol.

8. Some Kosovar villages base their myth of origin on flight from feuds and the adoption of new identities including religious conversions. The rationality behind such flight and identity changes is the same as in witness protection programmes guaranteed by state law, which, however, are at the time of writing (2003) non-functional in Albania and Kosovo.

9. The seven newly 'white-listed' countries included: Albania, Bulgaria, Jamaica, Macedonia, Moldova, Romania and Serbia/Montenegro (including Kosovo).

10. On some days I received three or more requests per day, a demand which could not be met.

11. Even if free movement between states should be understood as a human right (Hayter 2000: 1n), economic intentions do neither offer conventional nor humanitarian grounds for asylum and as of yet there are no alternative ways of gaining work permission for non-EU Europeans such as the Albanians, and such cases are therefore without any hope of being even admitted for appeal.

12. Cf. various BBC news postings, such as '"Killers still out there" says father' (21 March 2003; http://news.bbc.co.uk/1/hi/england/2873819.stm) and 'Father guilty of killing his sons' (25 March 2003; http://news.bbc.co.uk/1/hi/england/2885745.stm).

13. 'Beckham kidnap suspect is Albanian', Reuters (November 6, 2002; http://www.balkanpeace.org/hed/archive/nov02/hed5305.shtml).

14. One recent example among many: *McIntire investigates: Albanian Prostitution*, BBC 1, May 2002.
15. Most prominently known, the *kanun* of *Lekë Dukagjini* and of *Skanderbeg* in the north; or of *Labëria* and of *Idriz Suli* in the south (cf. Elezi 1994); variations best described in Hasluck (1954).
16. Methodological limitations include that Gjeçov used only one informant of a particular region, that he did not justify his preferences, selection and assemblage of information, that the author had a particular interest in codifying and standardising his findings as the basis of a future indigenous constitutional law, that he, as a Francisan priest, had an interest in promoting the role of the Church in the region, and there was a general nationalist patriot agenda leading to the construction of ideal-types out of previously orally transmitted, flexible norms.
17. All Home Office Letters of Refusal received in 2002 and 2003 cited this wording taken from the 2002 IND country assessment (2002: 43).
18. These have been extensively discussed elsewhere (cf. Schwandner-Sievers 2001, 2004).

# References

Alvarez, L. and J. Loucky. 1992. 'Inquiry and Advocacy: Attorney-Expert Collaboration in the Political Asylum Process', in R.F. Kandel (ed.) *Double Vision: Anthropologists at Law* (NAPA Bulletin No 11). Washington: American Anthropological Association, pp. 43–52.
Blumi, I. 1998. 'The Commodification of Otherness and the Ethnic Unit in the Balkans: How to Think About Albanians'. *East European Politics and Societies*, 12(3): 527–569.
Bolton, S. 2003. 'Profile: The Seven New Countries on the "White List"'. *The Guardian* (special report: refugees), 14 February.
Bonifazi, C. and D. Sabatino. 2003. 'Albanian Migration to Italy: What Official Data and Survey Results Can Reveal'. *Journal of Ethnic and Migration Studies* (special issues: Albanian Migration and New Transnationalisms), 29(6): 967–995.
Bourdieu, P. 2002[16] [1972, French original]. *Outline of a Theory of Practice*. Cambridge: Cambridge University Press.
Bourgois, P. 1995. *In Search of Respect: Selling Crack in El Barrio*. Cambridge: Cambridge University Press.
Byrne, C. 2003. 'Doubt Cast over Beckham Informer'. *The Guardian*, 2 June. http://media.guardian.co.uk/presspublishing/story/0,7495,968976,00.html, accessed 26 October 2003.
Clifford, J. 1988. *The Predicament of Culture: Twentieth-Century Ethnography, Literature, and Art*. Cambridge MA and London: Harvard University Press.
Donovan, J.M. and H.E. Anderson III. 2003. *Anthropology and Law*. Oxford: Berghahn.
Elezi, I. 1994. *E Drejta Zakonore e Laberise ne Planin Krahasues* [The Customary Law of Laberia in Comparative Perspective], Tirana: Libri Universitar.
Fishta, G. 2001 [1933]. 'Parathâne' [prescript], in S. Gjeçovi. *Kanuni i Lekë Dukagjinit*. Lezha. Albania: Kuvendi.
Foreign and Commonwealth Office. 2003. *Travel Information*. London: FCO, www.fco.gov.uk, accessed 7 November 2003.
Giordano, C. 2000. 'Inkompatibilität von Normen – der Ethnologe als Forensischer Gutachter'. *Ethnoscripts*, 2(2): 9–22.
Gjeçov, S. 1989 [1933[1]]. *Kanuni i Lekë Dukagjinit* (with English translation and introduction by Leonard Fox). New York: GjonLekaj.

Good, A. 2003a. 'Anthropologists as Expert Witnesses: Political Asylum Cases Involving Sri Lankan Tamils', in R. Wilson and J. Mitchell (eds) *Human Rights in a Global Perspective: Anthropological Studies of Rights, Claims and Entitlements*. London: Routledge, pp. 93–117.
———. 2003b. 'Anthropologists as Experts: Asylum Appeals in British Courts'. *Anthropology Today*, 19(5): 3–7.
Hart, L. 1999. 'Culture, Civilization and Demarcation at the Northwest Borders of Greece'. *American Ethnologist*, 26(1): 196–220.
Hayter, T. 2000. *Open Borders: The Case against Immigration Controls*. London: Pluto.
Hasluck, M. 1954. *The Unwritten Law in Albania*. Cambridge: Cambridge University Press.
Igric, G. 1999. 'Kosovo Rape Victims Suffer Twice'. *Balkan Crisis Report* 48 (ed.) IWPR (Institute for War and Peace Reporting), http://www.iwpr.net/index.pl?archive/bcr/bcr_19990618_2_eng.txt, accessed 12 February 2002.
IND (Immigration and Nationality Directorate). 1998. *Asylum Directorate Instructions*. London: Home Office.
———. 2002. *Country Assessment Albania*, London: Home Office, Country Information and Policy Unit, www.ind.homeoffice.gov.uk, accessed 12 February 2003.
———. 2003. Country Assessment Serbia and Montenegro. London: Home Office, Country Information and Policy Unit, www.ind.homeoffice.gov.uk, accessed 28 September 2003.
Kikia, M. 1999. 'Gjakmarrja, lufta mes shqipatareve qe nuk do the shuhet' [Blood Feud, the War among Albanians which Does Not Fade], *Koha Jone*, 10 October.
Kokot, W. 2000. '"Forensische Ethnolgie" – zum Themenschwerpunkt dieser Ausgabe'. *Ethnoscripts*, 2(2): 1–9.
Koptiuch, K. 1996. '"Cultural Defense" and Criminological Displacements: Gender, Race and (Trans)Nation in the Legal Surveillance of U.S. Diaspora Asians', in S. Lavie and T. Swedenburg (eds) *Displacement, Diaspora, and Geographies of Identity*. Durham, London: Duke University Press, pp. 215–233.
Kretsi, G. 2002. '"Shkelqen" oder "Giannis"? Namenswechsel und Identitätsstrategien zwischen Heimatkultur und Migration' ['S' or 'G'? Name Changing and Identity Strategies between Home Culture and Migration], in K. Kaser, R. Pichler and S. Schwandner-Sievers (eds) *Die weite Welt und das Dorf: Albanische Emigration am Ende des 20. Jahrhunderts*. Vienna: Boehlau, pp. 263–289.
Kuper, A. 2001. *Culture: The Anthropologists' Account*. Cambridge, MA: Harvard University Press.
Kurkiala, M. 2003. 'Interpreting Honour Killings: The Story of Fadime Sahindal (1975 – 2002) in the Swedish Press'. *Anthropology Today*, 19(1): 6–7.
Mai, N. and S. Schwandner-Sievers. 2003. 'Albanian Migration and New Transnationalisms' (Introduction to Special Issue: Albanian Migration and New Transnationalisms). *Journal of Ethnic and Migration Studies*, 29(6): 939–948.
Milner, H. and B. Schmidt (Womankind Worldwide) 1999. 'Rape as a Weapon of War'. *British Council Newsletter*, October, (http://www.womankind.org.uk/5b%20rape.htm), accessed 6 June 2003.
Morris, S. 2003. 'Press Whips Up Asylum Hysteria: Editors dub Britain a Gangsters' Haven as They Make Direct Links between Refugees and Terrorism'. *The Guardian*, 24 January, http://www.guardian.co.uk/Refugees_in_Britain/Story/0,2763,881251,00.html, accessed 26 October 2003.
NCIS (National Criminal Intelligence Services). 2003. *U.K. Threat Assessments of Serious and Organised Crime 2002*. www.ncis.gov.uk/press/2002/261102.asp, accessed 22 May 2003.
OSCE and UNHCR 2003. *Tenth Assessment of the Situation of Ethnic Minorities in Kosovo*, March. www.osce.org/kosovo/publications/pdf/minrep/pdf, accessed 16 April 2003.
Pandolfi, M. 2002. 'Myth and New Forms of Governance in Contemporary Albania', in S. Schwandner-Sievers, S. and B. Fischer (eds) *Albanian Identities: Myth and History*. London: Hurst, pp. 203–214.

Refugee Council. 2002. *Returns Policy Background Paper A: International Principles of Protection*, February, www.refugeecouncil.org.uk/publications/pub007.htm, accessed 5 March 2003.

Refugee Women's Resource Project. 2002. *Refugee Women and Domestic Violence: Country Studies Kosovo*. London: Asylum Aid. www.asylumaid.org/publications, accessed 13 December 2002.

—— 2003. [update], *Refugee Women and Domestic Violence: Country Studies Albania*. London: Asylum Aid. www.asylumaid.org/publications, accessed 5 October 2003.

Reineck, J. 1993. 'Seizing the Past, Forging the Present: Changing Visions of Self and Nation among the Kosova Albanians' (Special Issue: War among the Yugoslavs). *Anthropology of East Europe Review*, 11(1–2), http://condor.depaul.edu/~rrotenbe/aeer/aeer11_1/reineck.html, accessed 25 January 2003.

Robinson, V. and J. Segrott. 2002. *Understanding the Decision-making of Asylum Seekers*, Home Office Research Study 243. London: Home Office Research, Development and Statistics Directorate, July.

Rosen, L. 1977. 'The Anthropologist as Expert Witness'. *American Anthropologist*, 79: 555–578.

Schwandner-Sievers, S. 2001. 'The Enactment of "Tradition": Albanian Constructions of Identity, Violence and Power in Times of Crisis', in B.E. Schmidt, I.W. Schröder (eds) *Anthropology of Violence and Conflict*. London: Routledge, pp. 97–120.

——. 2004. 'Albanians, "Albanianism" and the Strategic Subversion of Stereotypes', in A. Hammond (ed.) *The Balkans and the West: Constructing the European Other, 1945–2003*. Aldershot: Ashgate, pp. 110–126.

Shore, C. and S. Wright. 1997. 'Policy: A New Field of Anthropology', in C. Shore and S. Wright (eds) *Anthropology of Policy: Critical Perspectives on Governance and Power*. London, New York: Routledge, pp. 3–39.

Smith, H. 2000. '"Rape victims" Babies Pay the Price of War'. *The Observer*, 16 April.

Stewart, P.J. and A. Strathern. 2002. *Violence: Theory and Ethnography*. London, New York: Continuum.

Stoppel, W. 2003. *Die Strafgesetze Albaniens*. Tirana: K&B.

'The Kanun Bastardized, Dossier: the Blood Feud / Kanuni i Bastarduar, Dosje: Hakmarrja' *Reviste Periodike per te Drejtat e Njeriut* 2. 2000 – 2001.

UNDP. 2000. *Albanian Human Development Report*, Tirana: United Nations Development Projects.

UNHCR. 2002. *Position on the Continued Protection Needs of Individuals from Kosovo* (April), www.unhcr.ch/world/euro/seo/protect/minoritymenu, accessed 15 November 2002.

# NOTES ON CONTRIBUTORS

**Adam Drazin** has worked primarily on material culture and mass consumption in Romania. Prior to his Ph.D., he worked for several years in market and opinion research with MORI Ltd., using a variety of non-anthropological commercial research techniques and has also conducted assorted freelance work. He is currently IRCHSS Government of Ireland Postdoctoral Research Fellow at Trinity College Dublin, funded by the Irish Research Council for the Humanities and Social Sciences, and has also worked in hi-tech design, most recently in the Industrial Design department of the University of Eindhoven, Holland, and at Hewlett-Packard Laboratories in the UK.

**Maia Green** studied social anthropology at the London School of Economics. She conducted fieldwork in Southern Tanzania and has published extensively on religion, political socialities, and gender. Since 1997 Maia Green has been involved in social development activities in Kenya and Tanzania, providing social analytical input to the development planning process and working of project design across a range of sectors. She has worked on public sector reforms in health and local government and on civil society issues in east Africa.

**Elizabeth Hart** is Senior Lecturer in Social Anthropology at the University of Nottingham. Her doctoral research at the London School of Economics was with pottery workers in Stoke-on-Trent and since then she has conducted ethnographic research in a wide range of organisations, including hospitals and nursing homes. She established the Centre for Social and Cultural Research in Stroke and runs a course on the anthropology of organisations for health professionals studying for masters and research degrees. Her main research interest continues to be in women, work and ritual. She is a member of the Medical Committee of the Royal Anthropological Institute.

**Paul Henley** has been Director of the Granada Centre for Visual Anthropology at the University of Manchester since it was founded in 1987. As an anthropologist, he trained at the University of Cambridge (1969–79) and as a film-maker at the National Film and Television School at Beaconsfield (1984–87). He has published extensively on the indigenous societies of Amazonia, and as a film-maker has worked both in South America and Europe. Whilst some of these films have been for academic audiences, others have been for British television. At the Granada Centre, he has supervised well over 100 Masters and Doctoral students. He has also given seminars or run workshops in several countries of Latin America, Africa and Asia, as well as in a number of European countries. In 2001, he was appointed Professor of Visual Anthropology.

**Mils Hills** read for a doctorate in the Department of Social Anthropology at the University of St. Andrews. He joined the Centre for Human Sciences of the Defence Evaluation and Research Agency (DERA) of the U.K. Ministry of Defence in 1998. Initially contributing technical input to Information Operations research, he rapidly came to be deployed on a range of research and consultancy activies across the organisation. In 2000 Mils was appointed Task Manager and in the following year Capability Group Leader as DERA moved towards privatisation (as QinetiQ). Mils left QinetiQ in 2002, and joined DERA's successor organisation the Defence Science and Technology Laboratory (DSTL). At the same time, Mils was seconded to the Civil Contingencies Secretariat of the Cabinet Office. Mils has also served as a member of the Department of Trade and Industry Taskforce on Future Society and Crime and Secretary of a Defence Scientific Advisory Committee Working Party on Information Operations and Information Technology.

**Garry Marvin** is Reader in Social Anthropology at Roehampron University. He has a particular interest in human/animal relations and has conducted research into bullfighting, cockfighting, circuses, zoos and hunting. His present research centres on two main areas – an ethnographic study of foxhunting and a study of the relationships between humans and wolves. He started on the path of a traditional academic career after completing his doctorate on bullfighting in southern Spain in 1982. However, in 1986 he was asked, because of his knowledge of bullfighting and his contacts in that world, to work on a series of television programmes about modern Spain, one of which was to deal with the bullfight. Thus began a ten-year period of working as a freelance researcher/producer of television documentaries. In 1996, dissatisfied with the decreasing possibilities of documentary-making of the kind he hoped to make, he applied for and was offered a lectureship at the Roehampton Institute (now Roehampton University). Since his appointment he has maintained close relationships with the documentary companies with whom he previously worked and continues to develop programme ideas with them.

**David Mills** is an academic co-ordinator at Sociology, Anthropology and Politics (C-SAP), part of the Higher Education Academy, and a lecturer at the University of Birmingham. As well as carrying out research on disciplinarity in the social sciences, he is writing a political history of social anthropology. He is co-editor of 'Teaching Rites and Wrongs: Universities and the making of Anthropologists' (C-SAP, 2005) and the forthcoming volume 'African Anthropologies: History, Practice and Critique'.

**Sarah Pink** has a Ph.D. in Social Anthropology from the University of Kent and an M.A. in Visual Anthropology from the University of Manchester. Her first applied anthropology project was directly after graduating with a B.A. in Anthropology from the University of Kent, on a project about parcels service customers, followed by other consultancies. Since being awarded her Ph.D. in 1996 (published as *Women and Bullfighting* in 1997), she has worked at the University of Derby and from 2000 in the Department of Social Sciences at Loughborough University. Her second book *Doing Visual Ethnography* was published in 2001. During this period she has also worked with Unilever Research on a range of consumer ethnography projects using her skills as a visual anthropologist, as a consultant to a health project in West Africa and with photographers using anthropological approaches and visual ethnographic methods to inform their practice. Her book *Home Truths*, based on a comparative visual ethnography of gender and home in England and Spain, developed with Unilever, was published in 2004. She has also guest-edited a special issue of *Visual Anthropology Review* on the topic of Applied Visual Anthropology.

**Simon Roberts** is the Director of Ideas Bazaar, a research consultancy he started in 2002. He read anthropology at The University of Edinburgh, his Ph.D. research examined the cultural impact of the satellite TV revolution in India. His research at Ideas Bazaar, in the public and private sectors, has focused on technology, media and organisations. Simon is an associate of iSociety at The Work Foundation where he led the use of ethnography in a research programme on technology and everyday life. He has published work based on his thesis, on broadband, mobiles, media, technology at work and the application of anthropology.

**Stephanie Schwandner-Sievers** studied and taught Social Anthropology and Balkan Studies at the Berlin Free University (1985–1997). From 1997 until 2003 she was the Nash Fellow for Albanian Studies, founding the Albanian Studies Programme at the School of Slavonic and East European Studies, University College London, and since 2003 she has worked as a freelance researcher, writer and anthropological consultant. Since 1992 she has conducted anthropological fieldwork in Albania and Kosovo for several months each year. Her research and publications focus on ethnicity movements, nationalism, political culture, Balkan image and representation, politics of tradition including blood feuding, gender and various aspects of development and crisis both in contemporary Albanian and Kosovar society. She has regularly acted as a consultant for the World Bank, OSCE, FCO, German Government, NATO, the ICTY , the UN, and for police, solicitors and courts investigating criminal and asylum cases.

**Susan Wright** is Professor of Educational Anthropology at the Danish University of Education. Previously she was Director of C-SAP, the Higher Education Academy's Centre for Learning and Teaching in Sociology, Anthropology and Politics. She has been senior lecturer in Cultural Studies at Birmingham University and lecturer in anthropology at Sussex University. In a voluntary capacity she was convenor of GAPP (Group for Anthropology in Policy and Practice) from 1987 to 1991. She was co-founder and convenor of BASAPP, renamed Anthropology in Action, in 1988–90 and in 1994 and a committee member in between. She established the National Network for Teaching and Learning Anthropology and directed its educational development programme from 1994 to 1999 (the precursor of C-SAP). Her own research is on processes of political transformation in neo-liberal Britain and in pre- and post-revolutionary Iran. With Cris Shore she edited Anthropology of Policy: Critical Perspectives on Governance and Power (Routledge 1997) and has published numerous articles on university reform and higher education.

# INDEX